£12.95

By the same author

THE OLD SHRUB ROSES
COLOUR IN THE WINTER GARDEN
SHRUB ROSES OF TODAY
CLIMBING ROSES OLD AND NEW
PERENNIAL GARDEN PLANTS
THREE GARDENS
TREES IN THE LANDSCAPE

PLANTS FOR GROUND-COVER

WRITTEN AND ILLUSTRATED
BY

GRAHAM STUART THOMAS,
O.B.E., V.M.H., D.H.M., V.M.M.

Gardens Consultant to the National Trust

With 32 plates in colour and
79 in black-and-white

J. M. DENT & SONS LTD
LONDON & MELBOURNE

Printed in Great Britain
by Biddles Ltd, Guildford, Surrey
for
J. M. DENT & SONS LTD
Aldine House, Welbeck Street, London W1M 8LX
© Graham Stuart Thomas, 1970
First published 1970
Reprinted 1970
Reprinted 1971
Revised edition 1977
Reprinted (with revisions) 1984

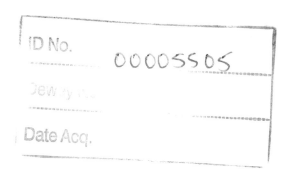
ISBN 0 460 03994 6

CONTENTS

Illustrations vii
Acknowledgments xii
Introduction xiii

1 Natural and Scientific   1

2 Preparation, Cultivation, Planting and Maintenance   5

3 A Guide to the Alphabetical Tables and Rules for
   Planting   16

4 Shrubs   26
   Alphabetical table   52

5 Climbing Plants   96
   Alphabetical table   102

6 Conifers   108
   Alphabetical list   112

7 Herbaceous Plants   116
   Alphabetical table   136

8 Grasses and Rushes   202
   Alphabetical table   204

9 Ferns   208
   Alphabetical table   212

10 Ground-Cover Plants for Large Areas   216

11 Annuals and Biennials   228

Appendix I. Weeds, Weedkillers, Fertilizers and Soils 231
Appendix II. Lists of Plants for Special Conditions 244
Addenda 1977 255
Books for Further Study 262
General Index, including Common Names of Plants 263
Index of Latin Names of Plants 266

ILLUSTRATIONS

PLATES IN COLOUR

Between pages 134 and 135

I(A) The heather garden in the University of Liverpool's botanic garden at Ness, Cheshire
(B) A small-scale heath garden in Cornwall

II(A) *Hebe pinguifolia* 'Pagei'
(B) *Erica carnea* 'Springwood Pink' and 'Springwood White' at the Royal Horticultural Society's garden at Wisley, Surrey

III(A) Labour-saving beds in the National Trust garden at Killerton, Devon
(B) *Helianthemum* 'Rhodanthe Carneum' in Norfolk

IV(A) *Potentilla fruticosa* 'Tangerine'
(B) Dwarf 'social' shrubs, etc. in a sunny border

V(A) *Salvia officinalis* 'Icterina'
(B) *Salvia officinalis* 'Purpurascens' and *Santolina chamae-cyparissus*

VI(A) *Genista pilosa* 'Procumbens'
(B) *Genista sagittalis*

VII(A) *Rosa* 'Max Graf'
(B) *Lonicera pileata*

VIII(A) *Hedera helix* 'Buttercup'
(B) *Hedera colchica* 'Dentato-variegata'
Both photographed in the University Botanic Garden, Oxford

IX(A) *Vaccinium oxycoccus* in the Royal Botanic Garden, Kew
(B) *Vinca major* 'Elegantissima'
(C) *Vinca minor* 'Bowles' Variety'

X(A) *Juniperus communis* 'Hornibrookii' in Mr Maurice Mason's garden at Fincham, Norfolk
(B) *Juniperus horizontalis*
(C) *Picea abies* 'Reflexa'

vii

XI(A) *Hosta fortunei* 'Albopicta'
    (B) *Hosta fortunei* 'Aurea' and the hybrid 'Thomas Hogg'

XII(A) *Hosta sieboldiana* 'Elegans'
     (B) *Hosta crispula*

XIII(A) *Hosta crispula* surrounded by *Saxifraga umbrosa*
      (B) A September border in the author's garden

XIV(A) *Anaphalis triplinervis* contrasted with bergenias
     (B) *Bergenia* 'Sunningdale'
     (C) *Bergenia ligulata*
     (D) *Bergenia* 'Silberlicht'

XV *Alchemilla mollis* and *Rosa polliniana*

XVI(A) *Geranium macrorrhizum*
     (B) *Geranium* 'Russell Prichard'

XVII(A) *Geranium endressii*
      (B) *Geranium × magnificum* (*G. ibericum* or *G. platypetalum* of gardens)

XVIII(A) *Origanum vulgare* 'Aureum'
       (B) *Stachys olympica* (*S. lanata*) 'Silver Carpet'

XIX(A) *Primula florindae* in the Royal Botanic Garden' Edinburgh
     (B) *Astilbe* 'Rheinland' at Kew

XX(A) *Lysichitum americanum* in flower in the National Trust garden, Hidcote, Gloucestershire
    (B) *Rodgersia podophylla* at Wisley, Surrey

XXI The stream garden at Hidcote

XXII(A) *Oxalis oregana*
      (B) *Waldsteinia ternata*

XXIII(A) *Symphytum grandiflorum*
       (B) *Polygonum affine*

XXIV(A) Ferns, pulmonarias and hostas
      (B) *Lamium maculatum*

XXV(A) Epimediums and *Tiarella cordifolia*
     (B) *Glyceria aquatica* 'Variegata'

XXVI *Centaurea hypoleuca* 'John Coutts'

XXVII(A) *Cornus* (*Chamaepericlymenum*) *canadensis*
       (B) *Lonicera periclymenum serotina*

XXVIII(A) *Cotoneaster dammeri*
      (B) *Penstemon newberryi*
  XXIX(A) Irish ivy at Kew
      (B) *Hedera helix hibernica*, Irish ivy
   XXX(A) *Heracleum mantegazzianum* in the University Botanic
          Garden, Cambridge
      (B) *Pachysandra terminalis*
  XXXI(A) *Rubus odoratus*
      (B) *Hypericum calycinum*
 XXXII *Geranium macrorrhizum*, flowing round other plants

PLATES IN MONOCHROME
Between pages 6 and 7

1 *Viburnum plicatum tomentosum* 'Mariesii'
2 *Hydrangea macrophylla*
3 *Prunus laurocerasus* 'Zabeliana'
4 *Salix lanata* 'Stuartii' backed by *Juniperus × media* 'Pfitzerana' in the Royal Botanic Garden, Edinburgh
5 Japanese Azalea
6 *Rhododendron pemakoense*
7 *Rhododendron* (Azalea) 'Mucronatum Bulstrode'
8 *Senecio laxifolius* backed by ceanothus and rhododendrons
9 *Ephedra gerardiana*
10 *Juniperus sabina* 'Tamariscifolia'
11 *Iberis sempervirens* 'Snowflake'
12 *Arctostaphylos nevadensis* (of gardens) at the Royal Botanic Garden, Kew
13 *Rubus tricolor*
14 *Vinca major hirsuta* in the National Trust garden at Hidcote
15 *Cotoneaster microphyllus*
16 *Rosmarinus lavandulaceus* (R. *officinalis prostratus*)
17 *Euonymus fortunei vegetus* at Hidcote
18 *Rosa × paulii* 'Rosea'
19 *Pachysandra terminalis*. Courtesy Elsa M. Megson
20 *Hedera canariensis* 'Variegata' and *H. helix* 'Sagittaefolia variegata'

21 *Hedera colchica* 'Dentata'

22 *Leucothöe fontanesiana* (*L. catesbaei*)

23 *Xanthorhiza simplicissima* (*X. apiifolia*)

24 *Gaultheria shallon*

25 *Rodgersia aesculifolia*

26 *Rheum palmatum* 'Atrosanguineum'

27 *Hosta undulata univittata*

28 *Hosta lancifolia*

29 *Hosta albomarginata*

30 *Hosta fortunei* 'Marginato Alba'

31 *Hosta fortunei* 'Obscura Marginata' ('Yellow Edge')

32 *Hosta sieboldiana* 'Elegans' and *H. fortunei hyacinthina*

33 *Hosta sieboldiana* 'Frances Williams' ('Gold Edge')

34 *Hosta ventricosa* 'Variegata' and *H. plantaginea grandiflora*

35 *Hosta plantaginea grandiflora*

Between pages 38 and 39

36 *Pachyphragma macrophyllum* (see note page 135)

37 *Iris innominata* hybrid

38 *Salvia officinalis* 'Purpurascens', *Geranium renardii* and *Calamintha nepetoides*

39 *Alyssum saxatile*

40 *Alchemilla mollis*

41 *Alchemilla mollis* foliage with *Ruta graveolens* 'Jackman's Blue'

42 *Geranium psilostemon* (*G. armenum*)

43 *Viola septentrionalis*

44 *Bergenia cordifolia* 'Purpurea'

45 *Helleborus foetidus*

46 *Saxifraga geum* 'Monstrosa'

47 *Asarum europaeum*

48 *Oxalis acetosella* 'Rosea'

49 *Tiarella cordifolia*

50 *Epimedium pinnatum colchicum*

51 *Vancouveria hexandra*

52 *Lamium galeobdolon* 'Variegatum' at Hidcote

53 *Lamium maculatum*

54 *Phlox douglasii* 'Boothman's Variety' at Kew

55 *Gypsophila repens* at Kew

56 *Geranium himalayense* (*G. grandiflorum* of gardens)

57 *Potentilla alba*

58 *Brunnera macrophylla* (*Anchusa myosotidiflora*) at Hidcote

59 *Luzula maxima* (*L. sylvatica*)

60 *Festuca eskia* (*F. crinum-ursi*) with sun roses, thymes, etc.

61 *Hemerocallis fulva* 'Kwanso Flore Pleno'

62 *Stachys macrantha, Geranium psilostemon* and *Symphytum* ×
uplandicum 'Variegatum'

63 *Maianthemum bifolium*

64 *Asperula odorata*

65 Labour-saving borders

Between pages 230 and 231

66 *Polypodium vulgare*

67 *Blechnum penna-marina*

68 *Gymnocarpium dryopteris*

69 *Athyrium filix-femina* 'Minor'

70 *Trachystemon orientale*

71 *Anemone tomentosa* (*A. vitifolia* of gardens)

72 *Juniperus* × *media* 'Pfitzerana' in the National Trust garden at
Polesden Lacey, Surrey

73 *Taxus baccata* 'Dovastonii Aurea' in the National Trust garden
at Sizergh Castle, Westmorland

74 *Petasites hybridus*

75 *Petasites albus*

76 A bank covered with *Lithospermum diffusum* 'Heavenly Blue'
and *Erigeron mucronatus*. Courtesy H. J. Brusca Nursery, Inc.,
Philadelphia

77 *Coronilla varia*, the 'Penngift Crownvetch'

78 *Sagina glabra* used as a lawn in the rock garden at the École
d'Horticulture near Paris, France

79 *Helxine soleirolii* in the Jardins Kalm, near Paris. Courtesy
M. Littledale, Esq.

ACKNOWLEDGMENTS

ALTHOUGH this is the first page of this book it has been written last. Having completed the various chapters I can look back over two years' work and try to recall all the help and kindness I have received from many friends and correspondents. First and foremost I have pleasure in recording my gratitude and indebtedness to Mr C. D. Brickell, who has patiently guided me through many taxonomic tangles, has made many useful suggestions and has exercised his great knowledge of plants both in gardens and in the wild for the benefit of this book.

Little has been written on this subject, which is indeed a comparatively new form of garden study, occasioned as much by economic conditions as by the desire to create garden pictures. If one cannot grow every plant in one's own garden one must see them established elsewhere before daring to write about them and recommend them to others. Many visits have accordingly been made to national and university botanic gardens, and at Edinburgh Dr H. R. Fletcher has been kind enough to elucidate several knotty problems. I also want to express best thanks to Mr H. G. Hillier, Mr A. H. V. Bloom and Mr H. J. Welch for sparing much time in shewing me their collections of plants. Mr David Pyecraft has been kind enough to help with revision of Appendix I on weeds and weedkillers, for which I am very grateful.

In short, once again I must record that one cannot write a book without the help of others, and I hope that what I have written may give them all some increase of leisure to recompense them for the time they have given to my self-appointed quest.

G. S. THOMAS

Woking, Surrey, 1969
Revised 1977

Introduction

'A LAZY gardener' would undoubtedly be the verdict given by many who were superficially acquainted with my ideas on gardening. Up to a point they might be right, but as a rule a lazy man's garden would show evidence of neglect. I do not pretend that my garden is perfect by any means, but my friends have so far been kind enough to remark on the general absence of weeds. Their presence (the weeds, not the friends) is something I simply cannot stand; any weed that finds a roothold or space to grow is removed at the first opportunity, and certainly before it seeds. By keeping abreast of the general maintenance from spring to autumn we can avoid the worry and distress occasioned by neglect. Over a period of about twenty years I have made a lot of mistakes, but have learnt many lessons by experience and by watching other gardeners' methods; the object of this book is to help others to arrive earlier at that state of bliss during the summer when one actually walks round *looking* for weeds, and avoiding thereby a deal of hard work.

In our daily contact with other gardeners we come across some vastly different ideas. There are those who say they will surround their garden with a brick wall, cover the whole area with concrete, first planting a tree to give shade for sitting and snoozing—and doing no gardening at all. The use of gravel instead of concrete with occasional application of weedkillers would provide a little more work annually. Others decide to have practically nothing but lawn: they are probably the mechanically minded who rather love the smell of a hot engine, the noise and the oil; I do not personally enjoy walking behind a noisy mower. Yet others will cast aside all caution and aim at growing every popular flower. A steadily increasing number will pin their faith on a selection of trees, shrubs and plants with which they can create a lasting picture with living materials; my own approach is mainly this, but I try to make the plants maintain the garden for me. In addition I suppose I might well be branded a 'plant collector'; it gives me pleasure to assemble many examples of particular genera, such as snowdrops, roses, miniature daffodils, hardy geraniums, hostas and ferns. I take comfort in knowing that this is a very prevalent failing among gardeners today. It does not necessarily contribute to a garden picture.

By growing suitable permanencies we can avoid annual planting, lifting, dividing and also staking; by judicious use of the right plants we can avoid digging, hoeing, spraying, watering and weeding. There is little left but the deck-chair or 'li-lo' during the growing months, while during the winter some manual labour comes not amiss in a few movings, rearrangings and replantings, the major prunings and general surveillance; and the exciting moment is liable to occur at any time when one realizes that by subtle changes, or perhaps the choice of a new shrub, or by the completion of a colour-scheme or texture-group, one can immeasurably improve a portion of border.

THE VALUE OF LEAVES

If you would like to follow me further up this realizable dream-path let me first put to you a few fundamentals, without which we shall not be able to proceed amicably. If you are like me you wish for a large garden where you can rest and gain refreshment for the mind, with a constant succession of beauty in one form or another throughout the twelve months; in spite of all this the garden should cause the least work. To achieve this I ask you to think on these precepts:

1. That leaves are more important than flowers.

2. That green in its many variations is a colour that deserves the closest attention and appraisal in a garden.

3. That a plant or shrub should be assessed on all its points— its stance and character (usually known in horticulture as its 'habit'), its foliage (colour, shape, size, texture), as well as the colour of its flowers, its flowering period and its fruiting propensities.

4. That a mulch of dead leaves or other decomposing vegetable matter is an asset of incalculable value in regard to fertility and is not to be eschewed on account of untidiness.

5. That it is unnecessary to dig and hoe to ensure the good health of your plants.

As further explanation and qualification I would stress the value of leaves throughout the year. Evergreens possess their foliage for the full twelve months while the deciduous kinds hold their foliage during four to seven months, and even the short life of a deciduous leaf is longer than the period over which any one tree, shrub or plant will hold its flowers. Flowers come and go but the leaves are always with us, and the whole success of my argument and persuasion rests upon your idea of garden values; whether you wish to grow 'flowers' or 'plants'; whether you prefer the production of fine flowers (with all the attendant work required) to the creation of a garden picture; whether you look upon gardening as a science or an art. I cannot help you to decide, but even if you differ wholeheartedly from me over the above paragraphs I should be surprised if no portion of your garden could be devoted to the carefree permanent plants of which there is such an astonishing variety to choose from in cultivation today.

I think the above remarks help to amplify my first three points. These refer to the art side of the matter; for amplification of points 4 and 5, which are essentially scientific, I will refer you to Chapter 2, to avoid a lengthy interruption here. But I will now assert that if you garden hand in hand with leaves—either green and growing, or brown and decaying—you will find gardening much easier. I write from Surrey, a county that is by no means as clement as is popularly supposed. In this area of the county great fluctuations of temperature occur and we experience severe winter frost and torrid summer heat (for brief periods); both are occasioned partly by the large areas of commons, whose sand cools quickly and whose heathery wastes develop a hot breath after some hours of continuous sunshine, a phenomenon experienced also in arable country. Naturally I write of my experiences in one small plot in this area, but I am fortunate enough to be intimately concerned with the climates and difficulties experienced in almost all counties of England and Wales through my work as Gardens Adviser to the National Trust. In these gardens—some great, some small—are found the same basic needs to reduce work and save labour, though of necessity each garden is completely different from the next and no general rule can be laid down about what economies should be made. Observing the behaviour of plants all over the country has, however, given me an insight into the possible climatic problems that may have to be studied as a preliminary to successful gardening.

AN EARLIER BOOK

It is my aim to shew you how you can maintain your garden without a lot of digging and hoeing. If you have read thus far, you may quite likely be on the point of returning the book to the shelf on the grounds that I am just another 'crank'. If so my crankiness started during a long friendship with a great gardener —one who did most of his own work and knew and grew a host of beautiful things in his garden in North Wales. During the 1930's, and until his death in 1956, he wrote profusely of his findings and methods (to say nothing of his plants) both in the horticultural press and in several books. He was Arthur Tysilio Johnson, a schoolmaster who became a horticultural journalist, aided and abetted by his wife Nora, who was equally gifted in growing and knowing plants. Between them they created a small garden of limitless charm and interest. In his later years A. T. J. sought to encourage us all to let plants do much of the 'daily round', realizing as we all do that the time comes when we shall prefer sitting to stooping. Here are some of his thoughts from a booklet called *Labour-Saving Plants and how to Use Them*, published by that successful little periodical *My Garden*, shortly after the Second World War. It soon went out of print.

Garden economy is a matter that deeply concerns us all. For a quarter-century and more most of us have been faced by the problem as to how to reduce the rising expenses of maintenance, and the solving of this problem has now become an acute necessity. Everything we handle has increased in price, but the biggest bogy of all is labour. The wages that have to be paid for any sort of help have advanced several hundreds per cent, and, realizing with every justification that our garden, if it is to fulfil its destiny, must not be a drain on our resources and a disturber of our peace, we are confronted with the cold truth that it will have to be run on less money or given up.

It may, of course, be argued that to do without paid labour is possible in a small garden. Very true. But, even so, one's own labour has to be considered. Our lives are so much fuller these days than they were, that the time available for the tending of even the most modest garden is too often wholly insufficient, and physical capacity has to be taken into account. Most garden folk are on the wrong side of middle age, and they discover soon enough, especially if they have been caught up by the pace of horticultural advance today, that their garden, instead of being a recreation and comfort, has become an anxiety and care.

It is with the object of reducing the weekly wage bill, or doing away with it altogether, as well as of relieving the owner-gardener of that fear of failure over upkeep which so frequently haunts his efforts, a grim shadow, that these pages are written. The conclusions that I have arrived at are the outcome of fifty years in close touch with the soil, and our own three-acre garden, worked by our two selves (full days rarely being given to it) with a man only one and a half days a week, does, I think, prove that those conclusions are sound. I am not contending that this garden is a model garden, that it will appeal to everyone. But in its informality it suits us and evidently delights our visitors, who cannot be convinced that we have not got an efficient 'staff' hidden somewhere away behind the tool-shed.

His garden was almost entirely composed of permanent things —trees and shrubs, herbaceous plants which were limited to the stalwart clump-formers and the ground-coverers, and bulbs. Though A. T. J. and his 'Lady of the Garden' scarcely ever picked flowers for the house, I know that except during prolonged spells of severe frost and snow a bunch could always be found. It is my ideal also, and indeed I count it a failing in a garden of any size to be unable to furnish two or three vases with beauty throughout the year, even though it may be nothing but leaf, berry and twig during the darkest part of winter.

It is possible to establish permanent plants and shrubs in a garden of about an acre so that during the growing season, from April to October, two working days a month are ample to keep it clean and tidy, inclusive of cutting the areas of grass. This is apart from the clipping of a surrounding hedge and all winter work such as pruning and occasional transplanting. With three working days a month many extras could be attended to such as the transplanting of congested clumps of bulbs immediately after flowering (the best time), the removing of dead heads (where they are not part of the decorative scheme) and certain necessary summer pruning and clipping of interior hedges.

AN HISTORICAL APPROACH

In short, to my mind, there is no doubt that for the smaller gardens of today a combination of mown lawns, paths of weed-proof materials or of gravel treated regularly with weedkiller, and borders filled with ground-covering shrubs and perennial plants is the most conducive to a restful enjoyment of the area under control. But we cannot leave it there; what I have written outlines only briefly one special type of modern gardening, and I should like before getting to the uses and abuses of ground-cover plants to make a little historical survey to see why we have more or less automatically arrived at this point in the story of gardening in this country.

Very briefly we may visualize the growing of herbs for medicine and the pot in medieval times widening into greater collections of plants—many cultivated solely for beauty—during the Renaissance period; though design had begun to take its place, to label it we might call this long awakening the day of the herbalists. Severe formality of design, avenues and much clipping of bushes and hedges came into this country at the Restoration, Charles II bringing with him many fresh ideas from the Continent. The beauty of plants was not so much to the fore, though a number of specialist 'crazes' started. The eighteenth century saw a revulsion against this excessive formality, and 'gardening' was relegated to the park, where the great landscapists cut down the vast radial avenues and destroyed formal designs in order to create scenes reminiscent of idyllic pictures by continental artists. Trees, grass, water and classical buildings gave place eventually to more artificial schemes, where grottoes and fantasy reigned. Flowers and herbs were the care of the cottager.

With the period of Victorian opulence arriving, and heated greenhouses becoming fashionable, the numerous exotic plants assumed great importance. For a long time, until 1914, great pleasure gardens and ornamental vegetable and fruit gardens were created by the very rich, and labour was cheap. Fortunately, vast quantities of hardy plants, shrubs and trees were being discovered throughout the world and imported, particularly during the nine-teenth and early part of the twentieth centuries, which caused the next fashion to arise—the arboretum. By the end of the nineteenth century the time was ripe for the gradual demise of the lead given by the all-powerful architect and the great head gardeners; the spearhead of a new fashion in gardening was brought about by noted amateur plantsmen and women of the day, the most famous among many being William Robinson, Gertrude Jekyll, Ellen Willmott, G. F. Wilson, E. A. Bowles, Lawrence Johnston and A. T. Johnson, whom I have already mentioned. Between them they altered the whole trend of gardening through their examples and writing, focusing the attention on the trees, shrubs, bulbs and plants, both the old kinds fostered through decades by their de-votees, and also all the new material that was pouring in from the temperate zones. Each was an expert in one way or another, either botanist-plantsman, or garden-artist, often a combination of both.

THE GARDEN OF TODAY

Gradually the influence exerted and the examples formed by these and other owner-gardeners brought about a trend towards informal gardening. Apart from this trend, the small householder of this century can have found no sure and single-minded thesis to follow, when he discovered he was to be his own designer, head gardener and staff all rolled into one. All of us are influenced by inherited ideas, which we can elaborate or throw aside, and the choice of the whole field of horticulture is before us. At one end of the scale is the scientist-technician-gardener who treats his plants as a series of 'cases', and his garden shed as a laboratory, revelling in all the latest 'chemicals', gadgets and machinery. Far away, at the other end, is the landscape architect who uses his plants as so much material to offset the stark lines of his roads and blocks of flats. In between comes the great range of owner-gardeners—the amateurs, the rank-and-file, call them what you will—in short the multitude who make gardening what it is today: the foremost hobby in the land.

Among them are those who approach either of the extremes outlined above, the botanists, the collectors, the artist-plantsmen, the potterers and the flower-lovers, and the back-to-Mother-Earth gardener who grows simple things with the aid of compost and nature's methods. It is not surprising that no two gardens are ever alike, considering the tremendous influence the past has upon us, the vast numbers of plants in cultivation today and the mass of books and periodicals that literally flood our senses with gardening in one form or another.

So far what I have written applies almost entirely to gardens of small size and under private control. Even so there are still many great gardens in private hands, many of them open to the public, including those cared for by the National Trust and the old-established college gardens. A. T. Johnson's words quoted above, though written many years ago, seem every bit as topical today. In greater areas more reliance must be placed on machinery so that all jobs such as mowing, edging and hedge-clipping can be done in a minimum of time, and other work reduced by the right use of the right plants. As an example I would cite the gardens of Anglesey Abbey, Cambridgeshire, a property of the National Trust. This is surely an exceptional case of how, with a simple design and concentrating the floral displays into definite, controlled areas, a vast garden (a hundred acres) can be tended satisfactorily by a small staff (six men). Grass in various states of close- or rough-mowing, shrubs, trees and an unashamed acceptance of the value and beauty of common and Irish ivy as ground-cover under trees, minimize the maintenance.

Side by side with the general shrinkage in individual size of the private garden the area devoted to public gardening has grown beyond all conception. This is surely the biggest single trend in twentieth-century gardening. The park superintendents wield an enormous and increasing influence, particularly those who aim at more modern trends and fashions rather than slavishly carrying on with extravagant and sterile ideas. There are not only the public parks themselves, but the numerous big sites such as are found around factories, blocks of flats, hospitals, the new universities, schools and experimental stations. In addition there are the vast amenity areas under municipal or ministry control around our new towns and alongside new roads and motorways.

Collectively, here is a range of gardening of limitless variety. Gardening today opens out like a fan, extending, widening and spreading in every direction, and though none of us have the same ideals, we all suffer from the lack of one thing: TIME. Do we not all long for more time to tend our garden? Do not those in authority all say that they 'cannot get labour'? Or if they could get it that they cannot afford it? The same sort of cry meets us everywhere. The answer is, I am convinced, that in gardens great or small the plants themselves can be chosen and encouraged to do much of the work. This is the message I am trying to put over in this book. I suggest that as a preliminary you should walk round your garden or your neighbour's, or examine the borders of a public park, and make a note of how many square yards are so well covered with shrubs and plants that no cultivation is needed. The alternative is to note how many areas need digging and hoeing (or treating with weedkiller). Another exercise would be to try to assess the man-hours taken to mow a stretch of public lawn that is never walked upon and does not really contribute to the beauty of the design.

The planting of ground-cover might well be called the carpet bedding of today, but it is the antithesis of the Victorian concept, being concerned, as I have been at pains to shew, with avoiding work, creating a natural appearance and helping to maintain soil fertility. The history of gardening has ever been closely related to social and other fashions, and we can create a new approach to gardening today if we are ready to forget preconceived ideas and artificiality and to follow nature.

THE VALUE OF GRASS

To get back to the fundamentals suitable for an introductory chapter, we must consider the use of lawns. Where frequent access is to be given there is no doubt that mown grass is the best ground-cover. As far as I am aware there is no suitable alternative. In public gardens it is the most effective green covering and wears away only with excess traffic, and even this can often be minimized by controlling, or enticing to widely divergent routes, the traffic in general. In small and many large private gardens it provides the ideal restful contrast to other plantings.

It is when we start to cope with the bigger areas—public parks, roadside embankments and amenity areas around great modern buildings—that grass alone, or with trees and shrubs, begins to pall. Apart from the closeness of mowing there can be little variation—and I cannot stress too strongly the delight and relief obtained when close-mown walks lead one practically and aesthetically through a large rough-mown area. Lawns bring with them monotony and the noise of the motor mower. I long for the day when silent machines are within reach of us all, leaving us with the gentle whirring of the blades and the unadulterated smell of cut grass.

Repeating, therefore, that where traffic is heavy there is no real substitute for grass, with only the variation of close-mown and rough-mown areas, I would put in a plea for areas of ground-cover plants in our bigger schemes of public gardening or roadside embellishment. This plea would fall under several headings; to be considered are the steep banks, the marshy ground and areas where tree roots or rocks make mowing difficult; and also the places where soil conditions and lack of light make lawns a poor proposition. Ground-cover would be welcome in such places, and would, surely, be the obvious and the practical solution. It would provide total cover and also serve as a complete contrast to the areas where mown grass would be successful.

It is this contrast which is so important and gives an aesthetic, though practical, twist to what is often considered only in a practical way. We need contrast of surface in gardening just as we do in architecture. Brick, stone, wood, concrete or other materials are satisfying when used skilfully in contrast, and I see no reason why mown grass should be considered the only flat surface to set off our ornamental borders. There must be many acres of land set aside for public use which are put down to grass simply because it is green and thought to be economical, though seldom used to walk upon. Rampageous ground-cover plants could be used instead; they create satisfying contrasts to mown grass in height, colour and texture and require far less upkeep when once established. They need far less in the way of fertilizers, because if the right plants are chosen they will continue in robust health for many years, feeding themselves with their own dead leaves and others which collect among their foliage. If any rejuvenation is found necessary, certain fertilizers can be applied among them, and the plants do not suffer if occasionally walked upon to do the winter shrub-pruning.

THE DISADVANTAGES OF GROUND-COVER PLANTS

There are no disadvantages connected with ground-cover plants in borders if chosen with circumspection. They are comparatively cheap to buy, slow or quick to increase according to variety, and easy to plant.

As a substitute for grass it must be admitted that they have some drawbacks. The initial cost would be greater; the planting by hand would also be more costly, though robot transplanters would cope easily with large areas, the rows disappearing eventually, and especially with the spreading types of plants. The cleaning during the first season or two is best done by hand. In all such work of cleaning, whether by hand, machine or weedkiller, in big areas or small, a study of the habit and life-cycle of prevalent weeds is the best aid to quick and effective control. After establishment, and having achieved a close uniform cover, the two possible disadvantages are tree seedlings and vermin. Mice are a nuisance in established gardens anyway; under high cover rabbits could find homes. Occasional cutting of the plants almost to ground level by machines would make control of vermin easier, the application of fertilizers more practicable, and very speedily a new carpet or thicket would develop.

Tree seedlings cannot be disposed of except by hand work. Seedlings of oak, ash, beech, horse chestnut and other trees spring up with remarkable speed when they find a humus-laden soil to foster them, and brambles are also a source of trouble. But an annual examination of affected areas should keep this matter under control.

'Friends' often offer surplus ground-cover plants to those starting with an empty garden. My advice is always to accept clump-formers, but avoid like poison *Veronica filiformis*, and take care where you put *Fragaria indica*, *Lamium galebodolon* 'Variegatum' and *Verbena corymbosa*, and also those which increase by underground shoots.

IN GENERAL, AND ABOUT THIS BOOK

Each and all of us have similar problems. Our gardens, unless run on very specialist lines, should be a setting for our houses.

In the great gardens of the past, and some of the bigger modern designs, the house acts as a focal point in the design of the garden; in the smaller schemes of today the garden becomes, as it were, an outdoor room, ready for careful and tasteful furnishing, to be in beauty throughout the year. Those which fall between the two sizes may often be likened to a series of rooms, each one furnished in a different style. Therefore we should decorate them with all our means and ability, though the fund of creative art varies in every one of us. We can experiment with our shrubs and plants to a certain extent, but it is by no means as easy to move an established shrub as to transfer the positions of the sideboard and the television set; patience and hope however are two invaluable characters which I find can be increased in even the most impatient of us by cultivating the garden and growing plants.

This book is directed entirely to ornamental gardening. Other books have been written about the production of high-quality fruit and vegetables by the aid of mulching with many and indeed any forms of compost or decaying vegetation, though obviously not with the use of ground-covering plants. My arguments are addressed as much to young gardeners as to the old; the young, perhaps, who are creating new gardens but who want time for other recreations, and the old who are possibly finding their garden is getting too much for them.

The following chapters attempt first to see where this ground-cover idea stands in relation to natural laws, or shall we call it the more scientific approach; how to prepare for planting and an outline of the details of cultivation, and thus on to the classification of the plants themselves, examining each one in detail and considering its merits and uses—or limitations and disadvantages—in our gardens, and finally the use of ground-cover in our public areas.

Postscriptum. Readers have been kind enough in the past to write appreciative letters about my earlier books with special reference to the hand-drawn plates and the occasional literary flourishes and snatches of poetry, among other things. This book is aimed rather differently; I have tried to make it a reference book, not only for those already started in the pursuit and cultivation of ground-cover plants, but also for those who are new to the idea and perhaps new to gardening. Therefore I have chosen photographic illustrations which convey the appearance of a mass of foliage rather than the individual leaf, however beautiful it may be.

Similarly, hoping that I have written a book of reference, I have deliberately avoided filling the pages with irrelevant botanical asides, and have tried to keep my pen concentrated on practical points connected with cultivation and also with the aesthetic uses of the plants enumerated. Only time and readers' letters will prove whether I have been successful and I hope that *kind* readers will send me a note of errors and omissions, for which I tender apologies and thanks in advance.

It occurs to me that a verse from *The Indian Emperor* by John Dryden (1631–1700) is apposite:

> See how on every bough the Birds express
>   In the sweet notes their happiness.
> They all enjoy and nothing spare;
> But on their Mother Nature lay their care:
> Why then should Man, the Lord of all below
>   Such troubles chuse to know
> As none of all his Subjects undergo?

I

Natural and Scientific

EXCEPT for arid sandy wastes and rocky hills the whole of the
surface of the earth uncovered by snow and ice is clothed by
nature with verdure of one kind or another. Even the oceans
support a varied sea-bed flora. Fed by decaying leaves, dying
roots and the detritus of animal life, a permanent covering is
maintained, though it may vary in composition and be influenced
by fundamental changes over periods of time.

Nature's ground-cover is infinitely varied. It may be high or
low. As we go about the country we see many untouched
examples. High ground-cover is provided by thick woods of
beech or fir; they support little else but a few mosses and fungi,
the beech wood in spite of its luxuriant and excellent mulch of
leaves and because of its dense and greedy surface roots, and the
fir wood mainly because of the permanent gloom, but also because
of the mat of decaying needles which, unlike leaves, remain where
they fall. At the other extreme are the estuary banks and marshes
or the mountain slopes, or the floor of thin mixed woodland, each
covered with a company of plants that can best maintain themselves in the local conditions, related closely to climate and soil.
Or our acid heathy commons may be cited, supporting a well-
recognized and fairly limited number of plants: pine and birch,
gorse, heather and bracken, and sundry small grasses, lichens and
mosses. Similarly an area on a chalk slope would have guelder
rose, wayfaring tree, dogwood and spindle growing up to some
ten feet while beneath is a rich mixture of grasses, scabious,
knapweed, bedstraw, thyme and harebells. Either of these last
examples emphasizes how ground-cover fosters the fertility of the
soil and completes the picture; the selection of suitable denizens
has been going on for millions of years and any intruding plants
that cannot stand the conditions and company languish and die.

Everywhere leaves—alive or dead—prevent the sun from baking the soil, and the roots of the plants prevent erosion; natural compost is supplied to the surface of the soil and nature does no digging (except through the agency of worms and moles), nor hoeing, staking, tying and clipping. Diseases and pests are seldom rife until the balance is upset.

Our gardens are rather different. In each little plot we try to grow plants that are likely to be hardy from even more diverse homes than the few suggested above, from all over the world, regardless of the chemical content of our natural soil and the vagaries of our climate; we try to coax them into thriving by applying 'goodness' in one form or another to the soil, and as often as not we bury this material. We dig and hoe open spaces, have to stake and tie our tall plants, vitiate the health of many of our most popular plants by excessive inbreeding, remove and often burn all decaying matter; and, in short, we try to grow what would normally not be found in our gardens and at the same time to remove almost everything that tries to grow of its own accord.

We gardeners are as a consequence very apt to live in a kind of artificial world. We try to impose our will on the plants, which is another way of saying on nature. We have to resort to all sorts of fungicides and insecticides simply because the plants we grow are unsuited to the culture we give them. There is no doubt that the highly bred strains of plants are infinitely more prone to disease and insects than the wild species, and this is due not only to the breeding but also to the shortcomings of the microclimate of our gardens and our soil. We are getting a 'pest and disease' complex, which is increasing yearly. There is no doubt that gardening is in some ways becoming a battle against nature rather than developing along the lines she uses. Fortunately pioneer spirits in farming are now turning back to the infinite value of humus, looking towards sowing without reversing the topsoil; the danger of wholesale spraying against pests and disease is at last being brought to the fore and research is being directed to establish the cause of these troubles rather than to curing them regardless of the consequences.

If we were to take any row of a dozen gardens, where trees, shrubs, perennial plants, bulbs and lawns are the main characters, and remove all the fences and the few paths, we should be left with something much like nature's arrangements envisaged in the second paragraph of this chapter. In general effect, according to the height of the trees, it could be called thin forest or open woodland. This is in any case what obtains in the large plantsmen's gardens of today. It is what may be called gardening in four layers, the trees anything from twelve to fifty feet perhaps, casting their dappling of shade gently across the open areas during the day, the shrubs acting as screens and shaping the views, while around them flow the clusters of dwarf bushes and ground-cover plants interspersed with bulbs, all individuals being placed carefully, depending on whether they grow best in sun or shade. This would be an approach to gardening close to nature's methods, and if the entire area of soil is covered with some form of verdure, and the dead leaves are not removed from it, fertility in my experience is maintained. If our imaginary garden is filled with a suitable selection of hardy shrubs and plants from the wild, as opposed to highly bred strains of popular plants, we shall find that diseases and pests seldom trouble us—apart from the birds, which every year seem to find one more kind of toothsome bud or berry to devour prematurely.

It will be seen from the above that ground-cover can be of any height in nature or in the garden. The prerequisite is to produce leaves—leaves everywhere, and plenty of them. They may be provided by quite high trees or low ones like fruit trees, and under them can be grown shrubs which may cover the soil themselves by widespread branches, or be erect in growth providing places for yet smaller shade-loving shrubs or perennial plants beneath them, or the area may be open to sun and wind and covered with a sun-loving sward of heather or creeping plants, or yet again quite high herbaceous plants can be used, of kinds that make thickets and do not need frequent division and staking. Every shrub or plant must thrive; it must be chosen as probably suitable for its position, and it must be tried elsewhere if it does not thrive. Plants are contrary things sometimes, and do not always grow just where we choose. Any plant or shrub mentioned in this book, if it is thriving, will make a satisfactory, dense, weed-proof cover; if it does not thrive it will grow thin, with the result that weeds will find space to pierce it.

Fortunately gardeners in this country have such a wide variety of plants to select from, made available by numerous excellent nurseries, to say nothing of friends' surpluses, that none need despair of covering his ground and filling his garden with beauty, no matter what the soil, climate or aspect. If he goes about the job in the right way and selects plants suitable for his conditions he will achieve success, but if he doggedly persists in growing dahlias in a marsh, rhododendrons on chalk, or daphnes on poor sand, he will find gardening an uphill task—and an expensive one. If he goes hand in hand with nature all will be well.

At the same time we must not let natural ideas run away with all formal design. Even though the use of ground-cover plants may be the epitome of natural gardening, a great number of the shrubs and plants are of neat appearance, creating a level carpet of greenery of almost any height, perfect for formal as well as for informal schemes. In large gardens and parks where there are walls and steps of substantial masonry, coupled with steep grass banks, grass mowing is often particularly difficult. Suitable ground-cover plants are available for every possible site, and well-designed formality can be as restful as the best informal planting —very often more so, though the fact that it is formal generally necessitates a tidier state of upkeep and the choice of neater plants.

2

Preparation, Cultivation, Planting and Maintenance

THERE are a few very vigorous ground-cover plants, such as petasites, trachystemon and peltiphyllum, and shrubs such as *Viburnum plicatum tomentosum*, which, when once established in conditions to their liking, will gradually spread over a sward of weeds of all but the most persistent kinds, and smother them. It may as well be placed on record, however, that it is of little use expecting cover-plants to thrive when planted in holes in grassy, weedy areas. It is essential to give the plants as good a start as anything else, planting them in clean, well-dug ground. But read a little further please, before you consign the book to the dustbin in despair.

In the old days, starting a new garden was a back-breaking job. Today those who dislike digging can hire machines—or even buy them—but they are not likely to need them again if they adopt the scheme of work I am outlining. Machines, quite small ones or really big tractors, are available for clearing and ploughing and harrowing. There are excellent weedkillers such as simazine and paraquat which spell death to all normal weeds, and another invaluable discovery, amitrole (aminotriazole), which in one application will destroy persistent things like couch-grass and ground-elder; both this and paraquat are neutralized immediately on contact with the soil and leave no deleterious effect, nor will they injure the underground roots of trees and shrubs—though damage will be caused if the spray reaches the bark or exposed roots. They are all available in brands with proprietary names. In areas where there is nothing of any value growing at all the old sodium chlorate is highly effective, but remains active in the soil, particularly if heavy, for a year or more, and it is dangerous to

5

use on slopes, is corrosive and inflammable. Simazine is safer.
Both are apt to wash down into other areas in heavy rains. It will
be obvious that paraquat and aminotriazole do not do this. (For
proprietary brands, see Appendix I.)

If machines can be brought into use they will destroy all annual
weeds and turn over the soil in one operation; where persistent
weeds are present it is better to use weedkiller first, and then to
cultivate the entire area by machinery or digging. For in spite of
all the no-digging ideas with which these chapters are concerned
I am still of the opinion that a thorough initial cultivation is the
best preparation for a garden, and there is no doubt that digging
is better than mechanical cultivation. By digging we can remove
brickbats and other buried treasure and readily see when too much
subsoil is being brought to the top, and we avoid the weight of the
tractor rolling down the subsoil. Because I like to keep the bulk
of humus in the top layer of soil I consider that turning the soil
over by one spade's depth is sufficient, but if the subsoil is clay or
chalk or gravel it is better to loosen it if possible, letting in some
grit or humus to encourage rooting.

I think it is hardly necessary to stress the importance of making
the top layer of soil fertile with the addition of some form of
humus, used together with long-lasting organic fertilizers such
as bonemeal or hoof-and-horn meal. Ground-cover plants respond
quickly to good soil and will increase fast if this extra care is
given at the outset.

LIMY SOILS

Likewise it is vital to know whether the soil is alkaline (limy)
or not, and if not, whether it is neutral or downright acid. These
terms can confuse beginners, but, as I have been at pains to
indicate in this book soil preferences of the various plants, I think
a little space devoted briefly to this matter may be advisable.
Rhododendrons, azaleas, all ericaceous plants, camellias, kalmias
and *Hydrangea macrophylla*, *H. serrata* and the Hortensia varieties
and many lesser things will thrive only in acid or at least neutral
soil. (It is true that these hydrangeas will grow in limy soils, but
they seldom luxuriate in them.) It is usually possible by examining
local gardens or neighbouring native plants to be tolerably certain

1 *Viburnum plicatum tomentosum* 'Mariesii' is undoubtedly the ideal tall shrub for covering the ground.

2 Several of the lace-cap forms of *Hydrangea macrophylla* such as 'Blue Wave', 'Lilacina' and 'Mariesii' provide a high cover of greenery, clothed to the ground.

3 A variety of the cherry laurel, *Prunus laurocerasus*, 'Zabeliana', with conspicuous, nearly horizontal habit and narrow leaves.

4 A wide border filled with the grey-leafed dwarf willow *Salix lanata* 'Stuartii', backed by the Pfitzer juniper and surrounded by heaths.

5 All the Japanese evergreen azaleas provide admirable cover for the ground as well as a scintillating floral display and autumn tints.

6 *Rhododendron pemakoense*, a dense, spring-flowering evergreen which spreads slowly by underground shoots.

7 A single plant of *Rhododendron* (Azalea) 'Mucronatum Bulstrode'. All of these require lime-free soil.

8   A mass of grey *Senecio laxifolius* in front of blue ceanothus, backed by rhododendrons. Evergreens.

9   The grey-green wiry stems of *Ephedra gerardiana* bring an unusual texture to a sunny or shady border.

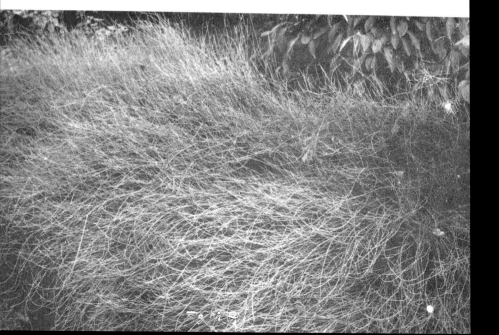

10   The slow-growing but dense *Juniperus sabina* 'Tamariscifolia'.

11   Evergreen perennial candytuft, *Iberis sempervirens* 'Snowflake', a sheet of white in spring.

12 The perfect evergreen carpeting shrub for sun or part shade in lime-free soil, *Arctostaphylos nevadensis* (of gardens).

13 *Rubus tricolor*, the most rapid carpeting shrub for woodland conditions, eventually mounding itself up to 3 ft. Glittering evergreen leaves on stems covered with red-brown hairs. Grows 10 ft in a season.

14 *Vinca major hirsuta* (*V. m. pubescens*) is less ornamental in flower than the species itself, but is a more successful colonizer. *Vinca minor* and its varieties are better for small gardens. Evergreen.

15 *Cotoneaster microphyllus*, with very dark green, tiny leaves, white flowers, and crimson berries in autumn. A vigorous carpeter for sun or shade. Evergreen.

16 The prostrate rosemary, *Rosmarinus lavandulaceus* (R. *officinalis prostratus*). For sheltered maritime gardens it is an admirable evergreen ground-cover.

17 The carpeting or sprawling shrub, *Euonymus fortunei vegetus*, which thrives in shade or sun. Evergreen.

18   *Rosa* × *paulii* 'Rosea'. Clear pink flowers—or white in the type—cover a fast-spreading mound, proof against weeds and trespassers.

19   Although it does not establish itself as quickly as some plants, *Pachysandra terminalis* is splendid where a dense evergreen cover is needed for large areas.

20 Contrast in size. *Hedera canariensis* 'Variegata', whose large, dark leaves are marked with grey-green and creamy white, and *H. helix* 'Sagittaefolia variegata'.

21 *Hedera colchica* 'Dentata' has large, dull green leaves and is a rapid carpeter for shady places. Ivies are excellent carpeters.

22 *Leucothöe fontanesiana* (*L. catesbaei* of gardens). Hung with white flowers in summer; the leaves become burnished in winter. For lime-free soil.

23 *Xanthorhiza simplicissima* (*X. apiifolia*), a high ground-cover whose leaves turn to rich colours in autumn.

24 *Gaultheria shallon*, a rampageous spreader, valuable for its evergreen leaves, pinky-white flowers and blue berries. All three spread by underground shoots.

25 *Left:* Creamy flower sprays overtop the magnificent rough foliage of *Rodgersia aesculifolia*. High deciduous cover for rich, moist soil.

26 *Below:* Rich green leaves of great size, red-purple beneath, smother all weeds around the ornamental rhubarb *Rheum palmatum* 'Atro-sanguineum'.

27　*Hosta undulata univittata* has dark green leaves striped with creamy white. The flowers are pale lilac.

28　*Hosta lancifolia* produces its showers of rich lilac flowers in September over dark green leaves.

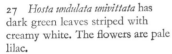

29　*Hosta albomarginata* has a white edge to its leaves, and particularly showy lavender blooms in summer.

30 *Left:* Flat grey-green leaves edged with white and pale green are found in *Hosta fortunei* 'Marginato-alba'. The flowers are soft lilac.

31 *Below:* Greyish-green leaves edged with yellow. *Hosta fortunei* 'Obscura Marginata'. The flowers are soft lilac.

32 *Right: Hosta sieboldiana* 'Elegans' (*left*), and *H. fortunei hyacinthina*, which has glaucous blue-grey leaves not quite so large as 'Elegans', but a far better display of rich lilac flowers. The creeping *Geranium macrorrhizum* does not choke the hostas.

33 *Below: Hosta sieboldiana* 'Frances Williams'. Leaves blue-grey broadly edged with yellow. Lilac-white flowers; the photograph shews seed pods which in all *H. sieboldiana* varieties are extremely ornamental in winter.

34 Violet-purple, bell-shaped flowers of *Hosta ventricosa* 'Variegata', whose dark, shining leaves are edged with creamy yellow, growing alongside the pale green *H. plantaginea grandiflora* with a foreground covering of purple-leafed ajuga.

35 *Hosta plantaginea grandiflora*, with pale green leaves and fragrant, pure white flowers in October.

whether a soil will grow these genera or not, but there are many neutral soils which—with a little encouragement from acid peat and other humus—can be made to support them. To the contrary there are excessively acid areas of the country where lime and other important ingredients should be added before the general run of shrubs and plants can be luxuriant—even those that cannot thrive in limy soils. I have known rhododendrons on extremely acid soil (pH 3·5–5·0) benefit remarkably from a dressing of nitro-chalk in showery weather in spring.

It is one thing to test the soil for lime content by use of a small readily purchased outfit [1] and another to have the possible lack or superabundance of important trace elements revealed by complete analysis. This is always best if serious gardening is contemplated in an area with which one is not familiar, and may save a lot of worry and trouble later. In short, the soil and its quality and content are extremely important matters for any kind of gardening, and should receive careful attention from the start.

DRAINAGE

When taking over a new garden one of the most important things is to consider the drainage. More plants are killed or linger in poor health through bad drainage than through anything else. It is indeed a good idea to watch the garden for a year, inquiring about neighbours' troubles and difficulties, cleaning and tidying whatever may be on the ground, digging a few essential areas to act as nurseries for gifts, propagating ground-cover and allowing bulbs to increase, and generally getting used to the area, climate and soil. Weedkillers can be applied where necessary. Such a delay is never waste of time. During this period the temporarily planted things can easily be moved, the ground-cover and bulbs will have increased at least twofold, and ideas will have crystallized. Drainage can be attended to before any planting is done, and it can be seen which areas, if any, are moister or drier than others. This all refers to a virgin plot as much as to an old-established garden, where there may be the usual signs of neglect, bad design and plants which do not appeal to us. Areas should be cleared piecemeal, one at a time; the most interesting work in gardening is the designing and planting, not the maintenance,

[1] B.D.H. Soil Testing Outfit.

and so I should counsel a gradual bringing under control of the area, year by year. Another good reason for proceeding slowly is the enormous difference in light and shade occasioned by the changing seasons; areas which may be bright and sunny in June may be dark and shady in autumn, and anything planted in them will not be lighted by a low sun. This all needs careful study to achieve the maximum results.

WHEN AND HOW TO PLANT

If I were starting a garden today I should try to decide on the main features and overall design and if possible plant whatever trees might be needed during the first winter where the ground is clean. I should like, too, to plant important shrubs, particularly evergreens, which will govern views and give reasons for bends in paths or bulges in borders, or that may be needed for screening purposes. As mentioned above I should also want a nursery bed for increasing ground-cover plants, so that I could have available a goodly number of each when ready for them. When the ground is satisfactory in regard to drainage, fertility and weeds, it is time to prepare and plant the borders and then dig and sow the grass areas. The bulk of shrubs can then be planted. If perennial weeds may still be present, the placing of the ground-cover plants should be delayed and the area should be fallowed and cleaned for a whole summer, forking out any remaining roots. Then in September or October the accumulated cover-plants can go in, divided into small rooted pieces; they can be interplanted with bulbs—where required and suitable—a year later or at the same time.

A far better cover, uniform and attractive, is achieved more quickly by pulling plants apart and putting in quite small pieces fairly closely than by setting out bigger clumps and waiting for them to meet.

Until the shrubs and ground-cover have spread and linked together there will be some hoeing and hand-weeding to be done, unless we have at our command plenty of humus. This can be partly rotted leaves (including freshly fallen ones), chopped bracken or straw, general compost, grass mowings, wood shavings and sawdust, peat, spent hops, in fact any form of vegetable refuse that is weed-free. (See also Appendix I.) It is worth noting here that sawdust is apt to 'cake' and needs stirring now and again, and that both this and wood shavings are liable to absorb nitrogen out of the soil; this can, however, be readily reinforced by a teacupful of sulphate of ammonia per square yard in late spring; on acid soils, but where lime-haters are not to be grown, a better alternative is nitro-chalk. A trap for the uninitiated is in the collecting of leaf-mould. If raked off limy ground it will obviously contain a certain amount of limy soil, but what is not always realized is that the leaves off trees growing on limy soil contain an appreciable amount of lime; annual application of these leaves or the resulting leaf-mould to beds specially prepared with lime-free ingredients may cause trouble.

Those who find humus too difficult or costly to obtain because of their dwelling in towns can resort once again to the selective weedkillers, skilfully applying them between the plants until they have linked together. On impoverished soils this is also the moment to apply a good mulch of farmyard manure, if necessary and if obtainable, between the ground-cover; the shrubs should be well rooted and able to benefit from the added nourishment. Deciduous herbaceous plants (apart from those with woolly leaves) do not suffer if manure is applied among them in autumn, the rains washing the goodness through. The alternative is the use of a general fertilizer, sprinkled around them in showery weather in spring, or, better still, bonemeal used in autumn or winter. On an acid soil, away from lime-haters, nitro-chalk is very beneficial and easy to apply, being granular; on neutral or limy soils a balanced fertilizer is ideal. All fertilizers should be used in conjunction with humus of some kind. Spent mushroom-bed manure, with its admixture of chalk, is ideal for lime-tolerant plants. If it is feasible and desired, nutrition can be given through an appliance fixed to a garden hose, or simply used in a watering-can if the area is small.

These points all call for common sense, and I think I have written enough to shew that fertility of the soil should be con-firmed at the outset and can be maintained in after years. This book does not pretend to give a complete guide to cultivation; there are many practical how-to-do-it gardening books available. These few notes may be of interest to those who want a little initial guidance, and further details will be found in the Appendix.

NUTRITION

Although out of place in our sequence of work in preparing and planting ground-cover, in order to keep fertilizers together in one chapter I feel it necessary to digress here a little. After some years certain plantings may fail from want of nutrition. As a rule, if reasonably suited to the conditions, the solid-clump-forming plants last indefinitely, but the colonizers are apt to grow thin. This is natural and quite understandable: a colonizing plant, whether its shoots grow over or through the soil, is by nature destined to move on to fresh ground, and its most vigorous growth is usually at the perimeter of the area, where its roots come into contact with soil on which it has not fed before. When these plants grow bare they should be given a top-dressing of humus together with a slow-acting organic fertilizer such as equal portions of bonemeal and hoof-and-horn meal. Together the humus and fertilizers are the next best thing to farmyard manure and are easier to apply. If such dressings fail to rejuvenate the plants, there is no alternative but to plant something else.

To return, having achieved our planting, we now have to wait for the ground-cover plants to link up. As the years go by, those originally placed around the shrubs of spreading habit will need moving out, ready for dividing and planting in the next areas to be brought under control. As an example it is surprising how a hardy geranium increases: probably five- or sixfold yearly. Vast stocks can be quickly raised, to cover large areas of ground, and as our slower, choicer ground-cover increases, the coarser things having done their work nobly and ably can be consigned to the compost heap or passed on to other gardeners. This is not to say that I should ever tire of geraniums, for any plant that looks beautiful and saves work is to me a priceless asset in a garden, and as soon as the plants—of whatever kind they may be—have linked together and collected their own dead leaves and others that fall around, amplified by what we can sweep on to the borders, the tcp few inches of soil will begin to take on a new colour and texture. The rather hungry-looking lower soil that we brought to the top will become rich, dark and crumbly, thoroughly infused with humus. This is nature's way, and it is an example that any of us can find in our gardens, and one of the most convincing arguments why manures, compost and all kinds of 'goodness' should be applied to the surface rather than be buried.

Nevertheless, though I advocate this whole-heartedly, I still think it a good plan to mix fine crumbly humus of some kind in the soil at the start, particularly round the sides of the hole one makes to plant a shrub. Especially is this so with shrubs that depend on humus, such as the entire rhododendron tribe and all its relatives, the heaths, camellias, hydrangeas and many more. In general the finer the root the more is humus needed at the start; hairlike roots do not readily take hold of clods of heavy soil.

On heavy limy ground one seldom comes across the rich black layer of humus-laden topsoil experienced on the acid sands. On lime the decomposition is hastened and thus the humus disappears quickly; more and more humus can be applied, but even then it is not as successful as that supplied by growing plants. Therefore planting should be closer on limy soils to hasten the eventual cover.

Heavy clay soils are usually too sticky to touch in winter. Early autumn or spring planting is therefore best, and subsequent cracking of the soil in periods of extreme drought can be minimized by a covering of humus to the depth of three inches or so. Deep cracking of soil with the consequent tearing and drying of roots causes havoc among plants and shrubs, large and small.

PLANTING BANKS AND SLOPES

The above remarks apply to normal gardens, reasonably level, on soils varying from light to heavy, limy or acid. On steep banks there are methods to overcome the disadvantages. If a bank is freed of weeds or plants and thoroughly dug, there may be some danger of having the soil washed down in a heavy storm, particularly if it is of a light, sandy nature. The best way of bringing such a bank under permanent trouble-free cultivation is to use weedkillers first, and when all is clear to plant the bank without the wholesale disturbance of digging. If it is a dry bank it is best to leave around each shrub or ground-cover plant a small hollow, so that rain is collected and directed to the roots. For greater areas where the ground slopes steeply coarse coconut matting can be pegged down after the initial cleaning and shrub planting; small 'sets' of cover plants can be dibbled through the netting and will have covered the entire area satisfactorily by the time the matting has rotted. Flat brushwood, such as is pruned off spruce fir trees, will serve the same purpose. Plants that trail will obviously be helped if pegged down here and there, and all these suggestions are of prime importance in windswept areas, and where soil is loose or light and subject to storm damage.

There is a comparatively new method of treating slopes of chalk or shale or similar poorly nourished soils where grass is the ultimate aim. First the bank is graded, then spread with a few inches of sludge or compost. Grass is sown directly on to this surface, and then sprayed with bitumen, through which it quickly germinates. On extra steep banks chicken wire or fibrous strands of various materials are sometimes used to hold the humus in position. The result is a good grass bank, but it is possible that some of the many plants mentioned in this book might achieve the ground-holding and ground-covering desired as easily, though not so quickly.

Ground-cover plants are also valuable in preventing erosion of banks by streams and rivers. For the smaller schemes any of the deep-rooting larger bog plants will help in wet areas and those with spreading roots will bind the higher reaches of the banks. Where the scale is vast, and large growing plants can be welcomed, a method of overcoming the further loosening of banks by normal planting is to insert long cuttings of shrubs closely over the area. Dry banks can be colonized in this way with yard-long cuttings of common privet (*Ligustrum vulgare*) inserted in holes made by a soil-auger; for damper positions dogwood (*Cornus alba*) and various willows, particularly bushy kinds like *Salix gracilistyla*, are useful. This method has been successful on banks which tend to become eroded by wind or by seepage of water from above.

VARIEGATED LEAVES

It is not generally appreciated that leaf colouring is affected by sunshine and shade. In considering the placing of plants and shrubs other than plain green, we have the category of densely felted—'silvery'—foliage and those of glaucous hue almost invariably preferring full sunshine. Both coverings are an antidote to hot sunshine. Even the glaucous hostas can tolerate more sun than the green kinds. Equally sun-loving are the purplish-leaved plants: the depth of colouring is enhanced by sunshine and they fade to dirty green tints in shade. As a general rule all yellow variegated leaves enjoy full sunshine, while yellow-flushed leaves (as opposed to those which are striped or otherwise marked) and all white variegated leaves are at their best in partial or full shade, according to the needs of the species.

SHADE IN THE GARDEN

In deciding on the number of trees we want in our gardens we need never be afraid of the amount of shade they will cast over the borders, though we may resent having insufficient sunny places for seats. There is such a wealth of plants to choose from that we can be confident of filling all shady borders with beauty to their fullest. There are certainly as many shade-loving ground-cover plants as there are sun-loving kinds. A lot depends on the soil. A garden on a cool retentive soil may provide admirable homes for a vast number of good plants without much shade, but a light sandy soil can support a greater variety of plants if shadows pass over it during the day, breaking the heat of the sun. And newly laid out lawns and borders will suffer much more from hot sunshine than those that are old established. Once again we can see how leaves help—on the trees, on the shrubs or on the ground, conserving moisture and cooling the air.

BULBS IN CONJUNCTION WITH GROUND-COVER

Any bulb that is known to thrive and persist, even increase, when planted in grass may be expected to grow well under certain ground-cover plants. The general rule is that the foliage of the cover-plants should not exceed one-third of the height of the foliage of the bulb. For instance, the small species crocuses and scillas would be excellent growing among cotulas and acaenas, and bluebells and the larger daffodils could pierce and grow well through a plant as high as common ivy. So long as the cover plants are of an insignificant kind, or their foliage and flower do not assume importance before June, bulbs can combine with them towards the picture of beauty. The smaller bulbs benefit from the anti-splash effect of the carpet of greenery. It just depends upon whether we can tolerate the limp dying leaves of the bulbs lying over the cover-plants for a few weeks or months after flowering. The only bulbs that should be used among the big clump-formers are such as snowdrops and aconites and other really early bulbs, which will derive strength from their leaves for the next season before the bigger plants smother them with foliage. I am firmly of the opinion that it is easier to plant bulbs immediately after flowering, with their leaves on, rather than in the autumn. To be able to do this we must have the bulbs growing in the garden, having set them out in nursery rows a year or two before. All kinds of spring-flowering bulbs have responded to this treatment in my experience, and one can visualize the effect so much better by having the position of each bulb marked above ground by its leaves, and also having their heights, colours and seasons fresh in one's mind.

PRUNING

None of the shrubs listed requires pruning in the ordinary sense of the word, but a number tend to become 'leggy' if they are not clipped or cut down once a year. Where this is advisable a note has been added to the introductory remarks following the name of the genus in the Alphabetical Table.

Most of the deciduous herbaceous plants will need an annual tidying, between autumn and spring. The evergreen types require practically no attention.

THE VERGES OF BORDERS AND BEDS

The treatment of the edges of a planted area can make or mar a garden. Except where the scheme is obviously 'wild' or 'natural' there is nothing that gives a garden so well tended an appearance as trim verges, and the furnishing of a border with quite small plants in front. In a small garden this gives us scope for yet a further selection of plants, while in a large garden a reiterated planting of verge-plants where the bigger things do not come right forward quietens the most diverse collection. Where the border or bed has a path defining it, it is a simple matter to encourage low plants to flow forward and soften the line; grass verges on the other hand have several problems, and one of he best solutions is to lay paving stones 1–2 feet wide just below the level of the grass—so that mowing is not made difficult—and over which the verge plants can grow forward here and there. But we cannot all afford this luxury, and in any case it gives a rather artificial and smart appearance.

Many of us prefer a mown edge, and this is where difficulties of maintenance occur. It is fatal to use a half-moon edging iron every spring: gradually the verge is cut away. Instead, edging shears should be used, and if on a light soil the verge gets out of line owing to the crumbling away of soil, a slit can be cut with the half-moon tool and the verge pushed forward, the slit being filled with soil and sown with grass. Good verge plants like bergenias, *Stachys* 'Silver Carpet', London Pride, *Geranium macrorrhizum*, tiarella, waldsteinia and others will grow forward till they meet the verge, avoiding that tiresome verge-weeding, and the grass fringe cut with shears can be left under the plants out of sight, avoiding all hand work. Where something much smaller is required we should use acaenas, cotulas, ajugas and *Sedum* 'Green Mantle'. The first two in particular will fill the hand-weeded edge and may grow into the lawn, but this will not matter. What is of vital importance is to have a lawn verge *composed only of non-running grasses*, and of course no running weeds, so that the lawn cannot grow into the border!

As shrubs and the bigger verge plants grow, one is tempted to cut away the grass so that they can go on spreading and increasing in beauty. This can usually be done on convex curves but seldom, without destroying the line, on concave ones. Where the verge is straight only a really big bush is important enough to stand out and dominate a broken line. Which brings us back to the old problem of choosing the right-sized plants from the start.

Starting a garden must therefore be, for all of us, a period of trial, and if we accept the conditions and work towards them we shall succeed—nature still rules, whatever we may do.

3

A Guide to the Alphabetical Tables and Rules for Planting

THANKS to the equable though often maligned British climate we are able to grow in these islands an astonishing number of plants, chiefly from widely differing latitudes of the northern temperate zone, and also quite a number from the southern. Apart from botanical curiosities and breeders' specialized strains, there must be well over thirty thousand different kinds of trees, shrubs, plants, bulbs and annuals in general cultivation today, with a great many more in the hands of specialists. By far the most distinct of these are species and geographical forms, the wild 'weeds' of other countries. In order that gardeners and botanists of any nationality may be conversant with their names, they are christened in Latin on discovery or later.

THE NAMES OF THE PLANTS

So far in these pages I have scarcely troubled you with Latin nomenclature, but from now onwards it will be the staple diet. There is no other. We are very little concerned with the breeders' strains and fancy varieties—plants recognized by such names as milkwort, snapdragon and the like, or named 'Yellow Glory', 'Mrs Smith' or 'Magic Carpet'. Our wildlings from other countries are recognized by a name for the genus, another for the species, and perhaps a further one or two for a form or variety. I shall not have to ask you to twist your tongue around such teasers as *Echinofossulocactus zacatecasensis* or *Polystichum polyblepharum fibrillosopaleaceum* because they, fortunately, do not concern us here, but many of the plants I recommend are by no means well known and may bear unfamiliar names. On the other hand we accept in Latin such old friends as geranium, erica and del-

16

phinium without trouble, and without much practice anyone can enjoy such euphonious epithets as smilacina and leucothöe. They soon become acceptable. It does not really help, for example, to translate *Caryopteris* into 'winged-nut'; it means no more to us, especially as the 'nuts' borne by the plant, though winged, are as small as a pin's head. Such transatlantic so-called 'popular' names as 'Silky-leaf Woodwaxen' and 'Bunchberry', or 'Box Elder' (which is related neither to a box nor to an elder) and 'Creeping Snowberry' (which is not related to a snowberry) to my mind merely add confusion to a subject which requires considerable intelligence in the first place.

What is far more troublesome is the energy some botanists misapply to their studies, for ever coining new names or going back to older originals, or subdividing species or 'lumping' several similar species into one. Equally troublesome are the gardeners and nurserymen who do not check their names, do not hesitate to put a new name to an old plant when in doubt about its real name, and do not give synonymous names in their lists when they are known. For these reasons and others we have frequent changes in nomenclature, and to try to overcome all this I have followed the nomenclature adopted by various up-to-date works and have added well-known synonyms to the text and more obscure ones to the index. (It is very disconcerting to go to Kew, for instance, and see a plant that one knows perfectly well bearing a label with some other name; one is never sure if it is a case of a misplaced label or an over-busy botanist.)

Until still greater pressure can be brought to bear at one of the periodic International Botanical Congresses we shall continue to suffer from this state of confusion. Man tries to name all individuals of nature and to devise 'keys' for their recognition by elimination, regardless of the fact that they have developed and spread without man's help and do not need it to reveal their inexhaustible diversity and beauty.

GENERA AND SPECIES

Each genus has a few general notes in regard to the main characters and uses of the various species selected, with further notes on

closely allied varieties or man-made forms or hybrids not mentioned in the main alphabetical column.

I have tried to give an indication also of the needs of the genus
or of separate species, such as good drainage, moisture, lime,
shade or other particulars. The suggestions are very cursory and
should only be regarded as the briefest of hints. A well-drained
soil can be moist or dry, cool or hot, even at the margin of a
stream. Areas which are geologically limy can provide acid soil
over magnesian limestone or soil with high alkaline content on
the Cotswolds or chalk downs, and even on these heights certain
areas of acid soil occur. A cool woodland can have hot sunny
patches in it. A heavy soil can be soggy or well drained. Many
more examples and extremes obtain, but with a little initial forethought, examination or advice, some idea can be obtained of
what we should concentrate on or cast aside in our gardens,
bearing in mind that the heavier soils will prove the more
difficult. Plants take longer to establish in these, whereas in a
light soil one can grow almost anything, though very often without the eventual luxuriance and opulence of those on heavy soils.

Because I think it interesting and often helpful from a cultivation point of view, I have given very briefly the country of
origin of each species. This can be useful after a little studying
of the world's varying rainfall and temperature.

DIMENSIONS

The heights next given apply somewhat differently to shrubs
and herbaceous plants. The figure given for a shrub indicates its
height in maturity, whether in flower or not. With a herbaceous
plant it is the height achieved by the main basal leaves when it is
established. It will be understood that the flowers ascend higher
than the leaves on most plants, while on a shrub they add little if
anything to the height of the branches. The 'distance apart for
planting' is the dimension I should use myself, to be fairly certain
that the plants would link up in, say, three years or so in a normal
fertile soil. It does not, obviously, indicate the eventual spread of
any static plant or shrub, which may root as it goes, nor of a
colonizer like lily-of-the-valley; both will spread indefinitely. The
heights, then, are fairly definite, depending on soil and climate,

while the distance apart is added to give a little idea of the speed of spread; again much depends on local conditions. These dimensions, so often omitted from publications, should be of special value to landscape architects and all who design gardens, but must be used with a little 'give and take'. With these figures anyone can assess how many plants are needed to cover a given area in a reasonable time.

A further qualification must be made here. Any recognized garden 'clone', or what we often call 'variety', is usually propagated vegetatively and is constant in every garden, apart from the latitude mentioned above. A species when raised from seed may vary considerably in character; many selected forms of species are also propagated vegetatively, and thus a certain type may be distributed by one nursery which is quite different from the stock of another. As a rule, however, variable species or species liable to hybridization are not raised from seed by reliable nurserymen. I mention all this because in a book like this, which seeks to be a general guide, the provision of measurements, times of flowering and other variable criteria is fraught with difficulty and liable to be misunderstood or taken too literally.

LEAVES

Being the most important factor in our scheme, leaves come next. They form the background and foreground and scenery, against which the actors—the flowers and fruits—display themselves for a short while. A well-designed 'set' on the stage can satisfy without the presence of actors. So much depends on the leaves; it has been difficult to describe them briefly without cluttering up the column with dimensions. Therefore we must take into consideration the height of the leaves when assessing what may be meant by 'large' or 'small', and of course the better the soil the larger will be the leaves, and indeed the plants as a whole. They may be rounded or long and grassy, entire or lobed, pinnate or ferny; smooth or hairy, shining or dull, light green, dark green, waxy, glaucous and grey, or velvety and covered with silvery hairs; variegated with white or yellow, or flushed all over with yellow or coppery purple. Furthermore their tints may vary

with the season. What an infinite wealth of material to have on
our palette, ready for the transformation scene!

DURATION

As evergreens are so essential in any garden my next column
concerns this character; thus we may visualize the effect of the
leaves for the whole twelve months of the year or for only five
or six. If autumn colour is provided by any of the deciduous
kinds it is mentioned in the notes concerning the genus or the
description of the foliage.

HEIGHT AND COLOUR OF FLOWERS AND FRUITS (IF ANY)

Next comes the height of the plant in flower if it is a herbaceous
perennial; from an earlier paragraph it will be obvious why this
figure is omitted from the shrub list. Some indication follows of
the colour, form and size of the flowers, though necessarily very
curtailed, together with a reference to the fruits. This term is
used to cover berries, pods, seed-heads and the like. The time of
flowering is naturally very approximate, varying with the district
and season. A plant in Aberdeen might flower two months later
than one in Cornwall, and the seasons especially in the spring will
vary in one district as much as three or four weeks from year to
year, though by midsummer this has usually become less noticeable.

MODE OF GROWTH

The effect given by the growth and foliage in the mass next
concerns us, usually known as the 'habit' of the plant. This is
highly important in planning. The following terms are used.

Hummock. A bun-shaped bush, large or small, suitable for ground-
cover when planted fairly closely together. The fact that they
need one another eventually to make a carpet, high or low, has
prompted me to call them 'social' shrubs. Examples: *Erica*
(heath), *Potentilla* (shrubby kinds).

Clump. Herbaceous plants which gradually increase in size from a fairly static rootstock. This term has been used in the tables also for plants which increase slowly but which are not, strictly speaking, either carpeters or spreaders. Examples: *Hosta (Funkia), Peltiphyllum.*

Sprawler. A loose-growing shrub which flops on the ground, but also produces irregularly erect shoots. Examples: *Jasminum nudiflorum, Fatshedera.*

Carpet. A plant or shrub increasing by surface runners or prostrate growths, sometimes rooting as they grow, the leaves or shoots rising to a uniform height above ground, or lying more or less flat. Examples: Strawberry, prostrate junipers.

Spreader. Extending its hold by what are best described as underground shoots or questing roots; above ground the stems generally rise to a uniform height. Examples: Lily-of-the-valley, *Xanthorhiza.*

Tuberous. Having swollen bulbous or tuberous rootstock which spreads in the soil or by the scratching of birds. Example: *Claytonia sibirica, Arisarum proboscideum.*

The term 'rooting' is applied to those plants whose stems often take root as they go, extending their colonies the more rapidly.

PLANTING TIME

Originally I intended to give a further column indicating the best planting time, but came to the conclusion this was unnecessary. Certain broad rules apply: evergreens are best moved in early autumn or in spring; deciduous plants can be moved at any time between autumn and spring; those which are described as tender or needing sheltered conditions, and those which have woolly leaves, are best moved in spring, also those needing particularly well-drained soil, so that they can become established before the autumn rains start to fall.

As there are many gardeners in Britain who like a purely shrub garden, I have thought it best to divide the Alphabetical Tables into shrubs and herbaceous plants. This arrangement also makes it easier to select a shrub or a plant from the lists. To these divisions are added the sub-divisions of climbing plants, conifers, ferns, grasses and annuals.

PROPAGATION

Propagation assumes high importance when one requires large quantities of cover-plants to fill new borders and hence in the last column I have hinted at the best methods of increase.

C = cuttings, which may be rooted in a sandy mixture in frames.

D = division. All rooting carpets and spreading plants are easy to lift and pull to pieces. Some big clumps are a man's job. A good method of increasing established hostas and other dense clumps is to take a sharp spade and cut one or two triangular sections out of them, like slices out of a round cake, filling in the gaps with good soil. The clumps will not suffer. Divisions can be made from looser-knit plants, after lifting a clump, by inserting two forks back to back and levering the roots apart. It will be found that different genera need different techniques and no rules can be laid down.

L = layers; a term denoting the bending of a shoot into the soil with its apex free, and keeping it in place with a peg or a stone. The operation takes several months, even a year or two. All plants described as 'rooting' do this without assistance, but produce roots more quickly with assistance.

R = root cutting; roots cut into short lengths in January and placed in a frame or cool greenhouse in boxes or beds of sandy soil will start life on their own. Portions of outlying roots can often be removed without lifting the parent plants.

S = seeds, which should be sown in pots or boxes in frames or glasshouse.

RULES FOR PLANTING

Although I have given some suggestions for planting at the beginning of each of the following chapters, there are a few main rules which apply throughout and I think therefore that they should be included here, for ease of reference and to govern all plans.

We can all cope easily with what I term the 'social' shrubs—those which make small or fairly large hummocks and join into a dense carpet, high or low, like the potentillas, the heaths, iberis, santolinas, to name but a few. We need not be afraid, either, of the spread of clump-forming perennials. Even the rapid creeping stems of *Duchesnea* (*Fragaria*) *indica*, *Rubus tricolor* and the invaluable ivies can easily be pulled up if they extend too far. But those plants which spread by underground shoots can be a trouble to the unwary and to those who plant indiscriminately.

Apart from trying to provide a rough-and-ready vignette of each plant in the Alphabetical Tables, the description of the growth or habit of each plant is intended also to act as a guide to planting. The stalwart dense clumps of herbaceous perennials, such as hostas, and the dense ground-covering shrubs, the dense hummock-forming shrubs, and also those whose rate of growth is shewn as gradual, may be regarded as 'buffers' against the rapid spreaders. The golden rule is to use these 'buffers' to separate the invasive kinds, and furthermore never to plant two rapid colonizers next to each other. A glance down the column of figures will speedily pick out the plants of rapid growth.

For instance, at the back of the border we might establish lily-of-the-valley—which could run to its heart's content, be out of mind except at flowering time, and cover the ground effectively —being prevented from spreading by big dense bushes and stalwart coverers *of greater stature*. A dense cover of greater height will always discourage a lower though rapid spreader. Occasionally one might plant for experiment two runners of similar height together; for a time the effect might be the high light of the garden, but one would always win. So my counsel is to go easy with the underground rooters like lily-of-the-valley and the thicket-forming shrubs; they can be a nuisance when their rampaging, questing roots spread into something else. Try them by all means; among them are some invaluable and beautiful ground-covers, but keep a watchful eye on their progress in your particular soil. In light soil they are apt to spread extra quickly, while from heavy soil they are difficult to remove.

Another source of trouble is found in the more vigorous carpeters—those bouncing, sub-shrubby plants whose stems arch over and root where they touch, like *Lamium galeobdolon* 'Variegatum' and the larger periwinkles or vincas. These need controlling by dense clumpy plants of greater height, and even then may find their way through them; they also clamber through the bases of shrubs and the lamium in particular can make an unsightly tangle in this way. In fact I should only plant them on bare ground under trees, where they are safe and admirable performers.

The main rules, I suggest, are that all plants which make any pretence at running, either over the ground or below it, should be kept in check by dense plants or shrubs of greater height; no two runners should be planted near each other; certainly always avoid planting an underground spreader next to a vigorous carpeter. These rules can be modified as experience increases.

Fortunately, even if we defy the above rules, we have a remedy today in the use of new weedkillers. A mere spray carefully applied from a tiny nozzle will banish them, should we have mistakenly given too much latitude to anything which is inclined to envelop the whole garden.

A further counsel concerns the mixing of herbaceous ground-cover with shrubs of any sort. Invariably I think we can success-fully carpet the foreground of shrubs with either dwarf shrubs or herbaceous cover. It always looks well, is obviously within the laws of nature, and is horticulturally pleasing. The reverse is not so acceptable. Though dwarf shrubs may look perfectly well in front of tall perennials in the summer, when winter comes the area will have an empty appearance. Therefore I should always prefer to use herbaceous ground-cover in front of taller perennials.

Terms and Abbreviations used in the Tables and Elsewhere

The different printer's type faces used in the names of plants in the Tables indicate as follows:

CAPITALS, bold face, for the genus or generic name.
small letters, bold face, for the species or specific name, or recognized botanical variety, form or strain.
'Single quotes' for a fancy name given to a cultivar or garden form or variety.

While single quotes are retained for fancy names in the text, generic and specific names are set in *italic* face.

×. A sign used to denote a recognized hybrid.

Cultivar (contraction of 'cultivated variety'). The vegetatively reproduced progeny of a hybrid, garden form, or sport variety, or of a strain of natural or hybrid origin which when raised from seed breeds reasonably true to type. The term 'clone' is also used and refers specially to vegetatively reproduced garden form, sport or hybrid.

Habit. Mode or style of growth.

Sport ('mutation' in genetic parlance). A shoot which is different in growth from the parent plant; these shoots usually remain constant when vegetatively propagated, and are then termed a garden variety or form or cultivar.

Annual. A plant living for one year only.

Biennial. A plant flowering and dying in its second year.

Perennial. A plant living for more than two years.

4

Shrubs

THE explanations given in the previous chapter are designed to help prospective planters to find their way through the Alphabetical Tables following, while the selected lists at the end of the book may help them to choose plants for their particular problems and positions. But it is one thing to describe or to select a shrub, and another to know how to use it, and I think therefore that as ground-cover is as much part of the design of the garden as of its economy a little examination of the uses of shrubs and plants in gardens may not come amiss.

Paradoxically I shall start my observations by harking back to the historical chapter and considering the herbaceous border. This was a style of gardening which waxed and waned during, roughly, the first fifty years of this century. It was fostered by such eminent writers and exponents as Gertrude Jekyll because it gave an opportunity for artistry in the arranging of plants and also because garden staff was available for such a time-consuming speciality; time-consuming, I should add, if developed to its best with the class of plants then used. The quantity of new shrubs coming into cultivation during the same period and earlier was immense, and the fashion for them and the desire to grow them took the gardening world by storm. They were used more as collectors' pieces than as colours on one's palette. Though there were many exponents of the shrub border, where each shrub was grown for its own interest, there was, so far as I know, nobody who gave us serious thoughts about artistry in the arrangement of shrubs.

The inevitable result was that the technique of herbaceous border design was adapted to shrub-planting schemes by the designers of large gardens. The same thing obtained when public parks were started. The cunning shapes of the groups of herbaceous plants—looking charming on paper and perfectly adapted to the provision of colour in graduated heights—were magnified into great groups and patches of shrubs. Examples can be seen throughout the country; many borders are still designed on these lines. Not only do the shrubs tend to be overcrowded, but they lose their individuality. From a herbaceous border point of view the popular plants (most of which have foliage lacking in diversity and character) are measured simply by height and colour, their stems being held erect by pea-sticks. Shrubs, on the other hand, are mostly individuals with height, width, 'line' and deportment, quality of foliage and seasonal displays of flower, fruit and foliage. If, as some do, they tend to fail on the score of line, deportment and perhaps fine foliage, they can be treated as 'social' shrubs, in which case it is not sacrilege to plant them in groups. Wide borders filled with first-class shrubs in which those in front obscure those behind—the whole becoming an interlocked thicket or 'shrubbery'—is what we should try to avoid, though each shrub in its turn may produce good flowers over its summit.

I am not going to suggest that the widest and largest borders of shrubs should necessarily have only one of each specimen, widely spaced; to gain the greatest beauty from them we must first study their height and width, and as there are many shrubs which in maturity will measure twelve feet across it is manifest that even a border forty feet wide and three hundred feet long— sufficient in size for most major schemes—is not difficult to fill.

The grouping of shrubs should depend on the value we place on the beauty of the individual plant. It may be said that every shrub has some beauty of line, and a well-grown isolated specimen will be satisfying, but some fulfil what is required of them better than others. Those whose branches arch over gracefully, or grow out horizontally, are particularly those which are most appreciated in isolation. And it is these which are ground-covers in their own right, so to speak. Many other shrubs tend to make V-shaped bushes, bare at the base, and need the presence of dwarf shrubs or plants as ground-cover beneath them. Well-known and popular examples of these erect shrubs are *Philadelphus* 'Virginal' and *Rosa moyesii*; it will be my task to select a few of the big rounded shrubs in a later paragraph.

The area to be planted, then, can be roughly divided into several sections each providing homes for different but complementary planting. At the back, but coming forward here and there, would be the less characterful shrubs, arranged in groups of varying numbers; in large borders each plant would be so placed that every group would present a bow-front, not a zigzag line, much like the effect of an individual bush in a smaller border. Under them would be shade-loving ground-cover plants, either dwarf shrubs or perennials. In the wider, empty parts of the foreground isolated shrubs of fine deportment would stand, either graceful and open, to be seen through, or great hummocks clothed to the ground and governing the view along the border. The remaining spaces—some wide, some narrow—would be filled with dwarf shrubs, mostly of the 'social' type: potentillas, ericas, etc., or perennial ground-cover, all varying from four feet down to six inches, and the whole a weed-proof cover of infinitely varied greens and textures, each shrub or plant providing its floral attraction in its turn. The main difference in this type of planting as opposed to the herbaceous border type is that, though punctuated here and there by high shrubs right in the front, the planting is lower over most of the border, if it is to be viewed close at hand. Borders seen mainly at a distance will require higher planting—and this brings me back to ground-cover again, as we can have high or low cover, either being equally effective.

A garden can be a very artificial thing. So often it includes a great range of the owner's favourite plants and they have to be fused, somehow, into a homogeneous whole. I shall conclude therefore that though some of us may be purists and desire to create a special effect in our gardens, some striving for a woodland scene, others for the open heath, and yet others for the 'glorious June' touch of roses and herbaceous plants or a tropical feeling with great leaves and exotic blooms, there will be many who are happy to plant heaths with roses, shrubs with herbaceous plants and bamboos with escallonias—the riches of all the world gathered together to satisfy our craving for variety in the furnishing of the garden, which will give beauty through the year, regardless of the origins or special qualities of each individual. It is this kind of garden that is sometimes called 'restless': there are so many different plants in it that it lacks cohesion, and the borders become collecting places. If a garden-owner desires to grow numerous different kinds of shrubs and plants I cannot see any reason why he should not; it simply makes his garden different from his neighbours'; but where a large collection of shrubs is planted there is no doubt that broad, frontal patches of lowly ground-cover plants do a lot towards linking the bigger shrubs together and giving a quietening effect.

LARGE, ROUNDED SHRUBS WHICH DO THEIR OWN GROUND-COVERING

Before examining in some detail the numerous shrubs in the Alphabetical Table let us see what is available in these large rounded shrubs. They are not included in the Table for two good reasons. They mature slowly, and are such grand shrubs by themselves that they should not be used collectively. Ample space should be given them and indeed they deserve in every way to stand on their own, or at least to be planted so that, although several of a kind may be together, the eventual aim is to give the impression of one good shrub. We sometimes have to cheat a bit in order to achieve quick results, but we should try to avoid planting large spectacular shrubs *in depth*, because this takes up space, usually, where something taller would be more telling.

These noble shrubs will become the most important pieces in the scheme, but they will all need temporary, lowly ground-cover while they are achieving their maximum spread, which may take ten years or more. Perhaps the best example to start with is one that is well known, *Viburnum plicatum tomentosum* in its varieties 'Mariesii' (Fig. 1) and 'Lanarth'; the stems are erect, giving forth horizontal fan-like branches, dense to the ground, often rooting where they touch, and providing in May spreads of white flowers like tablecloths, followed by rich autumn colour and sometimes red berries in October. A shrub like this will be the dominant plant wherever it is placed (Fig. 1).

Among evergreens there are *Garrya elliptica*, whose pale green catkins start to elongate in January; *Mahonia japonica*, of very slow growth but magnificent in foliage and of exquisite fragrance from its pale yellow bells throughout the winter; and the early-flowering, fragrant, yellow *Berberis sargentiana*. All are evergreens of considerable size, conforming to our requirements, and of

dominant character. Less characterful, but equally good at ground-
covering, are those two hardy escallonias 'Edinensis' and 'Langleyensis', their graceful branches and small leaves covered by
light and dark pink stars respectively at midsummer. They, like
the garrya, thrive best in the warmer counties. Known usually
in its variegated form—and thus called the 'spotted laurel'—the
splendid, rich green foliage of *Aucuba japonica* 'Crassifolia' has
few rivals. It is a male form; for the scarlet berries we must put
with it one of the green-leafed female forms, such as 'Hillieri'.
The berries do not colour until the spring and are ideal for
assorting with orange-cupped narcissus. About 1930 a new style
of wallpaper appeared; the design was of overlapping leaves and
berries, and I believe the aucuba was the model. The Victorian
overtones of this plant are slowly giving place to reasoned
appraisal of its sterling virtues, growing as it will in dark corners
in town or country. Equally hardy and easy-going is *Phillyrea
decora*, of dark, leaden green; the female has blue-purple berries
and both sexes bear sweetly scented, small, creamy flowers in
spring. Two of the most magnificent evergreens are *Elaeagnus
macrophylla* and its hybrid × *ebbingei*. The former is more splendid,
graceful and silvery in its foliage than the latter, but is not quite
so hardy; they thrive best in light soil in full sun, and bear
tiny, fragrant, silvery bells among the leaves in autumn. The
scent is free in the air and it is a great joy to pass by a bush on a
mild autumn day. *Choisya ternata*, the Mexican Orange, quick-
growing, and *Osmanthus delavayi*, slow-growing, are both noted
for their fragrant white flowers in spring, and complete this little
survey of a few large evergreens for our purpose. All will achieve
more than six feet in height and width when mature.

Turning now to the greater deciduous shrubs other than the
viburnum which do their own ground-covering, I find *Hydrangea
macrophylla* 'Blue Wave' first class (Fig. 2). This of all the hydrangeas provides a great dome of growth covered over with pink,
lilac or blue 'lace-cap' flowers for weeks in late summer and
autumn. It grows best in lime-free soils. Even larger, on the
ideal retentive acid or limy soil in shade, is *H. villosa*, but it is not
so dense. In frost-free places and very mild climates the wonderful
leaves of *Melianthus major*, grey-green, pinnate and magnificent,
will provide the same cover. In the sheltered coombes of Cornwall

and in Ireland this should be a popular plant. Rose 'Nevada', covered with scented cream flowers over its whole nine-foot diameter in June, and seldom without a bloom later, and *Philadelphus* 'Beauclerk', exceedingly fragrant with a small mauve eye, both qualify; very often *Rhus cotinus*, now called *Cotinus coggygria*, will grow similarly, or can be made to do so by cutting it to the ground and encouraging it to produce many shoots instead of one. *Cytisus* × *praecox*, with some clipping after flowering, also makes a fine rounded bush.

There are some conspicuous omissions from the above paragraphs—shrubs which demand at least a lime-free soil and preferably a good admixture of humus in one form or another, and the sort of semi-woodland conditions which we should give to rhododendrons. *Rhododendron* 'Britannia' is our yard-stick; this forms a most admirable dome of light green leaves in addition to being the most splendid of the scarlet varieties among the hardy hybrids, which will all stand full sun if necessary except on very dry soils. 'Blue Peter' is a good second, and others are 'Snow Queen', 'Harvest Moon' and 'Vulcan'. R. × *nobleanum* 'Venustum' and 'Christmas Cheer' are two compact winter-flowering varieties of similar value, and of smaller, slower growth we can select 'Temple Belle', 'Cowslip' and 'Humming Bird', in pink, cream and scarlet respectively. With striking, tabular growth, reminiscent of *Viburnum plicatum tomentosum* but of less size, is the Japanese azalea, *Rhododendron obtusum* 'Amoenum Coccineum', in flaming magenta. This is so handsome in growth that it should be grown in splendid isolation, but with creamy or pale yellow rhododendrons near by to quench its overpowering magenta-purple colouring. (Varieties that usually flower at about the same time are R. 'Damaris Logan', 'Butterfly', 'Dairymaid' and 'Cowslip', together with the species R. *ambiguum*.) The bulk of the Japanese azaleas have less majesty and are best relegated to our main list later.

Certain varieties of *Camellia japonica* make large dome-like shapes in time, clothed to the ground. Good examples of spreading habit are 'Lady Clare' and 'Tsukimiguruma'. The following are usually densely branched at the base of the plant: 'Nagasaki', 'Elegans', 'Latifolia', 'Apple Blossom', 'Asuniyovense', 'Preston Rose' and 'Gloire de Nantes'. Their glossy, dark leaves are of enormous value in the garden through the year, to say nothing of their glorious flowers. Less glossy in the leaf are the varieties of *C. sasanqua*, the fragrant, autumn-flowering species, successful in the south-west. There are several distinct colours available in named Japanese forms from white to crimson. In the United States of America 'Shishi-gashira' and others have their leading shoots nipped out to encourage them to grow horizontally. I have not tried this.

Varieties of *Camellia japonica* and *C.* × *williamsii* will thrive in much drier positions than rhododendrons, although it is often stated that the two genera require similar conditions. Camellias often appear quite fresh and unaffected by a long drought while rhododendrons near by are limp and drooping. A camellia does need, however, to be thoroughly established before it can sustain such trials. The same may be said about their hardiness: they are often claimed to be as hardy as a laurel, but the severe winter of 1962–3 proved that young plants are more tender than laurels, although little damage was done to big established bushes.

The slow-growing evergreen *Pieris taiwanensis* is magnificent with its lily-of-the-valley-like white bells in April, contrasting well with its dark, dull green leaves.

GROUND-COVER SHRUBS IN THE ALPHABETICAL TABLE

Notes on Some of the Best Kinds

It has been difficult to find a dividing line in order to make a fresh start here, but in the main the subjects of the following paragraphs are either quicker in growth or smaller than those I have already mentioned; and apart from a few they are far less dominant in habit. Following the arrangement of the Alphabetical Tables, in which all the shrubs are divided into various categories—hummock or 'social' shrubs, carpeters, sprawlers and spreaders—we have first to consider the numerous rounded bushes or hummocks.

Some are valuable evergreens for any fertile soil. There are two excellent laurels: the variant with the smallest leaves, *Prunus laurocerasus* 'Zabeliana', is an unusual shrub and very free-flowering, with narrow, glossy leaves borne on flat, fan-like branches (Fig. 3). It is one of the most attractive of evergreens and excellent for cutting. If there is no lasting winter snowfall to weigh them down the branches need a peg or two to keep them low, when they form excellent cover. The newer 'Otto Luyken' is a low, rounded bush for much closer planting; both are happy in sun or shade.

Some berberis are useful, although the dense-growing species are slow to achieve cover; they are long-term projects and of heavy value in design. *Berberis verruculosa* is a magnificent evergreen, impenetrably thick and sturdy, with glittering, small, dark leaves. *B. hookeri* is a size larger and *B. candidula* a size smaller; all these have pretty little pale yellow flowers and bloom-covered dark berries in autumn. Of similar colour in flower is *B. wilsoniae*, but it is almost deciduous. The species of *Berberis* gave a great fillip to the autumn shrub garden in the thirties on account of their free-fruiting capacity. Nowadays (when the garden-owner does his *own* gardening), these prickly shrubs are not so popular; but the coral berries of *B. wilsoniae* and allied species contribute uniquely to the autumn scene.

On account of its broad, ribbed, shining, evergreen leaves, *Viburnum davidii* approaches the value of a *Bergenia* for contrast with shrubs of lesser character. One male will be sufficient to pollinate several females, which have the added attraction of bearing vivid blue berries in autumn, though the male is more showy in flower. In part or full shade there are few better social shrubs than the skimmias. Their rich green leaves are smooth and satisfying, and the male varieties of *Skimmia japonica* are highly attractive to the eye and nose when in flower, *S. j.* 'Rubella' (*S. reevesiana* 'Rubella') being my favourite and highly ornamental in winter, decorated with heads of ruddy brown buds, opening in spring to tiny, starry, white flowers. As with the viburnum, the females are less ornamental in flower, but good forms bear brilliant scarlet berries in bunches throughout the winter.

Now we can consider some deciduous bushes. In utter contrast to all the above comfortable, rounded plants is *Ephedra gerardiana* (Fig. 9); it bears no leaves that could be recognized as such, but creates dense, dwarf or tall thickets of erect twigs like nothing so much as green wire. No other plant except perhaps *Cytisus* × *praecox* gives such an unusual and effective contrast in texture. Most forsythias are too large for the small gardens of today—

though they are not usually excluded—and I am reserving *Forsythia suspensa* for consideration later. Here I will simply include the short-growing, dense *F. ovata*; while its flowers are not by any means as showy as those of its larger relatives, it has the merit of flowering earlier than they do and also of covering the ground satisfactorily, being usually broader than high when established. Care should be taken to obtain the genuine low type; there are several tall-growing hybrid forms in gardens and nurseries. It is easily grown, likewise *Ribes alpinum* 'Aureum', a study in soft yellowish green in spring, and *Stephanandra incisa* 'Prostrata', whose arching, rooting stems are covered with prettily cut leaves turning to rich tints in autumn. The bushy dwarf willow, *Salix lanata* 'Stuartii', slowly makes a dome-shaped bush three or four feet across or more, gay with yellow catkins in spring and covered all summer with broad, woolly-grey leaves (Fig. 4). It is particularly useful as it is one of the few grey-leaved shrubs that grow equally as well in sun or in shade, but objects to excessive dryness at the root. All of the above are easy to satisfy, like the shrubby spiraeas from the miniature *Spiraea decumbens* to the taller variants of *S. japonica* and the hybrid *S.* × *bumalda*. They produce their large, flat heads of tiny crimson, pink or white flowers all through the summer months; *S. j.* 'Ruberrima' is a dense, bun-like little shrub of considerable charm. All of these look particularly well growing near to the dwarf, coppery-leafed *Berberis thunbergii* 'Atropurpurea Nana' or the variegated dwarf forms of *Euonymus fortunei radicans*.

While rhododendrons fit best with the smaller social shrubs in a later paragraph, we must now consider an extremely valuable group of popular and showy garden shrubs, the Japanese ever-green azaleas—valuable for flower, foliage and general garden furnishing (Fig. 5). Botanically they are, like the deciduous azaleas, all rhododendrons, but for our present purpose they are completely distinct, forming low-branching, twiggy bushes covered densely in small leaves, and, while the scene at flowering time is as brilliant as anyone could desire, the autumn colouring is varied and attractive too. It is not usual to find evergreens providing autumn colour: the terms are contradictory; but the fact remains that all the new leaves stay on the bush and are wholly evergreen, while older leaves turn colour at the approach of autumn and either fall after a few weeks' brilliance, or may even stay on in burnished tones and revert to green in the spring. Some turn yellow, some red, flame and orange, but all are linked together by the russet, maroon and metallic shades of the majority.

In planting these azaleas we can aim at bringing out their value in many ways; their floral colour and their autumn leaf colour are fairly obvious, but there is also a prolonged floral season between the early cultivars and the late, because some bloom in late April and some, like the hardy varieties of R. *indicum*, do not finish until mid or late July. There is also their growth to consider; we have already placed R. *obtusum* among the greater bushes because of its splendid and characteristic growth, but many, such as the ever-popular clear pink 'Hinomayo' (the first to be introduced from Japan), will grow almost as large. They range in scale down to the semi-prostrate R. *indicum* varieties and the lowly Gumpo group. Between these there is a huge range of charming tints and differing habits, low, lacy bushes one of whose inestimable values is that they can be transplanted at any age, in common with most rhododendrons of more accepted style. This means that small plants can be put fairly closely together at the start; it is not a crime because they can be thinned out as they grow, starting new colonies elsewhere; in the meanwhile they will have provided cover and beauty.

Everyone should make his own personal choice to accord with his taste in colours; they range from creamy-white through pale pink to deep pink, magenta and crimson in the true Kurume race; from white, pink to crimson in the R. *simsii* (Gumpo), and white, pink, crimson and coppery-orange in the R. *indicum* varieties; further, there are white, pale and rich mauve, pink, crimson, salmon and terra-cotta in yet another race, descended chiefly from R. *kaempferi* and R. 'Mucronatum' and the garden plant known as 'Malvatica'. These three last groups have larger flowers than the first; in addition, those in the fourth group have larger leaves and growth (Fig. 7).

Now, having written about them in the 'social' shrub category I am beset by doubts. Are they not, nearly all of them, sufficiently beautiful in growth to qualify for use as specimen shrubs? Many of them indeed are, but they also knit together easily and pleasantly in groups of one variety. This perhaps is the answer:

use them singly, well spaced, if you want a collection, but do not set yourself against close planting when several of a kind are to be used for greater effect. This is no new dictum; it applies to almost everything, but should be borne in mind especially when dealing with a range of cultivars such as these Japanese azaleas or with heathers, both so tempting to one's 'collector's spirit'!

Several shrub roses are useful, but, as their habits and sizes are considered fully in my books *Shrub Roses of Today* and *Climbing Roses, Old and New*,[1] I will not go deeply into them here. The prostrate kinds are included later in this chapter and vigorous suckering species and varieties are mentioned in Chapter 10.

The above few paragraphs will serve to indicate the great wealth of shrubs of fair size that provide reliable ground-cover. I could lengthen the list considerably, but that would merely take up space at the expense of our main subject: the numerous dwarf bushes which can be planted *en masse*.

I feel sure there are many intending planters of ground-cover who are rather chary about introducing the more rampant carpeters and spreaders for fear that they will gain the upper hand. So they will, if not chosen and planted with circumspection. As many of us have small gardens today it will be best to give special prominence to the smaller bushes. They are the kinds that can be happily planted knowing that, apart from the odd rooting branch or two that tries to start a colony of its own, they will complement the bigger shrubs and help to cover the ground and bring the eye down to the verge of the border here and there. There is a long list of these hummock makers, or 'social' shrubs, as will be seen from the Alphabetical Table; I will call attention to some of them in their various categories.

THE SMALLER 'SOCIAL' SHRUBS WHICH MAKE ROUNDED
HUMMOCKS

In many parts of Britain are sandy acid wastes where heathers luxuriate. With them we find the gorse, pine and birch, and many other small shrubs in mountainous districts. A planting of this style, in an open windswept garden on suitable soil, gives interest

---

[1] Phoenix House, London, and St Martin's Press, New York.

of as varied a nature and colouring as any. The big family of
heaths and heathers—*Erica*, *Calluna*, and including the Irish heath,
Daboecia—are all social shrubs of dwarf bushy habit seldom
exceeding two feet, and will knit together in a few years, making
a rich, dense, varied carpet (Pl. IB), rich and varied throughout
the year, as anyone will know who has visited the excellent heath
gardens at the Botanic Gardens at Edinburgh, Ness (Pl. IA) and
Kew, and also at Wisley and the Savill Garden in Windsor Great
Park. The different kinds flower through different months; *Erica
cinerea* starting in June, followed by *E. vagans* and other species,
with *Calluna vulgaris* going on into October; by November *E.* ×
darleyensis is opening, followed by *E. carnea*, which usually
finishes in April, when some of the larger shrubby kinds open to
link up with *E. cinerea* again in June. I do not wish to imply that
all are equal in ground-cover value, but, in addition to their floral
attractions, their brown or grey faded flowers add to the diversity
of colouring; in addition their foliage is infinitely varied, notably
through some recent additions to the genus *Calluna* or ling. Some
of these are as brilliant in their yellow, orange and red foliage
throughout the year as any patch of summer annuals. Their vivid
tones have to be seen to be believed, and make superb contrasts
with the burnished hue of *Mahonia aquifolium* and *Leucothöe
fontanesiana* (*L. catesbaei* of gardens), the shining coppery purple
winter leaves of a good form of *Rhododendron saluenense* or the deep
colouring of *Tellima grandiflora* 'Rubra' and *Bergenia purpurascens*
and 'Sunningdale'. These are but hints of winter contrast; when
summer comes the opportunities are no less great.

There is no doubt that *Erica carnea* (Pl. IIB) itself—and the form
'Springwood White' in particular—is the best heath for ground-
cover, closely rivalled by the taller *E.* × *darleyensis*—and its fine
variety 'Arthur Johnson'—with *E. vagans*, the Cornish heath, a
good third. I have extolled the virtues of the winter-flowering
kinds and their value for planting with witch hazels in my book
Colour in the Winter Garden,[1] but the scope for delightful schemes
in July, August and September from these three genera, *Erica*,
Calluna and the long-flowering *Daboecia*, is almost limitless. They
assort well with silvery-leafed plants, and their floral colours, in

[1] 1967, rev. ed. Phoenix House, London, and Charles T. Branford Co.,
Newton Center, Mass., U.S.A.

which purplish crimson and pink flowers predominate, blend with the varied cool greens and copper-leafed shrubs, light pink and pale yellow roses, the paler shrubby potentillas, *Spiraea japonica* and many more.

But if a heath garden, or one of the fashionable, terraced, peat-block gardens is intended, there are several other genera which will help to create nearly as much interest in a quiet way while they will thrive in the same conditions. Glossy-leafed *Gaultheria cuneata* with white berries, dark green *Vaccinium* species, *Cyathodes colensoi* with lilac-grey leaves and red-budded *Leiophyllum buxifolium* all add something through their evergreen foliage alone.

It must be admitted that these dense dwarf shrubs have tiny leaves and something with bigger leaves should be provided here and there, such as *Viburnum davidii* if the soil is not too sandy, bergenias or hostas in shady areas. This is obviously the place to mention rhododendrons. Subject to what I have written in the Table, there are species and varieties for full sun and others for shade. If they are to be kept dwarf, compact and healthy they should not be allowed to get cluttered with dead leaves in winter, and broken shade from daily passing shadows is better than trying to grow them actually under trees. Botanically the genus has been classified into Series and those which I have selected from the Lapponicum Series (R. *impeditum*, R. *scintillans* and hybrids like × 'Impeanum' and × *prostigiatum*) form bun-like shrublets, bearing violet and bluish small flowers in clusters, and are suitable for full exposure to sun. They are admirable for the very foreground of the border or heath garden and for adding height and solidity to the rock garden. Much the same can be said of the Saluenense Series (R. *calostrotum*, R. *saluenense*, R. *keleticum*); their flowers are larger, are borne like those of a viola, and are of reddish-purple colouring. For cooler conditions are the plum-coloured R. *campylogynum myrtilloides* and the pale yellow R. *hanceanum* 'Nanum' (both very slow growing), and the white R. *leucaspis*, with striking brown anthers. Gorgeous rosy colouring and comparatively large bell-like flowers are found in some good though larger hybrids, such as 'Carmen' and 'Jenny' ('Creeping Jenny' or Elisabeth var. 'Jenny'). A very tough and hardy species for exposure is R. *ferrugineum*, the European Alpenrose. For those with patience the genus *Rhododendron* is full of possibilities and interest. My difficulty

36 After a very early spring display of white flowers, *Pachyphragma macrophyllum* provides glossy clumps for the rest of the season.

37 The colour forms and hybrids of *Iris innominata* are exquisite in flower and make hearty clumps of foliage.

38 *Left:* A sunny, well-covered border with (*right to left*) *Salvia officinalis* 'Purpurascens', *Geranium renardii* and *Calamintha nepetoides*.

40 *Right:* Greeny-yellow flowers and soft green, velvety leaves unite to make *Alchemilla mollis*, or lady's mantle, an indispensable plant for the garden or for cutting. It seeds itself freely.

39 *Left:* The spring-flowering yellow *Alyssum saxatile* provides good grey foliage for the rest of the season, useful for 'cooling down' bright roses, etc.

41 *Right:* A good contrast in colour and size: alchemilla leaves with the grey-blue filigree of *Ruta graveolens* 'Jackman's Blue'.

42　*Geranium psilostemon (G. armenum)*, whose flaming magenta-purple flowers contrast well with white astilbes. The geranium makes a large clump.

43　*Left:* Violets of all kinds make a good dwarf cover; *Viola septentrionalis* has particularly good foliage. *V. labradorica* has purplish foliage, and both spread freely.

44　*Right:* Still the most reliable and handsome in its large evergreen leaves, *Bergenia cordifolia* 'Purpurea' has magenta flowers on red stems.

45　*Top right:* The black-green leaves of *Helleborus foetidus* make excellent contrast to the pale-green flowers in earliest spring. It seeds itself.

46 *Left:* The evergreen rosettes of *Saxifraga umbrosa* (London Pride) and *S. × geum* 'Monstrosa' both make a crisp contrast against mown grass or paving. Best in part shade.

48 *Above: Oxalis acetosella* 'Rosea', the attractive pink form of Britain's native wood sorrel, is one of the prettiest of spring-flowering carpeters. The cool green leaves remain in beauty for most of the year. *Oxalis oregana* (see Plate XXIIIa) is more vigorous.

47 *Left:* The flowers of *Asarum europaeum* are of no garden value and are hidden by evergreen leaves. A spreader for shade.

49 *Below:* Its spring display of white flowers earns for *Tiarella cordifolia* the name of foam flower. Almost evergreen carpeter for shade.

50 *Epimedium pin-natum colchicum*, ever-green, with yellow flowers in spring.

51 *Vancouveria hexandra*, deciduous, cream flowers in spring. Both of these increase slowly.

52 The evergreen *Lamium galeobdolon* 'Variegatum' has white mottled leaves and spikes of yellow flowers in spring. Being very rampant it is recommended only for use under trees.

53 *Lamium maculatum*, with white-striped leaves and mauve or white flowers in spring. For rapid cover under shrubs and trees.

Left: Dwarf *Phlox douglasii* 'Boothman's Variety'. A dense, slow carpeting plant.

Right: Geranium himalayense (G. grandiflorum of gardens) excels in pretty leaves and rich Wedgwood-blue flowers in summer and spreads by underground shoots.

Left: Gypsophila repens (white or pink), a rapid carpeter. Weeding is unnecessary on a rock garden where carpeting plants are chosen.

Right: Smooth, grey-green leaves and white, orange-eyed flowers in spring and autumn are provided by *Potentilla alba*, a carpeter rooting as it spreads. Sun or shade.

58   *Top left:* Clouds of blue forget-me-not flowers from the large-leafed *Brunnera macro-phylla* (*Anchusa myosotidiflora*), which prefers shady conditions and spreads partly by seeds.

59   *Left:* A boon for steep banks and elsewhere in wood-land conditions where mowing is difficult: the evergreen woodland rush *Luzula maxima* (*L. sylvatica*). A rampageous surface spreader.

60   *Above:* The mat-forming *Festuca eskia* (*F. crinum-ursi*) growing in association with sun roses, thymes, *Achillea argentea* and other sun-loving plants.

61   A weed-proof mass of the orange *Hemerocallis fulva* 'Kwanso Flore
Pleno', one of the day lilies whose roots freely colonize.

62   A soft-coloured group on a sunny border: *Stachys macrantha*, mauve
pink with good basal foliage, *Geranium psilostemon* in magenta purple, and
a variegated comfrey, *Symphytum × uplandicum* 'Variegatum'.

63 *Maianthemum bifolium*, a spring-flowering relative of lily-of-the-valley.

64 Sweet woodruff, *Asperula odorata*. White flowers in spring. These both rapidly spread by means of underground shoots; for shade.

65   Borders in the author's garden where weeds find little chance to grow.

has been to limit the choice, to avoid overloading the chapter with what are normally very slow-growing plants.

However, we cannot all contemplate groups of heathers and dwarf rhododendrons in our gardens. They give the feeling of limitless space and the open air—no doubt through the association of ideas—and do not consort well with the summer flower garden and its roses; these to my mind are enjoyed best in a formal scheme as opposed to the natural. In addition the denizens of the heather garden require special lime-free soil conditions, but if we hanker after this style of gardening we need not despair as we have a most excellent further array of dwarf shrubs still to choose from, which can be welded into a heath-like mixture and yet are lime-tolerant. It is a blessing to us gardeners that while lime-haters will not grow on lime, many lime-tolerant plants will also thrive on acid sands. A link with the two groups is *Erica carnea* and its hybrid *E. × darleyensis*. All their forms and hybrids will grow splendidly in acid soils, but also in some soils containing lime provided there is plenty of humus present.

Here then is a collection of ardent sun-lovers for well-drained soils—headed by the shrubby potentillas (Pl. IVA). These range from one foot to five feet in height, all making dense bushes with fresh green or silvery, small, divided leaves and multitudes of small strawberry flowers borne continuously from early June until the frosts stop them. We are concerned only with the more dwarf, wider-than-high forms here, but fortunately they include all the floral tints from white to primrose, sulphur and brassy yellow to pale orange. So long as the soil does not become bone-dry they will continue to flower, and provided that we can tolerate their somewhat fussy appearance due to their miniature attractions, they are among the most valuable shrubs in the garden. 'Primrose Beauty' is a superb, cool contrast for grouping around that gaunt but glorious shrub *Rosa moyesii*, and I like the bright yellow 'Elizabeth' with the blue of *Ceanothus* and plants with coppery-purple leaves, while the white varieties charm us anywhere, assorting well with old roses.

All the potentillas are extremely hardy; where they will grow, so may we expect the following to be at home: the evergreen dense hummocks of *Iberis sempervirens* (Fig. 11) and *I. saxatilis*, so dazzling with their pure white flowers in early spring, a sharp contrast to the red 'japonicas', as forms of *Chaenomeles* are affectionately called; the brassy yellow dwarf Spanish gorse *Genista hispanica* and the dwarf broom *Cytisus × beanii* are useful additions for spring also. Noteworthy among grey-leaved dwarf shrubs is the Dutch lavender, longest lasting in flower and the greyest in leaf; the sages (Pl. V) provide the culinary sage, the 'English Broadleaf' form of *Salvia officinalis* itself, one of the best of soft grey-green plants; but the purplish-grey *S. o.* 'Purpurascens' (Fig. 38) and the pretty variegated forms are just as good for cooking.

Also of culinary as well as of garden value there is the very dark, almost black-green, of the common thyme, *Thymus vulgaris*; both this and its golden-green sport, *T. v.* 'Aureus', are low covers for the front of the border. The hebes, as we now have to call the evergreen Antipodean veronicas, are not sufficiently appreciated; I think we are inclined to forget them because the better known kinds, varieties and hybrids of *Hebe speciosa*, which are rich and lovely in flower over a long period, are only reliably hardy in our warmer coastal gardens. On the other hand there are many small-leaved, extremely hardy, dwarf, rounded or prostrate hebes—mostly with small white flowers it is true—which form admirable and distinctive cover in a variety of greens: bright grass-green in *H. rakaiensis* (*H. subalpina* of gardens); cool grey-green in *H. pinguifolia* 'Pagei' (Pl. IIA), *H.* 'Aoira' and *H. albicans*; and there are many shades in between.

Going a step further into the sunshine, so to speak, there are several good dwarf shrubs for really warm sunny banks, in our warmer countries and coastal districts. They savour of the *maquis* of the Mediterranean, where cistus and halimiums grow with other shrubs in close array, making a unique kind of local ground-cover, redolent of sweet oils. The *Halimium* species and the bigeneric hybrid, *Halimiocistus*, are of grey hue but brilliant yellow or white in flower; their foliage gives a soft smoky effect in winter when the contrast with dark evergreens becomes the more apparent. Like the *Cistus* species they drop their petals rather early in the afternoon but a new crop comes out the next morning, fresh and silky. Closely related and of great value are the garden forms of *Helianthemum*; so prodigal of short-lived blooms at midsummer (Pl. IIIB). The singles usually drop their petals by midday, but the double-flowered 'Mrs Earl', 'Jubilee' and 'Butter and Eggs' are worth much more to the daily worker, as they remain in flower until the evening. They all have dark green leaves—the last two being 'sports' of the first—and are apparently descended from *H. nummularium grandiflorum*, which has similar leaves. *H. nummularium* itself (*H. chamaecistus*) has downy leaves, and garden forms bred from this have good dense growth and larger, greyer, leaves. 'Rhodanthe Carneum' is one of the most vigorous and in good conditions in the milder parts of the country will grow to six feet across.

The silvery-leafed *Convolvulus cneorum*, with its silky-white trumpet flowers pink-touched outside, is one of the most decorative plants I know, and as a complete contrast we could grow next to it some hyssop. The spikes of flowers can be rich blue, pink or white, according to the colour form. The grey and pink *Dorycnium hirsutum*, *Satureia* or winter savory, the blue filigree of rue (*Ruta graveolens* 'Jackman's Blue') (Fig. 41) and the santolinas will all blend well. In the last, the hummocks of feathery soft foliage may be silvery or green, and the button-like flowers can be butter-, sulphur-, creamy- or golden-yellow. Many people object to the bright flowers of *Santolina chamaecyparissus* (*S. incana*), the commonest 'cotton lavender'—as it is misleadingly called—but a clip over in March prevents their flowering and creates nice bushy plants—as it does with the rue; the hyssop, like lavender, needs a clip in spring too, but this tends to ensure a good floral display.

Another good grey-leafed plant, a size larger than the above, is *Senecio laxifolius* (Fig. 8), which I believe to be the right name for the plant grown in gardens as *S. greyi*, which is quite a different species. Once again its brilliant yellow flowers can be prevented, if the prevailing colour scheme is soft, by shortening the main shoots in March.

Some plants usually seen on rock gardens are *Ptilotrichum spinosum* (*Alyssum spinosum*), grey, spiny little bushes covered with white in June, and also the erodiums. These are scarcely shrubs, but certainly are not herbaceous plants. *Erodium macradenum* and *E. trichomanifolium* both make low hummocks of feathery greenery, over which soft pink flowers are poised for the whole summer; those of the former have maroon centres. *E. chrysanthum* is pale

yellow with silvery leaves, not quite so reliable, and all of them
need well-drained slopes on the rock garden, as does the pretty
dwarf *Jasminum parkeri*, which bears tiny yellow flowers.

SHRUBS WHICH FORM CARPETS

We now have to consider shrubs of a different class, those which
are prostrate, often rooting as they go, and covering the ground
much more quickly as a consequence. It will be apparent that they
need more forethought in placing. Let us take the lime-hating
kinds first.

Rhododendron forrestii repens and its hybrids are slow and small,
but make a most lovely carpet of rich green, studded in due
course with remarkably large bell-shaped blooms of scarlet or red.
One of the most successful hybrids is 'Jenny', but as this throws
higher branches I have included it in an earlier paragraph. Invaluable in producing this rich colour in June or early July is 'Lava
Flow', which is rather more bushy. Quite small and nearly
prostrate are the magenta-purple species R. *radicans* and R.
prostratum with R. *imperator* a size larger, but they are scarcely
quick enough for ground-cover except on a small scale. There
are several dwarf vacciniums which might be included, particularly V. *oxycoccus* (Pl. IXA), but it is seldom seen in gardens; it
is a dwarf, rapid creeper with tiny pink bells in June and small
red fruits.

The best surface creepers I know for acid soil, in sun or shade,
are *Arctostaphylos uva-ursi* and the plant known in cultivation as
A. nevadensis (Fig. 12). I understand this is not the true species
but perhaps an American variant of *A. uva-ursi*. At Kew and at
the Savill Garden this *A. nevadensis* has made superb carpets of
small, glossy, dark green leaves; it is rapid growing and highly
effective. *A. uva-ursi* seems to be rather less rapid but is similarly
dense, with smaller leaves. They both thrive on well-drained soils.

There are several more little ericaceous and other choice shrubs
for lime-free soils: *Linnaea borealis, Cassiope lycopodioides, Gaultheria
nummularioides, Pernettya tasmanica, Epigaea repens, Mitchella repens*,
all specialists' plants for the treasured peat beds; and *Lithospermum
diffusum* (Fig. 76) ('Heavenly Blue' is the best form) and the hardy
Leptospermum humifusum. The last plant usually grows well, and

seems to be quite hardy, but does not flower very freely, whereas the lithospermum produces its pure blue flowers freely but will only grow in gentle climates. To see it cascading down banks in Ireland is to realize what it can do when luxuriating; in Surrey it needs a lot of attention. A close relative in equally good blue is the more compact *Moltkia × intermedia*. Another tricky true blue plant is *Ceanothus prostratus*. It may grow well in lime-free soil in sun. Although I included *Erica carnea* in the 'social' shrubs, it is equally a carpeter, and would assort well with the above. *Pachystima* species, *Coprosma petriei*, *Myrtus nummularia*, *Pimelia* species and *Helianthemum alpestre* are all very small dwarf, carpeting shrubs only a few inches high, for choice positions.

Cytisus decumbens and *C. × kewensis*, prostrate varieties of *C. scoparius* and *Genista pilosa* (Pl. VIA) all belong to the broom family, bearing yellow flowers of different tints freely when grown in full sun with good drainage. They are best above retaining walls or on the rock garden. Also for similar positions is a luxuriant thyme, *Thymus nummularius*, with dark green leaves and the usual small mauve flowers in heads. The Mountain Avens, *Dryas octopetala*, is somewhat slow, but with good drainage can be a most satisfying dense mat of pretty crinkled greenery and bearing white flowers on long stalks in early summer. I prefer *D. × suendermannii*, a hybrid of it, which is more vigorous and has larger creamy flowers.

Those who live in warm coastal areas should make good use of *Rosmarinus lavandulaceus* (*R. officinalis prostratus*), the prostrate rosemary (Fig. 16). It is a first-rate carpeter, rapidly creeping, and bespangled in spring with pale blue flowers nestling among the rich green, grey-backed, fragrant leaves. On warm sunny slopes it will give great satisfaction and beauty.

In our warmer counties and especially by the sea, the prostrate *Fuchsia* 'Exoniensis' ('Corallina') will remain shrubby, and cover large areas; in colder districts the stems die to the ground each winter. Owing to its pendant flowers it is seen to greatest advantage when it can hang over a wall or rock.

We have several more carpeters which do not demand shelter in cultivation, and among them many evergreen cotoneasters (Fig. 15); *C. microphyllus cochleatus* and *C. congestus* are rather slow, but are first-rate dark evergreens with surprisingly large berries.

C. dammeri (*C. humifusus*) (Pl. XXVIIIA) is undoubtedly the best carpeter and like all kinds thrives best in rather heavy soil in sun or facing north. This rapid creeper has good glossy leaves and bright red berries and will speedily cover anything. Considerably larger, *C.* 'Hybridus Pendulus', reputedly a hybrid between *C. dammeri* and *C. frigidus*, does not make perfect cover everywhere, seeming to prefer a cool position to become really dense, where it will grow a yard a year, and, if the birds refrain, is usually well covered with bunches of red berries throughout the winter. Occasionally a wayward shoot will grow more erect and should be pegged down. *C. horizontalis* is the well-known deciduous species whose flat, fan-like branches are studded with scarlet berries in autumn and winter. Though of horizontal growth it grows naturally up to two feet in height. It is apt to get insect troubles if in a starved condition, but is usually satisfactory.

The dwarf bush honeysuckle, *Lonicera pileata* (Pl. VIIB), bears no superficial resemblance to one of those delicious climbers, but is much nearer to the popular hedging shrub *Lonicera nitida*, except that it is not erect growing. The small glossy evergreen leaves are pleasant and in a good season it bears lovely purple berries. This is again a shade-lover, but will grow almost anywhere.

We may include some of the prostrate willows, which make good cover, though they are not of great interest from a floral point of view. They all bear catkins in the spring, but do not excel in leaf or autumn colour. The hybrid *Salix* × *gillotii* seems to be the strongest grower and will rapidly make dense cover. There is of course no reason why the 'Pendula' form of *Salix caprea*, the native sallow or goat willow, usually grafted high up on a straight stem to make a weeping tree, should not be grown from cuttings to make an excellent carpet. It is a female form with grey-green catkins; for the fine yellow pussy-willow of the male form 'Kilmarnock' should be sought. Likewise I long to see an area covered with the weeping holly, *Ilex aquifolium* 'Pendula'. This is usually a female tree, bearing berries, and it grows freely. Again it is usually grafted on a stem, but can be rooted from cuttings. It would be a great sight in winter, well set with berries and growing near to *Jasminum nudiflorum*.

The most vigorous evergreen prostrate cover that I know, even exceeding the rapid colonizing habit of the Irish Ivy, is a bramble, *Rubus tricolor* (Fig. 13). The leaves are ivy-shaped, of glossy rich green, borne on long furry brown stems; there are no prickles and it does not provide any noticeable contribution of flower or fruit. The long trails grow eight feet or more in a season and in time will mound themselves up to three feet. There is no doubt that this is of exceptional value where big, quick cover is needed. Of similar size and success are a few roses, notably *Rosa* × *paulii*, R. 'Max Graf' (Pl. VIIA) and the almost thornless R. *wichuraiana*. Seldom are roses considered for ground-cover; the bulk of the rambling varieties do not make sufficiently dense cover to combat all weeds, and I do not personally enjoy hand-weeding among prickly rose trails! The three mentioned are excellent, together with the exquisite clear pink R. × *paulii* 'Rosea' (Fig. 18), which is not quite so vigorous as the type. R. × *paulii* will grow to three or four feet in height with a limitless, dense spread, and is ideal for banks and large areas where it will be smothered in clematis-like white flowers at midsummer, and sometimes again later. It is deciduous, terribly prickly and is guaranteed to stop anything on two or four legs—short of an elephant—when established. R. *wichuraiana*, the original wild species from which many garden ramblers have originated, is practically thornless, bears small, dark green, glossy, almost evergreen leaves and small, very fragrant white flowers in clusters in August. It is therefore a rose entirely on its own, vigorous in growth—the trails exceeding ten feet in a season—and forms a very beautiful low cover. 'Max Graf' (Pl. VIIA) is a hybrid of it, rather higher and less glossy in leaf, bearing deep pink single flowers at midsummer. The shoots of all these roses root where they touch and extend their dominion continually. These roses and others are more fully discussed in my book *Shrub Roses of Today*.

Some of the best known ground-covers are found among the periwinkles; though in maturity they are both attractive and efficient it must be admitted that the common *Vinca major* and likewise the equally large but tender *V. difformis*, take some time to make dense growth. *V. difformis* is fit only for the warmer counties, in sheltered gardens, and is available in an exquisite pearly blue form as well as the darker *V. d. dubia*. Both are somewhat rare. This species and *V. major* spread by means of lax, arching shoots which take root where they touch the ground. If time can be spent at the end of the summer to peg down the trails by means of a stone or forked stick their job will be completed more quickly: if left alone, the wind by constantly moving the trails often prevents them from taking root. *V. major* and its beautiful, rather less vigorous, variegated form 'Elegantissima' (Pl. IXв) (*V. m.* 'Variegata') have fine large flowers that have so distinctive a tint that 'periwinkle blue' is an accepted term; it is a cool lavender-blue, or Michaelmas daisy shade. There is no doubt that *V. m. hirsuta* (*V. m. pubescens* or *oxyloba*) (Fig. 14), which has less glossy leaves and rather poor starry flowers of violet-purple, is a far quicker cover. At Hidcote it has preserved a really excellent cover over a large, poorly nourished area for many years; it will spread by three feet a year. All of these are too vigorous and high for use except under trees and very big shrubs; among lesser shrubs they are apt to make an untidy tangle.

V. minor on the other hand, the lesser periwinkle, is prostrate or nearly so; on young plants all the trails lie flat, and therefore no pegging down is necessary. As the plants become more filled and bushy the shorter shoots lie on top of one another, making a dense carpet some nine inches high. It is a much better garden plant, and some distinctive colour forms are available. The most luxuriant with the best flowers and leaves is *V. m.* 'Bowles' Variety' or 'La Graveana' (Pl. IXc), and the smallest is a white attributed to Miss Jekyll. In between are the double blue and semi-double plum-coloured forms, besides some pretty variegated forms, admirable for lighting dark corners. No soil seems too good or too poor for this genus, which will grow in sun almost as well as in shade, in soil of any quality except a bog.

SHRUBS WHICH SPREAD BY MEANS OF UNDERGROUND SHOOTS

Though I uttered a warning about the invasiveness of the foregoing surface runners, far more care is needed when using those with questing, spreading roots. Some produce short shoots, of more or less uniform height above ground, others make thickets of stems several feet in height; the latter I shall leave to consider later in the next group, which I call 'thicket-formers'. In spite of their invasiveness these underground spreaders are most valuable from our point of view, and provided they are well under the height of their more static neighbours they will do no harm. As with the carpeters, they have the great value of making a more or less level cover which links the bigger shrubs together and creates a natural effect.

Once again there are some for lime-free, humus-laden soils. *Gaultheria procumbens* makes a dense, dwarf carpet of broad rounded leaves bright with red berries in winter and white bells in summer. It is a steady spreader and makes an impenetrable turf, thriving in part or full shade. It is fragrant of 'wintergreen' when crushed and is indeed one of the principal sources of this unguent. Much quicker, running two to three feet in a season when once established, is *Cornus canadensis* (Pl. XXVIIA). It seems to thrive best in sandy soil in broken shade, and becomes quite dense when fully established. It is a great sight in May when every short erect shoot, bearing four rounded light green leaves, is topped by a flower-head of four white bracts; in September some turn to scarlet berries. The leaves become burnished and wine-coloured in later autumn and winter and are semi-evergreen. This is one of the very best spreaders, rampant when suited.

Of equal value, more adaptable, and a fine dwarf evergreen, is *Pachysandra terminalis* (Pl. XXXB). This gives richest greenery in shade and requires a neutral if not acid soil, and once started will be there for ever. The dark greenery is broken by small white spikes of scented flowers in spring. It is highly popular in the United States of America and great flats of it can be seen at Kew; it ranks with the very best, most luxuriant and satisfactory of evergreen covers.

Two most important spreaders for any fertile soil are the well-known St John's Wort, *Hypericum calycinum* (Pl. XXXIB), and the little dark-leafed, dark-wooded *Muehlenbeckia axillaris*. The latter forms a dense wiry carpet only a few inches high, contributing a distinctive colouring to any scheme, and is dense and a highly satisfactory cover for full sun. *Hypericum calycinum* is possibly the most adaptable ground-cover we have; it will grow luxuriantly in heavy or light soils, limy or acid, on chalk or peat, in sun or dense shade—anywhere except in a bog. Small wonder that it is the staple diet of planners! Apart from the beauty of its nearly evergreen covering, it produces large and lovely yellow flowers for many weeks in summer. After a severe winter it may need razing to the ground to encourage fresh growth. It is an outstanding feature in many great gardens.

THICKET-FORMERS

Each group so far has merged imperceptibly into the next and this is no exception. A thicket-former is simply a shrub with spreading underground shoots, whose stems give rise to an ever-widening clump of some height. While the spreaders in the immediately preceding paragraphs do not exceed a foot or so in height, the following will usually be over two feet in height. Still more vigorous kinds will be found in Chapter 10.

One of the best known is *Mahonia aquifolium*, whose holly-like leaves are beautiful the year round, burnished in winter, and the bunches of yellow flowers in spring are followed by blue berries in summer. Jam made from them is almost indistinguishable from blackcurrant jam. *M. nervosa* and *M. repens* are almost too slow-growing to be called ground-cover, but after several years' establishment can be very attractive.

Berberis calliantha, a glossy-leaved shrub with inch-wide pale yellow flowers, freely spreads underground and is so beautiful in leaf and flower that one is loath to pull it up. It thrives in sun or shade. *B. coxii* and *B. hookeri* are closely related. The winter-flowering sarcococcas, with which I dealt fairly fully in *Colour in the Winter Garden*, are unassuming small glossy-leaved bushes bearing mere tassels of flowers but powerfully fragrant; they like nothing so much as a shady position where they can slowly colonize the ground, achieving one to four feet in the different species.

I find *Xanthorhiza simplicissima* (*X. apiifolia*) (Fig. 23) equally adaptable, its stems achieving about three feet, and its fine spread of ferny foliage assuming rich purplish tones in the autumn. It is an excellent colonizer. For a sunny place the dwarf Russian almond *Prunus tenella* makes fairly good cover. There are two Japanese quinces for inclusion here, the compact *Chaenomeles japonica* (once called *Cydonia maulei*), with small bright orange flowers, and the much more vigorous dark red 'Crimson and

Gold'. This is so prolific of its suckers that I have ceased to recommend it for the average garden as a shrub, and it is therefore more suited to Chapter 10.

There is a little rose excelling in its autumn colour, *Rosa nitida*, which is admirable for sunny positions; other thicket-forming roses such as *R. virginiana* are in Chapter 10.

Although *Romneya coulteri*, the Californian Poppy, is grown and enjoyed in many gardens I think a word of warning must be given about its invasive habits. Too often it is troublesome to establish, but when once really well rooted into the ground in a sunny place—usually against a wall where the reflected heat helps to ripen the stems—it can become a nuisance. I have known it grow under the footings of a house and appear through cracks in the floorboards! It is so beautiful that many of us would give lots of space to it for the sake of its six-foot-high stems clothed in lovely grey foliage, bearing those great silky white flowers. *R. trichocalyx* is similar, and *R.* × *hybrida*, uniting both, is considered more free-flowering, particularly 'White Cloud'. They die to the ground in cold winters.

For lime-free soil, of slowly increasing tendency are *Leucothöe fontanesiana* (*L. catesbaei* of gardens) (Fig. 22) and its smaller relative *L. keiskei*. They have most beautiful leaves borne on graceful arching shoots, ideal for cutting, particularly in winter when, unless in deep shade, they take on rich coppery tints. Forming a prickly thicket in time, the *Pernettya mucronata* also will not tolerate lime. The reddish shoots and dark green tiny leaves make a dense array, and if you have good female or hermaphrodite forms, such as the Davis' Hybrids or 'Bell's Seedling', you may count on clusters of berries of real brilliance in autumn —white, pink, purple or red—produced with greatest abundance in sunny places. More rampageous in lime-free woodland conditions than anything so far mentioned is *Gaultheria shallon* (Fig. 24), but it is best omitted from the average garden; its handsome foliage, little pinky-white bell-flowers and succulent bloom-covered fruits all lead to a valuable shrub—and this it certainly is, when properly used. *Gaulnettya wisleyensis*—a bigeneric hybrid between the *Gaultheria* and the *Pernettya*—is a dense thicket-former up to two feet in height. It bears small white flowers and bunches of maroon fruits, but I have never been attracted by it.

Some slow colonizers not mentioned in the Alphabetical Table comprise a few more lime-haters, enjoying damp conditions. Some of the azalea species, *Rhododendron (Azalea) viscosum* and its varieties *nitidum* and *glaucum*, and also R. *atlanticum*, if established in the moist peaty soil—even boggy—which they love, will produce underground shoots and form a thicket. And anyone who has sniffed their dainty honeysuckle-scented flowers will go to a deal of trouble to establish them. The dwarf R. *pemakoense* (Fig. 6) is a slow colonizer, and both this and *Kalmia augustifolia* 'Rubra' will thrive in similar though drier ground; the latter has dark pink flowers in July.

SPRAWLERS

Once again this is a group of shrubs which might well have been included in other categories, but which I feel have enough uniformity between them to warrant a separate paragraph or two. The one thing that separates them from the carpeters, spreaders and the thicket-formers is that their height is not uniform. Odd branches will always grow up more strongly than others.

An ardent sun-lover is the common rosemary, *Rosmarinus officinalis*, a flopper if ever there was one, and if the upright shoots are pinched out a low rounded mass will result.

For shade we have *Euonymus fortunei* (E. *radicans*) (Fig. 17) in its more vigorous forms. E. *f. carrierei*, with broad ever-green leaves and E.*f.* 'Coloratus', whose foliage is metallic purple in winter, make large more or less flat trailing bushes and will mound themselves up to three or four feet without support, and root as they grow. When thoroughly established they produce elegant spindle-berries, orange seeds enclosed in creamy rounded envelopes. Both are quick-growing. More procumbent and equally at home in shade, or sun, is the strange hybrid between ivy and *Fatsia*, *Fatshedera lizei*. Its procumbent shoots bear large glossy, rich green, ivy-shaped leaves. It occasionally suffers in severe weather.

I wonder if anyone has thought of *Jasminum nudiflorum*, the popular yellow winter jasmine, for ground-cover? It is an ideal plant and I shall never forget seeing a large bank completely covered with this, *Cotoneaster horizontalis* and *Juniperus* × *media* 'Pfitzerana'. In the winter the yellow flowers of the jasmine and the red berries of the cotoneaster found their perfect foil in the grey-green plumy branches of the juniper. The jasmine roots extremely freely as it grows, rapidly mounding itself up in time to about four feet, and is in flower from October till spring, when weather permits. The jasmine, so often used as a climber, should not really be classed as such, for it is merely a sprawling shrub unless supported, but it is a suitable plant with which to end this long catalogue and leads us directly into the true climbers.

It is not until one begins to assemble all these low-growing shrubs that one begins to find new ones and hears of others. News has just reached me of *Pyracantha* 'Santa Cruz' from the United States, growing no higher than about eighteen inches but extending by rapid growth to twelve feet or more in diameter, and bearing a fine crop of scarlet berries in autumn. Perhaps we shall have it over here before long, but we must not necessarily expect it to be as hardy as the shrubby types we grow, for its name indicates a mild climate. Then there are the several low-growing *Cotoneaster* hybrids from the Continent, mostly hybrids of *C. salicifolius*. If they remain prostrate they will be invaluable, but so far they seem inclined to throw up rather erect shoots. Among them are 'Autumn Fire' ('Herbstfeuer'), 'Saldam', 'Repens', 'Skogholm', 'Gnome' and 'Park Carpet' ('Park-teppich'). So far 'Gnome', 'Repens' and 'Skogholm' seem to be the best and most densely prostrate. No doubt many prostrate forms and hybrids of shrubs will crop up and, now that there is a reason and desire for such things, they will be treasured and propagated.

SHRUBS

	Country of Origin	Height and Planting Distance	Leaf Colour and Shape
ARCTOSTAPHYLOS			

Full sun or part shade; lime-free light soil and some humus. The plant described as *A. nevadensis* may not be a true species but is accepted under this name in gardens. Both are excellent for sandy seashore gardens. The leaves of *A. uva-ursi* often become burnished with purplish tones in winter.

	Country of Origin	Height and Planting Distance	Leaf Colour and Shape
nevadensis	N. America	6″ × 4′	Dark green, small, poi.. glossy.
uva-ursi (*A. officinalis*)	N. America, Europe	5″ × 2′	Dark green, small, rounded, glossy.

ARISTOLOCHIA			

Full sun, well-drained soil; for the warmer counties. An intriguing plant with flowers like tobacco pipes.

	Country of Origin	Height and Planting Distance	Leaf Colour and Shape
sempervirens	Crete	6″ × 18″	Dark green, shining, pointed.

AUCUBA			

Will grow in any fertile soil; best in part or full shade, thriving even in dark corners in town gardens.

	Country of Origin	Height and Planting Distance	Leaf Colour and Shape
japonica	Japan		

As a high slow cover this has been mentioned on page 30. Here we should include the dwarf variety:

	Country of Origin	Height and Planting Distance	Leaf Colour and Shape
— 'Nana Rotundifolia'		2′ × 3′	Rich green, large, gloss..

AZALEA, *see* RHODODENDRON

BERBERIS			

Easily grown, preferably in sun. The genuine *B. wilsoniae* and *B. candidula* (and others) are very slow growing and their dense prickly growth makes them useful from another point of view, as a barrier. *B. coxii* and *B. hookeri* create good thickets also, up to four feet when established.

	Country of Origin	Height and Planting Distance	Leaf Colour and Shape
calliantha	SE. Tibet	3′ × 3′	Dark shining green, wh.. beneath.
candidula (*B. wallichiana pallida*)	W. Hupeh	1½–2′ × 1′	Dark green, narrow, w.. beneath.
coxii	SE. Tibet	3′ × 3′	Dark green, shining, w.. beneath.
hookeri	Himalaya	3′ × 3′	Mid green, grey benea..
× **stenophylla 'Corallina'**	Hybrid	18″ × 2′	Bright green, small.
— 'Prostrata' (*B. darwinii 'Prostrata'*)	Hybrid	18″ × 3′	Dark green, small.
thunbergii	China	6′ × 6′	Green, small, autumn colour.

Though this and its coppery-purple form, *B. thunbergii* 'Atropurpurea', are rather large for our classification, they do in maturity grow close to the ground. *B. t.* 'Atropurpurea Nana' is a dwarf form grown from cuttings, which when planted one foot apart will make a dense covering.

	Country of Origin	Height and Planting Distance	Leaf Colour and Shape
verruculosa	W. Szechuan	4′ × 3′	Dark shining green, sm.. white beneath.
wilsoniae	W. Szechuan	2½′ × 2′	Greyish-green, small, scarlet in autumn.

Deciduous or Evergreen	Flower Colour and Fruits	Flowering Season	Habit	Propagation
E	Tiny white bells, small red berries.	Spring	Carpet, rooting	CDL
E	Tiny pink bells, small red berries.	Spring	Carpet, rooting	CDLS
E	Small, purplish.	Summer	Carpet, rooting	CDS
E	nconspicuous; red berries in spring.	Spring	Hummock	CL
E	Pale yellow, large for a berberis.	Spring	Thicket	CD
E	Pale yellow, small.	Spring	Hummock	C
E	Pale yellow, small.	Spring	Thicket	CD
E	Pale yellow, small.	Spring	Thicket	CD
E	Orange, showy, in clusters.	Spring	Hummock	C
E	Orange, showy, in clusters.	Spring	Carpet	C
D	Small, pale yellow; red berries.	Spring	Hummock	CS
D	Pale yellow, small; coral berries.	Spring	Hummock	C
E	Pale yellow, small.	Spring	Hummock	CD

SHRUBS

	Country of Origin	Height and Planting Distance	Leaf Colour and Shape
BETULA			
nana	N. Hemisphere (Old World)	2′ × 4′	Dark green, rounded, small.

BRUCKENTHALIA
For the lime-free heather garden or rock garden. Same cultivation as for *Erica*.

spiculifolia	SE. Europe, Asia Minor	6″ × 18″	Yellowish-green, minute

BUPLEURUM
Tall growing shrub but usually seen about 3–4′ high, except in sheltered maritime districts, for which it is ideal. Sun; any fertile soil, withstanding wind.

fruticosum	S. Europe	4′ × 4′	Glossy leaden green, somewhat glaucous.

CALLUNA
Best in exposed positions, where dead leaves do not congregate; lime-free soil with humus. Full sun or partial shade. (See also notes under *Erica*.) Heather.

vulgaris (*Erica vulgaris*)	Europe, E. N. America	2′ × 20″	Dark green, moss-like.

There are numerous colour forms most of which grow too tall and 'leggy' for our purpose. 'Foxii Nana' is a hummock of mossy dark green, 6″ × 6″; 'Pyrenaica' or 'Minima' 9″ × 9″: these do not flower freely. Compact varieties, about 18″ × 18″: 'County Wicklow' and 'J. H. Hamilton', double, pink; 'Mullion', soft purplish pink; 'Sister Anne' and 'Rigida', mauve. 1′ × 1′: 'Multicolor' and 'Robert Chapman', vivid reddish foliage. 18″ × 18″: 'Blazeaway', 'Golden Feather', 'Sunset' and 'Goldhaze', brilliant orange-yellow foliage. The last five varieties are valuable for their winter foliage colour, together with the tall grey 'Hirsuta Typica', 2′ × 2′. Many others are available. All except the very dwarf varieties need clipping in spring to keep them compact.

CASSIOPE
All species are dense enough to be called ground-cover, but some are more upright than spreading. *C. hypnoides* is very small and spreading. *C. lycopodioides* is the most usually seen; all require moist peaty soil on shady slopes or thin woodland. Their leaves are appressed to the stem and give a mossy appearance.

lycopodioides	NE. Asia, NW. America	2″ × 9″	Dark rich green, minute
selaginoides	NE. Asia, NW. America	2″ × 9″	Dark rich green, minute
s ˈˈˈrana (*Harrimanella stellerana*)	NE. Asia, NW. America	3″ × 9″	Dark rich green, minute

CEANOTHUS
Good drainage, warm positions, full sun. *C. divergens* is quite hardy and easy, but poorly coloured; *C. prostratus* is a good blue but temperamental; occasionally does well on heavier soils. *C. gloriosus* is unproved as yet. *C. thyrsiflorus repens* is hardy, with pale blue flowers, making a large spreading bush, 2′ × 4′, and is thoroughly to be recommended.

Deciduous or Evergreen	Flower Colour and Fruits	Flowering Season	Habit	Propagation
D	Inconspicuous.		Hummock	LS
E	Tiny pink spikes, heath-like.	Summer	Hummock	CLS
E	Tiny, green, in flat heads.	Summer	Hummock	CS
E	Tiny, in tall branching sprays; white to purple.	Late summer	Hummock	CL
E	Tiny white bells on thread-like stalks.	Spring	Carpet	CS
E	Tiny creamy white bells on thread-like stalks.	Spring	Carpet	CS
E	Tiny white bells on thread-like stalks.	Spring	Carpet	CS

SHRUBS

	Country of Origin	Height and Planting Distance	Leaf Colour and Shape
CEANOTHUS *cont.*			
Many of the larger growing species are suitable for high cover on warm sunny banks in maritime and sheltered districts. Best on acid or neutral soils; short-lived on chalk.			
divergens	California	1′ × 4′	Dark green, small, glc
gloriosus	California	1′ × 3′	Dark green, small, glc
thyrsiflorus repens	California	3′ × 4′	Dark green, small, glc
CHAENOMELES			
The 'japonicas' are mostly too tall for general ground-cover, but *C. japonica* (which used to be called *Cydonia maulei*) is specially useful in its dwarf form *C. j. alpina*; this is only half the height of *C. japonica*. 'Crimson and Gold' is a first-rate cultivar whose freely suckering habit makes it a blessing for ground-cover but a nuisance otherwise.			
'Crimson and Gold'	Hybrid	5′ × 6′	Dark shining green.
japonica (*Cydonia maulei*)	Japan	3′ × 3′	Bright shining green.
CISTUS			
Somewhat tender shrubs, of which the first two are some of the most reliable, for full sun and well-drained soil. They suffer in cold winters but are suitable for the warmer counties. They only make dense cover when fully exposed to sun and air.			
× corbariensis	Hybrid	2′ × 3′	Dark green, crinkled, pointed.
lusitanicus decumbens		1′ × 2′	Dark green, long.
salviifolius	S. Europe	2′ × 2′	Rich green, small, hair
CONVOLVULUS			
This shrubby species enjoys a hot, sunny, well-drained position in our warmer counties.			
cneorum	S. Europe	1′ × 2′	Silvery silky, narrow, profuse.
COPROSMA			
Tiny dense carpeter for sunny slopes of rock garden. Seldom produces berries.			
petriei	New Zealand	2″ × 9″	Minute, olive green.
CORNUS			
Rapidly spreading by underground shoots in lime-free woodland soil in partial shade. Leaves turn wine colour in autumn and remain until severe frost. It is semi-herbaceous.			
canadensis (*Chamaepericlymenum canadense*)	N. America	6″ × 2′	In fours, rounded, dull green.

~ciduous or ~ergreen	Flower Colour and Fruits	Flowering Season	Habit	Propagation
E	Grey-blue, small, in fluffy heads.	Spring	Hummock	CS
E	Lavender-blue in fluffy heads.	Spring	Hummock	C
E	Blue, small, in fluffy heads.	Spring	Hummock	C
D	Orange, very free; yellow 'quinces'.	Early spring	Hummock	L
D	Dark red; yellow 'quinces'.	Early spring	Thicket	D
E	Large white, silky.	Summer	Hummock	C
E	Large white, crimson blotches.	Summer	Hummock	C
E	Small, white, profuse, silky.	Summer	Hummock	CS
E	Creamy white, trumpet-shaped.	Midsummer	Hummock	C
E	Inconspicuous; small purplish berries.		Carpet	CLS
D	White, 4-bracted flowers, sometimes developing scarlet berries.	May–June	Spreader	DS

SHRUBS

	Country of Origin	Height and Planting Distance	Leaf Colour and Shape

COTONEASTER

The following hardy, dwarf, creeping shrubs grow best in the heavier, limy soils, but are amenable to most soils; sun, or shade from buildings. The several new hybrid cotoneasters from the Continent, 'Herbstfeuer', 'Parkteppich', 'Repens', 'Saldam' and 'Skogholm', shew affinity to *C. salicifolius* and *C. dammeri* but are not yet fully tested.

adpressus		1' × 2'	Minute leaves.

C. adpressus praecox ('Nan Shan') is far more vigorous and more conspicuous in berry than the type species.

congestus (*C. pyrenaicus*, *C. microphyllus glacialis*)	Himalaya	4″ × 18″	Tiny, dark green.
conspicuus			

SE Tibet. Large rounded shrub achieving 7' × 12' or more; small dark leaves; scarlet berries lasting till spring. *C. c.* 'Decorus' seldom exceeds 5 ft, and grows more horizontally, covering large areas, with the same attractions.

dammeri (*C. humifusa*)	China	4″ × 2'	Small, glossy green, ide[..] carpet.
horizontalis	China	2' × 6'	Tiny dark green, autum[..] colour.

There are dwarf and compact forms, 'Little Gem' and 'Saxatilis', which do not berry freely but have good autumn colour and make dense hummocks. The white variegated form is less vigorous than the type, and leaves turn pink in autumn.

'Hybridus Pendulus'		1' × 6'	Small, dark, glossy gree[..]
microphyllus	Himalaya	18″ × 6'	Tiny, very dark green.
— cochleatus		9″ × 2'	Tiny, very dark green.

CYATHODES

Tiny heath-like shrub for peaty lime-free soil, in partial shade. Chiefly noted for its foliage tint.

colensoi	New Zealand	10″ × 18″	Grey-mauve, tiny.

CYTISUS

All brooms prefer well-drained soils, preferably lime-free, and full sun. The stems of the following kinds are so dense that though they are not evergreen they act as fairly successful ground-cover.

× **beanii**	Hybrid	1' × 1'	Erect green twigs.
decumbens (*C. prostratus*)	S. Europe	3″ × 1'	Small, hairy, soft green.
demissus (*C. hirsutus demissus*)	SE. Europe	3″ × 1'	Small, hairy, soft green.
× **kewensis**	Hybrid	1' × 4'	Small, grey-green, hairy[.]
leucanthus (*C. schipkaensis*)	SE. Europe	1' × 18″	Small, hairy, soft green.

58

Deciduous or evergreen	Flower Colour and Fruits	Flowering Season	Habit	Propagation
D	Small, white; seldom fruits.	Spring	Hummock	CL
E	Small, white; red berries.	Spring	Carpet	CLS
E	Small, white; red berries.	Spring	Carpet	CL
D	Small, white; red berries; fan-like branches.	Spring	Carpet	CS
E	Small, white; red berries, in bunches.	Spring	Arching	C
E	Small, white; crimson berries.	Spring	Carpet	CS
E	Small, white; crimson berries.	Spring	Carpet	C
E	Clusters of tiny white flowers.	Summer	Hummock	C
D	Golden yellow, small, profuse.	Early summer	Hummock	C
D	Small, bright yellow.	Midsummer	Carpet	CS
D	Small, yellow with brownish marks.	Midsummer	Carpet	CS
D	Primrose-yellow, small, prolific.	Spring	Carpet	C
D	Creamy sulphur-yellow.	Summer	Hummock	CS

59

SHRUBS

	Country of Origin	Height and Planting Distance	Leaf Colour and Shape
CYTISUS *cont.*			
scoparius			
(*Sarothamnus scoparius*)			

The common broom has two excellent vigorous prostrate forms, *C. scoparius maritimus* (*pendulus*) (*C. s. prostratus*), yellow, and *C. s.* 'Andreanus Prostratus', yellow and red flowers. These achieve 1–2 ft in height and should be planted 3–4 ft apart. They flower freely and their bright green twigs are attractive in winter.

DABOECIA

Closely resembling the heaths, and needing similar light humus-laden soil; making dense hummocks, and flowering profusely. The brown of the dead flowers is attractive in winter. *D. azorica* is hardy only in our warmer counties; *D. cantabrica* suffers sometimes in severe winters when old. *D. cantabrica* has several distinct forms in cultivation: 'Atropurpurea', rich reddish purple; 'Alba', pure white; 'Bicolor', flowers purple and white; 'Praegerae', coral pink, less vigorous. Clip in spring to encourage dense growth.

	Country of Origin	Height and Planting Distance	Leaf Colour and Shape
azorica	Azores	10" × 10"	Dark green, tiny, poin hairy.
cantabrica	SW. Europe,	2' × 2'	Dark green, tiny, poin
(*D.* or *Menziesia polifolia*)	Ireland		hairy.

DAPHNE

D. cneorum 'Eximia' is the most spectacular, prefers a well-drained, tacky, limy soil with humus, in full sun; occasionally seen 3 ft or more wide. *D.* × *burkwoodii* makes dense cover in maturity but is slow. 2' × 4'. All kinds will thrive in fertile, well-drained soil, but are not always easy to establish; exceedingly fragrant.

	Country of Origin	Height and Planting Distance	Leaf Colour and Shape
cneorum	S. and Central Europe	1' × 3'	Leaden green, dull, sm slow.
odora	Far East	1½' × 3'	Rich green, smooth; s

The form with the leaves edged with yellow, 'Aureo-marginata', is normally the most reliable in growth.

DORYCNIUM

Bushy, broom-like plant, whose stems die down in winter. Suitable for sunny places on light soil; associates well with heathers.

	Country of Origin	Height and Planting Distance	Leaf Colour and Shape
hirsutum	S. Europe	18" × 18"	Grey-green, woolly, sm

DRYAS

Sun, any well-drained soil. Carpeting shrubby plants for rock garden or border verge. The hybrid *D.* × *suendermannii* is the most effective.

	Country of Origin	Height and Planting Distance	Leaf Colour and Shape
octopetala	N. Europe, America	2" × 1'	Neat, crinkled, dark g
× **suendermanii**	Hybrid	3" × 18"	Neat, crinkled, dark g

EMPETRUM

Dense dwarf evergreen of heath-like appearance; requires moist peaty soil. Floral and fruiting assets limited.

	Country of Origin	Height and Planting Distance	Leaf Colour and Shape
nigrum	Temperate Zone	9" × 9"	Dark shining green, minute.

Deciduous or Evergreen	Flower Colour and Fruits	Flowering Season	Habit	Propagation
E	Small ruby-red bells.	Early to late summer	Hummock	CLS
E	Various.	Early to late summer	Hummock	CLS
E	Small, rich pink, in heads.	Late spring	Carpet	CD
E	Purplish buds, white flowers.	Late winter	Hummock	CL
D	Small pinkish-white; reddish pods.	Summer–autumn	Hummock	CS
D	5″. White, nodding, borne singly.	Early summer	Carpet, rooting	CD
D	6″. Cream, nodding, borne singly.	Early summer	Carpet, rooting	CD
E	Tiny, pink; purplish berries.	Spring	Hummock	CDS

	Country of Origin	Height and Planting Distance	Leaf Colour and Shape

EPHEDRA

Leaves inconspicuous, but the massed effect of the wire-like branches in various tones of green gives a unique texture.

gerardiana	E. Asia	2' × 2'	Blue-green stems.

E. *andina* and E. *distachya* are similar.

EPIGAEA

Shade, lime-free soil well mixed with humus. E. *repens* is rare and very difficult to move, and should be planted from pots, and is exceptionally fragrant. E. × *intermedia* 'Aurora' is a satisfactory hybrid between the two species. Though used as ground-cover in the U.S.A. they are seldom sufficiently available or tractable over here to be grown except as choice single items, though I remember seeing a carpet 10' × 10' of E. *repens* in Surrey in the thirties.

asiatica	Japan	4" × 10"	Rough, dark green, ov
repens	N. America	4" × 9"	Rough, dark green, ov

ERICA

All heaths thrive best in sandy soil with humus, fully in the sun, but will grow in most lime-free soils, so long as they are not smothered with dead leaves in autumn and spoiled by overhanging tree branches. E. *carnea*, E. *mediterranea* and their hybrid E. × *darleyensis* will also thrive in some soils where lime is present, with humus. As with *Calluna*, their dead flowers create a rich brown effect in winter, while E. *carnea* and E. × *darleyensis* start to flower in November and carry on until April. The best for cover are E. *carnea* in its many forms, particularly 'Springwood White', E. × *darleyensis*, E. × *d.* 'Arthur Johnson' and E. *vagans* varieties. E. *cinerea* is not so dense nor so hardy and reliable. E. *carnea* itself, E. *c.* 'Ruby Glow' and E. *c.* '*Vivellii*' are some dense, rich pink varieties; 'Myretoun Ruby' is richest in colour, E. *c.* 'Springwood Pink', pale pink. E. *ciliaris* is slightly tender and enjoys, with E. *tetralix*, moister conditions. Clip in spring to encourage dense growth.

carnea	Central and S. Europe	9" × 18"	Tiny, dark shining gre
cinerea	W. Europe	9" × 10"	Tiny, dark shining gre

Some good varieties: 'Alba Minor', white; 'Glasnevin Red', deep purplish; 'Rosea', pink; 'C. D. Eason', vivid deep pink; in addition, 'Golden Drop' and 'Golden Hue' bear yellowish foliage, but are less reliable.

× **darleyensis**	Hybrid	18" × 2'	Tiny, dark shining gre
— 'Arthur Johnson'		2' × 2½'	Tiny, dark shining gre
— 'Silberschmelze' ('Molten Silver')		1' × 2'	Tiny, dark shining gre
mediterranea			

SW. Europe. At times and in suitable climates achieves 6–8'. Usually 4–5'. Not reliably hardy but bushy and dense. Late spring flowering. Spring planting best, 3' apart. 'Brightness' and 'W. T. Rackliffe' are two compact hardy forms in pink and white respectively, about 18" × 18".

vagans	SW. Europe	2' × 2'	Tiny, dark shining gre

Noted colour forms are 'Mrs D. F. Maxwell', deep pink; 'St Keverne', bright pink; 'Cream', creamy-white; 'Pallida', palest lilac; 'Holden's Pink', clear bright pink.

× **williamsii**	Hybrid	1' × 2'	Tiny, dark green, tippe yellow.

Deciduous or Evergreen	Flower Colour and Fruits	Flowering Season	Habit	Propagation
E	Flowers inconspicuous; red berries.		Hummock	DS
E	Pink, hidden among leaves.	Spring	Carpet	CLS
E	Blush white, hidden among leaves.	Spring	Carpet	S
E	Various, pink or white, small, in spikes.	Winter–spring	Carpet	CDL
E	Various, pink or white, small, in spikes.	Midsummer	Hummock	CL
E	Lilac pink, small, in spikes.	Late autumn– spring	Hummock	CDL
E	Deep lilac pink, small, in long spikes.	Late autumn– spring	Hummock	CDL
E	White.	Late autumn– spring	Hummock	CDL
E	Tiny bells in spikes.	Late summer	Hummock	CL
E	Pink bells in clusters.	Late summer	Hummock	CL

63

SHRUBS

	Country of Origin	Height and Planting Distance	Leaf Colour and Shape

ERODIUM
Sub-shrubby; sun, well-drained soil. Ideal for the rock garden and border verges. *E. chrysanthum* needs a warm position.

chrysanthum	Greece	9″ × 1′	Grey-green, feathery.
guttatum	SW. Europe	9″ × 1′	Soft green, feathery.
macradenum	Pyrenees	9″ × 1′	Soft green, feathery.
trichomanifolium	Lebanon, Hermon	9″ × 18″	Soft green, feathery.

EUONYMUS
The ground-cover varieties are derived from *E. fortunei radicans* and thrive in any soil that is not boggy, in sun or shade. The variegated forms are whitest in shade, but take on pink tones in sun. *E. f.* 'Coloratus' develops darkest colouring in sun.

fortunei radicans   Japan
A lax trailer or climber. The following best-known forms have probably been propagated from sporting branches or flowering branches, and the latter sorts when well established produce good fruits, orange seeds enclosed in creamy covering. Flowers inconspicuous.
    E. f. 'Gracilis' is a good variegated form between 'Variegatus' and 'Silver Queen' in size.

— carrierei		2–3′ × 6–8′	Oval, dark dull green.
— 'Coloratus'			

Similar, but the leaves take on rich brown and purplish tints through the winter.

— 'Kewensis'		6″ × 9″	Minute, dull green, round
— 'Silver Queen'		2′ × 3′	Oval, green and cream white.
— 'Variegatus' and 'Emerald and Gold' and 'Emerald Gaiety'		15″ × 15″	Oval, variegated.
— vegetus. Similar to *E. f. carrierei*.			

Hybrid between *Fatsia japonica* 'Moseri' and *Hedera helix* 'Hibernica'. Suffers sometimes in extremely cold winters. Grows in any soil, sun or dense shade.

lizei		2′ × 4′	Large, ivy-like, rich glo green.

FICUS
This tiny-leafed evergreen fig might make good cover in our warmest counties.

pumila   China, Japan
'Minima' is a close carpeter, small evergreen leaves; no floral attractions; any soil.

FORSYTHIA
All forsythias are dense growers and make high cover, but *F. suspensa sieboldii* is the most prolific of all for covering ground; it is one of the most beautiful and is ideal for cutting. Any reasonably well-drained soil, sun or shade. 'Arnold Dwarf' is praised in U.S.A. for its excellent covering qualities, 3′ × 6′, but is poor in flower. I have not seen a successful example of this plant. 'Bronxensis' is smaller.

ovata	Korea	4′ × 6′	Rich green, smooth.
suspensa	China	8′ × 8′	Rich green, smooth.
— sieboldii			

This is a lax grower, rooting freely where branches touch the ground; semi-weeping habit. Long sprays of flower.

Deciduous or Evergreen	Flower Colour and Fruits	Flowering Season	Habit	Propagation
D	1'. Pale sulphur yellow.	Summer	Carpet	CDS
D	1'. White, maroon centre.	Summer	Carpet	CDS
D	1'. Lilac-pink, maroon centre.	Summer	Carpet	CDS
D	1'. Lilac-pink.	Summer	Carpet	CDS
E	Free fruiting form.	Autumn	Sprawling Sprawling	CL
E	Does not fruit.		Hummock	CDL
E	Seldom fruits. Slow growing.		Hummock	CDL
E	Do not fruit.		Hummock Sprawling	CDL CL
E	Pale green in umbels, inconspicuous.	Autumn	Sprawling	CL
E			Carpet	CD
D	Small, yellow.	Early spring	Hummock	CL
D	Small, yellow, profuse.	Spring	Hummock, rooting	CL

SHRUBS

	Country of Origin	Height and Planting Distance	Leaf Colour and Shape
FUCHSIA			

Sun or partial shade, good drainage but abundant moisture necessary for continuous production of flowers. *F. procumbens* for frost-free gardens only; *F.* 'Exoniensis' is hardy in most counties, and without frost will develop into a shrub. Both suitable for hanging over rocks, low walls, etc.

'Exoniensis' ('Corallina')	Hybrid	1′ × 3′	Dark green, handsome.
magellanica 'Prostrata'	Hybrid	9″ × 2′	Dark green, handsome.
procumbens	New Zealand	2″ × 2′	Dark green, tiny, smoot

GAULTHERIA

For lime-free, light soil, with humus, in shade. *G. shallon* and *G. procumbens* will tolerate considerable drought. The latter makes a dense turf-like carpet. *G. shallon* is very invasive and rampant. *G. adenothrix* suffers in severe winters; it is a miniature *G. shallon*. *G. nummularioides* is for warm gardens only.

adenothrix	Japan	9″ × 18″	Dark green, rough, broa small.
cuneata	W. China	1′ × 1′	Small, glossy, bright gre
nummularioides	Himalaya	4″ × 2	Oval, small, on long flat shoots.
procumbens	E. N. America	5″ × 18″	Dark glossy green.
shallon	W. N. America	4′ × 3′	Dark green, rough, broa

GAYLUSSACIA

Light, lime-free, peaty soil, partial or full shade.

brachycera	E. U.S.A.	9″ × 1′	Bright glossy green, sma

GENISTA

The genistas enjoy the same culture as *Cytisus*, and are useful for similar positions. Apart from *G. lydia*, their yellow is of a brassy tone. Though deciduous, they give an evergreen effect because of their densely packed twigs or spines. *G. hispanica* can be pruned hard back if it becomes straggly or open with age.

hispanica	SW. Europe	2′ × 2′	Leaves tiny, but many green spines.
lydia	SE. Europe	1′ × 2′	Leaves tiny, grey-green twigs.
pilosa	S. and W. Europe	9″ × 2′	Leaves tiny, dull grey-green.
sagittalis	Central and SE. Europe	1′ × 2′	Leaves tiny, deep green, hairy.
tinctoria	Europe	1 × 18″	Leaves tiny, deep green.
— 'Flore Pleno			This form is always dwar and a reliable cover; t species is variable.

uous green	Flower Colour and Fruits	Flowering Season	Habit	Propagation
D	Crimson and purple flowers, nodding.	Summer onwards	Carpet	C
D	Crimson and purple.	Summer onwards	Carpet	C
D	Tiny, purplish glaucous berries.	Summer onwards	Carpet	CS
E	Tiny white bells; reddish fruits.	Summer	Spreader	DLS
E	Tiny white bells; large white fruits.	Summer	Hummock	CDLS
E	White or pink tinted, tiny bells; fruit blue-black.	Summer	Carpet, rooting	CLS
E	Tiny white bells; scarlet fruits.	Summer	Spreader	DLS
E	Pinkish bells in sprays; indigo fruits.	Summer	Spreader	DLS
E	Tiny white or pink bells; small bluish fruit.	Summer	Spreader	CDLS
D	Yellow, small, in clusters.	Early summer	Hummock	CS
D	Clear yellow, small, in sprays.	Early summer	Hummock	CS
D	Yellow, small, in clusters.	Early summer	Carpet	CLS
D	Yellow, small, in clusters.	Summer	Hummock	CS
D	Yellow, small, in clusters, double.	Summer	Hummock	CL

SHRUBS

	Country of Origin	Height and Planting Distance	Leaf Colour and Shape
HALIMIOCISTUS			
Hybrids between *Halimium* and *Cistus*, and requiring the same conditions.			
ingwersenii		1′ × 2′	Leaves narrow, dark dull.
sahucii		1′ × 2′	Leaves narrow, dark dull.
HALIMIUM			
Needing full sun and warm positions, as for *Cistus*. Only hardy in warmer counties. The give a smoky-grey effect in winter.			
alyssoides	SW. Europe	18″ × 2′	Grey-green shoots a small leaves.
lasianthum formosum (*H. formosum*)	Portugal	18″ × 2′	Grey-green shoots a small leaves.
— **concolor** has pure yellow flowers without blotch.			
ocymoides (*H. algarvense*)	SW. Europe	1′ × 18″	Grey-green shoots a small leaves.
HEBE			
Sun-loving dwarf shrubs for well-drained soil; hardy in all but the coldest districts. Thes all blend well with heathers and other shrublets. Good town plants. Often called *Veronic* a generic name now reserved for the herbaceous species. 'Blue Gem', and particular! 'Autumn Glory', are rather tender.			
albicans	New Zealand	10″ × 18″	Glaucous grey, point
'Aoira'	New Zealand	9″ × 1′	Glaucous grey, point
'Autumn Glory'	Hybrid	1′ × 2′	Purplish-green, small rounded.
carnosula	New Zealand	9″ × 2′	Small, glaucous grey-
'Carl Teschner'	Hybrid	9″ × 15″	Small, dark green.
catarractae (*Parahebe catarractae*)	New Zealand	9″ × 1′	Small, toothed, dark
colensoi	New Zealand	1′ × 2′	Small, grey-green.
elliptica	S. Hemisphere		
— **'Blue Gem'**	Hybrid	2′ × 2½′	Fresh green, broad.
gibbsii	New Zealand	1′ × 2′	Small, grey-green.
pinguifolia	New Zealand		
— **'Pagei'** (*H. pageana*)		9″ × 18″	Small, glaucous blue-
rakaiensis (*H. subalpina* of gardens)	New Zealand	1′ × 2′	Bright grass-green, sr
vernicosa	New Zealand	18″ × 2′	Small, shining dark g

iduous or rgreen	Flower Colour and Fruits	Flowering Season	Habit	Propagation
E	White, silky, prolific, in clusters.	Summer	Hummock	C
E	White, silky, prolific, in clusters.	Summer	Hummock	C
E	Yellow, prolific.	Summer	Hummock	CS
E	Yellow, prolific, with crimson blotch.	Summer	Hummock	C
E	Yellow, small, prolific.	Summer	Hummock	CS
E	White, small, in short spikes.	Summer	Hummock	C
E	White, in small heads.	Summer	Hummock	C
E	Violet-blue, small, in short spikes.	Summer onwards	Hummock	C
E	Tiny white flowers in small spikes.	Summer	Hummock	CL
E	Violet-blue, small, in short spikes.	Summer	Hummock	C
E	Mauve, small, open sprays.	Summer	Hummock	C
E	Tiny white flowers in small spikes.	Summer	Hummock	CL
E	Lavender-blue, small, in spikes.	Summer onwards	Hummock	C
E	White, small, in short spikes.	Summer	Hummock	C
E	Tiny, white flowers in small spikes.	Early summer	Hummock	CL
E	White, small, in short spikes.	Summer	Hummock	C
E	White, small, in short spikes.	Summer	Hummock	C

SHRUBS

	Country of Origin	Height and Planting Distance	Leaf Colour and Shape

HEDERA

The ivies are mainly considered in Chapter 5, but the following dwarf forms of *H. helix* the common ivy, have attractive small leaves and thrive in sun or shade. 'Feastii', 'Sagit taefolia' and 'Très Coupé' may not be hardy in exposed positions.

helix	Europe		
— 'Conglomerata'		9″ × 18″	Small, dark green, rou
— 'Feastii'		9″ × 18″	Small, dark green, dee cut.
— 'Little Diamond'		9″ × 18″	Small, grey-green and white.
— 'Minima'		1′ × 18″	Small, dark green, pc
— 'Sagittaefolia'		9″ × 1′	Small, deeply cut, gre variegated.
— 'Très Coupé'		9″ × 18″	Small, dark green, dee cut.

HELIANTHEMUM

In sunny, sheltered, well-drained gardens, the garden hybrids between *H. apenninum*, *H* *nummularium*, etc., make good ground-cover, so long as they are open to the wind and no allowed to collect dead leaves around them in winter. In cold districts they are apt to be killed in winter, particularly when old. Sun Rose.

alpestre	Central and S. Europe	4″ × 9″	Small, grey-green, do
Garden Hybrids		1′ × 2′	Narrow, dark green o green.

Most kinds drop their petals by early afternoon. The double-flowered forms 'Mrs Earl' 'Jubilee' and 'Butter and Eggs' remain in beauty until evening. Some of the most dens and vigorous have broader, grey-green leaves, such as 'Rhodanthe Carneum' and 'Wisle Primrose'.

HYPERICUM

H. calycinum is one of the most reliable of covers, for sun or shade on any soil. *H. andro saemum* is effective in waste places but seeds itself freely. *H. rhodopeum* and *H. grandiflorum* are ideal for the rock garden or border verges. 'Sunspot' is a selected American form o *H. rhodopeum*. *H. buckleyi* and *H. × moserianum* are compact shrubs for full sun, the latte in the warmer counties. *H. calycinum* and *H. × moserianum* get cut to the ground in severe winters. St John's Wort.

androsaemum	Europe	3′ × 3′	Rich green, broad, sm
buckleyi	U.S.A.	1′ × 1′	Light green, reddish i autumn.
calycinum	SE. Europe, Asia Minor	1′ × 3′	Rich green, broad, sm
× moseranum	Hybrid	18″ × 18″	Deep green, broad.
olympicum grandiflorum (*H. polyphyllum* of gardens)	S. Europe	9′ × 1′	Grey-green, small, sm
rhodopeum	SE. Europe, Asia Minor	3″ × 1′	Grey, downy, small.

70

Deciduous or Evergreen	Flower Colour and Fruits	Flowering Season	Habit	Propagation
E			Carpet, rooting	CL
E			Carpet, rooting	CL
E			Carpet rooting	CL
E			Sprawler	CL
E			Carpet rooting	CL
E			Carpet rooting	CL
E	Yellow, small.	Summer	Carpet	CS
E	White, yellow, orange, pink, crimson.	Summer	Hummock	CS
D	Small, yellow; black berries.	Summer onwards	Clump	CS
D	Yellow, small.	Summer	Hummock	CS
E	Large, yellow.	Summer onwards	Spreader	CS
E	Large, yellow, reddish anthers.	Summer onwards	Hummock	C
E	Deep yellow, large.	Summer	Hummock	CS
E	Rich yellow, small.	Early summer	Carpet	CS

SHRUBS

	Country of Origin	Height and Planting Distance	Leaf Colour and Shape

HYSSOPUS
Full sun, well-drained soil; dense small bushes of the lavender persuasion, and good for associating with them or with the heaths. There are also pink (*ruber*) or white (*albus*) forms. Hyssop.

officinalis	Europe, Asia	18″ × 18″	Small, narrow, dark gre

H. aristatus is a richer colour and more compact.

IBERIS
Sun, well-drained soil. Excellent cover, eventually 3–4 ft across.

saxatilis	S. Europe	8″ × 12″	Dark green, small, narr
sempervirens	S. Europe	9″ × 18″	Dark green, small, narr
— 'Snowflake'		9″ × 18″	Dark green, small, narr

ILEX
Well-drained soil, preferably light; a sunny position will produce most berries. Holly.

aquifolium	Europe, etc.		

I. a. 'Pendula' is the weeping holly, usually grown on a stem, to weep down, but would make an excellent cover, though rather slow if grown as a bush.

— 'Pendula'		2′ × 4′	Dark shining green.

JASMINUM
J. parkeri is only hardy in our warmer counties. Full sun. *J. nudiflorum* is for sun or shade, away from overhanging branches; rooting as it spreads; there is a variegated variety. Neither is particular about soil.

nudiflorum	China	2′ × 6′	Dark shining green, dar green twigs.
parkeri	NW. India	1′ × 2′	Dark green, tiny. Slow growing.

LAVANDULA
(Lavender)
Best in full sun in well-drained soil. All the lavenders are more or less weed-proof but are apt to become rather open with age unless clipped over every spring. They often need replanting after ten years or so, and cuttings will root in the open ground in September if pulled off with a 'heel' and planted deeply. There are many garden forms and hybrids of which by far the most satisfactory is the 'Dutch Lavender', at once the most bushy, the greyest in leaf and the longest in flower. Much more compact and fairly weed-proof are 'Twickel Purple' and 'Hidcote Giant' (a giant only in size of flower spike).

'Dutch'		2′ × 3′	Profuse, grey-green.

LEIOPHYLLUM
Lime-free, well-drained soil, with humus. Excellent foreground bushlet, or for rock garden or heath garden. *L. b. hugeri* is similar. *L. b. prostratum* is more dwarf.

buxifolium	E. N. America	1′ × 18″	Tiny, dark, shining gre

Deciduous or Evergreen	Flower Colour and Fruits	Flowering Season	Habit	Propagation
D	Small, violet-blue, in spikes.	Summer	Hummock	CDS
E	Heads of pure white.	Late spring	Carpet	CLS
E	Heads of pure white.	Late spring	Carpet	CLS
E	More effective flowers.	Late spring	Carpet	CL
E	Inconspicuous; red berries.	Early summer	Carpet	CL
D	Yellow.	Autumn–spring	Sprawler	CL
E	Yellow, small.	Early summer	Hummock	CL
E	Lavender, in spikes.	Summer onwards	Hummock	C
E	White tipped pink, tiny, in heads.	Early summer	Hummock	CLS

SHRUBS

	Country of Origin	Height and Planting Distance	Leaf Colour and Shape
LEPTOSPERMUM			
Full sun, light or well-drained soil, lime-free. The hardy prostrate form described would be more valuable if it flowered more freely.			
humifusum		1′ × 3′	Greyish-green, small and profuse.
(*L. scoparium* 'Prostratum' of gardens)			
LEUCOTHÖE			
Lime-free soil with humus, well-drained; shade or partial shade. *L. fontanesiana* is a superb foliage plant of arching growth, also beautiful in flower.			
fontanesiana	SE. U.S.A.	3′ × 3′	Shining, pointed, deep green becoming burnished.
(*L. catesbaei* of gardens)			
keiskei	Japan	1′ × 2′	Shining, pointed, deep green, becoming burnished.
LINNAEA			
Lime-free soil with humus, partial shade. Makes a good carpet in good conditions, otherwise sparse. *L. b. americana* is a N. American form with larger flowers and stronger growth.			
borealis	N. Europe	1″ × 2′	Small, rounded, dull green on trailing stems.
LITHOSPERMUM			
Sun or part shade, lime-free soil with humus. Best in the milder, damper west. 'Heavenly Blue' and 'Grace Ward' are two good cultivars.			
diffusum	S. Europe	9″ × 2′	Dark green, small, hairy.
(*L. prostratum*)			
LONICERA			
Not particular about soil, thriving in sun or shade.			
pileata	China	2′ × 3′	Small, bright green; horizontal growths.
MAHONIA			
Extra handsome evergreens, thriving in any soil in shade; foliage becomes burnished in sun. *M. repens rotundifolia* is as tall as *M. aquifolium*; luxuriant. They spread very slowly.			
aquifolium	W. N. America	3′ × 2′	Shining dark green, pinnate.
nervosa	W. N. America	9″ × 1′	Dull, dark green, pinnate.
repens	W. N. America	1′ × 1′	Dull green, pinnate.
MITCHELLA			
For cool peaty positions on the rock garden or peat wall. *M. repens*, the 'Partridge Berry', has a white fruited variety, *leucocarpa*.			
repens	N. America	1″ × 1′	Small, rounded, dark green.
undulata	Japan	1″ × 1′	Small, rounded, dark green.

74

Deciduous or evergreen	Flower Colour and Fruits	Flowering Season	Habit	Propagation
E	Pale pink, small.	Summer	Carpet	CL
E	Small, white, in clusters.	Summer	Thicket	CLS
E	Small, white, in clusters.	Summer	Thicket	CLS
E	Dainty, tiny pinky-white bells.	Summer	Carpet, rooting	D
E	Vivid blue, small, in clusters.	Early summer	Carpet	CL
E	Inconspicuous; purple berries.		Hummock, rooting	CLS
E	Small, yellow, in clusters.	Early–late spring	Spreader	CDLS
E	Small, yellow, in clusters.	Spring	Spreader	CDS
E	Small, yellow, in clusters.	Spring	Spreader	CDS
E	Small, white; red fruits.	Spring	Carpet, rooting	CD
E	Small, white; red fruits.	Spring	Carpet, rooting	CD

75

SHRUBS

	Country of Origin	Height and Planting Distance	Leaf Colour and Shape
MOLTKIA			
Sun, well-drained soil. A dense carpet. M. × *intermedia* is a hybrid between *M. petraea* and *M. suffruticosa*.			
× **intermedia**	Hybrid	6″ × 18″	Dark green, grass-like
MUEHLENBECKIA			
Dense, of dark effect owing to its dark leaves and masses of maroon thread-like stems, creeping by underground shoots. Excellent where it cannot become a nuisance. Full sun for darkest colouring.			
axillaris	Australasia	8″ × 2′	Tiny dark green.
MYRTUS			
This tiny myrtle is hardy in our warmer counties, particularly in maritime districts, suitable for the rock garden.			
nummularia	S. America	1″ × 18″	Small, dark green on
PACHYSANDRA			
Shade, dense or partial; light, lime-free soil encourages rapid colonizing. Flowers scented. *P. axillaris* is very slow to spread.			
axillaris	China	9″ × 15″	Rich green, glossy, b handsome.
terminalis	Japan	10″ × 3′	Rich green, glossy, too dense.
PACHISTIMA			
Neat plants for peaty lime-free soil, in sun or shade. Dense only when in ideal conditions.			
canbyi	E. U.S.A.	1′ × 1′	Tiny, dark green, bro in winter.
myrsinites	W. U.S.A.	1′ × 2′	Small, dark green, glc
PENSTEMON			
Dwarf shrubs for sunny well-drained positions in our warmer counties. *P. newberryi* is suitable for the rock garden.			
newberryi	W. U.S.A.	6″ × 1′	Small, dull green.
scouleri	W. N. America	1′ × 18″	Small, dull green.
PERNETTYA			
P. mucronata makes dense-growing bushes for lime-free, humus-laden soil, preferably in sun, where they usually berry more freely. Male and female plants (or an interchange of pollen) are required to ensure a regular crop of berries. The berries vary from white to pink, mauve and crimson. Davis' Hybrids (several colours) and 'Bell's Seedling' (dark red) are prolific in berry and self-fertile. They may be cut down in spring if becoming too lanky and open in growth. *P. tasmanica* is hardy in our warmer counties in cool peat beds.			
mucronata	S. America	3′ × 2′	Dark green, smooth, s reddish twigs.
tasmanica	Tasmania	3″ × 10″	Dark green, tiny, den

Deciduous or evergreen	Flower Colour and Fruits	Flowering Season	Habit	Propagation
E	Vivid blue in nodding heads.	Summer	Carpet	C
D	Minute, greenish-brown.	Summer	Spreader	D
E	Small, white; pink fruits.	Spring	Carpet, rooting	CD
E	Small, white, in spikes.	Spring	Clump	D
E	Small, white, in spikes.	Spring	Spreader	CD
E	Inconspicuous; white fruits.	Summer	Hummock	CLS
E	Inconspicuous; white fruits.	Spring–summer	Carpet	CLS
E	Cerise-crimson, tubular, showy.	Spring–summer	Carpet	CLS
E	Lilac, tubular, showy.	Spring–summer	Hummock	CLS
E	Tiny white bells in clusters.	Early summer	Spreader	CD
E	Tiny white bells; fruits usually red.	Early summer	Carpet, rooting	CDS

77

SHRUBS

	Country of Origin	Height and Planting Distance	Leaf Colour and Shape

PHILESIA
Cool, moist, peaty soil in shade, in the warmer counties. Rare and choice plant, easy to grow when once established, but slow.

| magellanica | S. Chile | 18″ × 18″ | Narrow, dark green. |

PIMELIA
Lime-free soil, full sun, sheltered slopes of rock garden. Not for cold gardens.

| coarctata | New Zealand | 2″ × 1′ | Tiny, glaucous, grey-g |
| prostrata | New Zealand | 2″ × 1′ | Tiny, glaucous, grey-g |

POTENTILLA
Not particular about soil, but they thrive best in one that does not dry out, and continue to produce flowers from June to October if well nourished. Full sun if possible and preferably away from overhanging trees. As they do not respond to cutting back or reducing in height it is important to choose a variety of the right height of growth at the start. They respond to an occasional removal of old wood from the base. From a garden point of view these superlative low shrubs are best placed in one group under *Potentilla fruticosa*, though some are hybrids of a closely related species, *PP. arbuscula, davurica, glabra, parvifolia* and *rigida*. The following are some of the most pretty and spreading varieties, though many more which are taller and more erect will also make dense cover if planted at a suitable distance apart. From the nearly prostrate *P. fruticosa mandschurica*, 'Longacre' and 'Clotted Cream' to the much more upright 'Katherine Dykes' they are clumpy shrubs for associating with heathers collectively, or for furnishing the foreground of borders. The cultivar 'Elizabeth' has been known for many years as *P. arbuscula*, and *P. farreri* as *P. f. prostrata* both erroneously. 'Tangerine' holds its colour best when not in full sun, or in the cooler north.

fruticosa
The Shrubby Cinquefoil is a variable native of districts around the Northern Hemisphere, deciduous, with small pretty divided leaves, softly hairy, and dense twiggy growth. The rich brown seed heads of several varieties add to the winter scene.

— 'Abbotswood'		2½′ × 3′	Soft green, hairy.
— 'Beesii' ('Nana Argentea' of gardens)		1½′ × 2′	Silvery, silky.
— 'Clotted Cream'		2′ × 3′	Grey-green, silky.
— 'Elisabeth'		3′ × 4′	Bright green, downy.
— 'Farreri'		1½′ × 3′	Bright green, downy.
— 'Katherine Dykes'		4′ × 3′	Bright green, finely cu downy.
— 'Longacre'		2½′ × 3′	Bright green.
— mandschurica		1½′ × 2½′	Grey-green, downy.
— parvifolia 'Farreri'		3′ × 3′	Bright green, finely cu downy.
— 'Primrose Beauty'		3′ × 4′	Grey-green, downy.
— 'Red Ace'		?2′ × 2′	Bright green.

Deciduous or Evergreen	Flower Colour and Fruits	Flowering Season	Habit	Propagation
E	Crimson bells.	Summer	Spreader	D
E	White, tiny, in small heads; white fruits.	Late spring	Carpet	CL
E	White, tiny, in small heads; white fruits.	Late spring	Carpet	CL
D	White.	Early summer–autumn	Hummock	CL
D	Sulphur-yellow.	Early summer–autumn	Hummock	CL
D	Creamy-yellow.	Early summer–autumn	Hummock	CL
D	Sulphur-yellow.	Early summer–autumn	Hummock	CL
D	Bright yellow.	Early summer–autumn	Hummock	CL
D	Light clear yellow.	Early summer–autumn	Hummock	CL
D	Light clear yellow.	Early summer–autumn	Hummock	CL
D	White.	Early summer–autumn	Hummock	CL
D	Bright yellow.	Early summer–autumn	Hummock	CL
D	Primrose-yellow.	Early summer–autumn	Hummock	CL
D	Tomato-red.	Early summer–autumn	Hummock	CL

79

SHRUBS

	Country of Origin	Height and Planting Distance	Leaf Colour and Shape
POTENTILLA *cont.*			
fruticosa			
— 'Tangerine' ('Donard Orange')		3′ × 3	Bright green, downy.
— 'Walton Park'		1½′ × 2′	Bright green, downy.

PRUNUS

Although the two laurels listed are not prostrate, the new 'Otto Luyken' is very dense and bushy and P. *l.* 'Zabeliana' is wide-spreading, more or less horizontal if enough snow falls every year to keep it level! Otherwise its branches ascend slightly, radiating beautifully. It is elegant in flower. The most brilliant form of the sun-loving, root-spreading P. *tenella* is known as 'Fire Hill' or 'Gessleriana'.

laurocerasus			
Europe. The cherry laurel thrives in sun or shade in any soil, and in old woodlands is as much a nuisance as *Rhododendron ponticum*. The two forms listed are choice and attractive.			
— 'Otto Luyken'		3′ × 5′	Dark shining green, sɪ
— 'Zabeliana'		4′ × 8′	Dark shining green, nar. pretty.
tenella (*P. nana*)	SE. Europe	2′ × 3′	Shining leaden green, sɪ

PTILOTRICHUM

Full sun, well-drained soil. Spiny dense little bushes.

spinosum (*Alyssum spinosum*)	S. Europe	1′ × 1′	Grey, small.

RHODODENDRON

(including *Azalea*)

Lime-free soil well mixed with humus in partial shade suits the majority best, though all those listed with small leaves will stand full sun so long as they are cool and moist at the roots; a slope away from the sun suits them well, provided it is not exposed to cold spring winds. On limy soils some keen gardeners achieve success by the application of sequestrine to a soil well mixed with acid peat. Few rhododendron species or hybrids are quick enough in growth to be valued as practical ground-cover, except in the most favourable climates with reasonably high rainfall, though with time all the following knit together and make dense cover. Like heathers, the dwarf truly evergreen species do not appreciate being cluttered with dead leaves through the winter, though all will take a mulch of leaf-mould; on the other hand the nearly evergreen Japanese azaleas take no harm from fallen leaves provided they are not covered by them when small, and indeed, many of them being comparatively sparse in growth, they could not be classed as ground-cover were it not for the way they gather the fallen leaves around them.

Specially good forms of species and hybrids are propagated vegetatively by discerning nurserymen and Award forms or selected forms should always be sought; for this reason reproduction of species by seed is not recommended. R. *pemakoense* increases its bulk by underground shoots and is in a mild form a 'spreader'. The foliage of the Award of Merit form of R. *saluenense* turns to shining beetroot-purple in winter. The 'Cherry Red' form of R. *calostrotum* makes a specially good contrast with its grey leaves. R. *ovatum* is an obscure hybrid; R. 'Myrtifolium' and R. 'Wilsonii' of gardens are similar tough, hardy hybrids and all three will stand fullest exposure and flower after most of the small sorts are over. There is a good white form of R. *ferrugineum* in cultivation and the species is one of the parents of the preceding three.

Deciduous or Evergreen	Flower Colour and Fruits	Flowering Season	Habit	Propagation
D	Light orange.	Early summer–autumn	Hummock	CL
D	Bright yellow.	Early summer–autumn	Hummock	CL
E	White, small, in spikes.	Spring	Hummock	C
E	White, small, in spikes, very free.	Spring	Semi-horizontal	C
D	Pink, borne along the stems.	Spring	Spreader	D
D	White, tiny, in small heads; profuse.	Summer	Hummock	S

	Country of Origin	Height and Planting Distance	Leaf Colour and Shape

RHODODENDRON *cont.*

Of recent years a race of dwarf hybrids have come from Germany, raised by Dietrich Hobbie, using among many other parents R. *forrestii repens* and R. *williamsianum* crossed with certain hardy hybrids. These are not yet fully tested and are mostly of a dark or dull red colouring, but tough and hardy. The following are worth watching: 'Ems', 'Camillo Schneider', 'Elizabeth Hobbie', 'Gertrude Schale', 'Ursula Siems' and 'Moerheim's Scarlet'. The last is promising. Some of the hybrids of R. *yakusimanum* may also be valuable when proved.

When compared with the ordinary garden hybrid rhododendrons, all of the following have small leaves; few exceed three inches in length.

	Country of Origin	Height and Planting Distance	Leaf Colour and Shape
calostrotum	W. China	1½' × 2½'	Grey-green, small.
campylogynum myrtilloides	W. China	9" × 1'	Dark green, tiny.
'Carmen'	Hybrid	2' × 3'	Dark green.
ferrugineum	Europe	2' × 3'	Rich green, narrow.
forrestii repens	Himalaya, etc.	9" × 2'	Dark green.
hanceanum 'Nanum'	W. China	1' × 1½'	Dark green, small.
'Impeanum'	Hybrid	1' × 2'	Dark green, tiny.
impeditum	W. China	1' × 1½'	Blue-green, tiny.
imperator	Burma	6" × 1'	Dark green, tiny.
'Jenny'	Hybrid	4' × 6'	Dark green, veined.
('Creeping Jenny' or 'Elizabeth' var. 'Jenny')			
keleticum	Himalaya, etc.	9" × 1'	Tiny, dark green, shiny.
'Lava Flow'	Hybrid	2' × 2'	Dark green.
leucaspis	Burma, etc.	2' × 4'	Dark green, hairy.
'Mucronatum'	Japan	3' × 6'	Soft green, hairy.
(*Azalea*)			
'Ripense' is a pale mauve; 'Bulstrode' is a magnificent warm white, hardy and free.			
ovatum	Hybrid	4' × 4'	Dark green.
(of gardens)			
pemakoense	Tibet, etc.	1½' × 1½'	Dark green.
× prostigiatum	Hybrid	1' × 1½'	Dark blue-green, tiny.
prostratum	W. China, etc.	1' × 2'	Bright green, tiny.
radicans	Tibet	6" × 2'	Dark green, glossy, tiny.
saluenense	W. China	2' × 2'	Rich green, shiny, small.
scintillans	W. China	1½' × 2'	Mid-green, tiny.
williamsianum	W. China	3' × 4'	Rounded, light green, smooth.

JAPANESE AZALEAS

Requiring the same conditions as rhododendrons. Semi-evergreen, with varying rich tones of autumn colour, from yellow through orange and red to dark maroon tones. Descended mainly from R*hododendron kiusianum*, the true Japanese Kurume varieties are very suitable for our purpose and are available in every tint between white and crimson. R. *kiusianum* is particularly dense and of tabular growth like the much taller and more vigorous other parent R. *obtusum amoenum* (see page 31). Some good spreading or dense varieties: 'Azuma Kagami', salmon-pink, rather tender; 'Hana Asobi', rose-carmine; 'Haru no Kyoki', white; 'Hino Degiri', crimson-scarlet; 'Hinomayo', vigorous, clean pink; 'Kasume

Deciduous or Evergreen	Flower Colour and Fruits	Flowering Season	Habit	Propagation
E	Pale to dark cherry.	Spring	Hummock	CL
E	Plum colour.	Spring	Hummock	CL
E	Deep red.	Spring	Hummock	CL
E	Pink or white.	Summer	Hummock	CL
E	Scarlet, large, bell-shaped.	Spring	Carpet	CL
E	Pale yellow, bell-shaped.	Spring	Hummock	CL
E	Lilac, in starry heads.	Spring	Hummock	CL
E	Pale to dark lilac-blue.	Spring	Hummock	CL
E	Violet-purple.	Spring	Carpet	CL
E	Scarlet, large, bell-shaped.	Spring	Hummock	CL
E	Reddish-purple, saucer-shaped.	Summer	Hummock	CL
E	Scarlet, large, bell-shaped.	Summer	Carpet	CL
E	Ivory-white, saucer-shaped.	Spring	Hummock	CL
E	White or mauve.	Spring	Hummock	CL
E	Rosy-red, small, in clusters.	Summer	Hummock	CL
E	Pale lilac-pink, large.	Spring	Hummock (spreading)	CL
E	Violet-purple, small, in starry heads.	Spring	Hummock	CL
E	Rich magenta.	Spring	Carpet	CL
E	Magenta, saucer-shaped.	Summer	Carpet	CL
E	Magenta-purple, saucer-shaped.	Early summer	Hummock	CL
E	Violet-blue, small, in starry heads.	Spring	Hummock	CL
E	Soft rosy-pink, bells, large.	Spring	Hummock	CL

	Country of Origin	Height and Planting Distance	Leaf Colour and Shape

RHODODENDRON *cont.*

Gaseki', shell-pink; 'Kiritsubo', rosy-lavender; 'Kumo no Yue', salmon-pink; 'Nani Wagata', palest mauve; 'Yaye Hiriryu', rose-crimson. These flower over a long spring period.

R. *indicum* heads another group, flowering later into June and even July. They are of lower, more spreading habit: 'Bungonishiki', terra-cotta, very late; 'Caldwellii', vivid rose-pink; 'Crispiflorum' vivid pink, very late; 'Kokinshita', salmon-orange, low and slow.

R. *simsii* is a species concerned in the late, large-flowering 'Gumpo' race (white to crimson); all rather tender. R. *kaempferi*, R. 'Malvatica' (of gardens) and R. 'Mucronatum' have been hybridized to produce a brilliant large-flowered hardy race of larger growing plants often achieving five feet or more. Those leaning towards the mauve of R. 'Malvatica' are usually the most spreading. The following are a few suitable growers for our purpose: 'Addy Wery', scarlet; 'Atalanta', lavender-purple; 'Bengal Fire', orange-red; 'Leo', orange-red; 'Pippa', soft lavender; 'Pulchrum Maxwellii', crimson.

RIBES

Will thrive in any reasonable fertile soil; sun or shade. This, the Mountain Currant, is very hardy and is most desirable in its form R. *alpinum* 'Aureum', whose leaves are flushed with yellow. All forms are sweetly fragrant in flower.

	Country of Origin	Height and Planting Distance	Leaf Colour and Shape
alpinum	N. Europe	6' × 7'	Rich green, small.
— 'Aureum'		3' × 3'	Bright yellowish-green, small.
— 'Pumilum'		3' × 4'	Rich green, small.

ROMNEYA

Full sun, well-drained soil. When luxuriating as it does in mild districts, it can be an effective ground-cover but takes some years to establish. Once really started there is no holding it, and therefore it is best in a bed against a wall where it cannot spread in all directions. R. *trichocalyx* spreads less, and is better in cooler districts. R. × *hybrida* has R. *coulteri* and R. *trichocalyx* as parents, and is supposed to be better than either. Pot-grown plants are easiest to establish.

	Country of Origin	Height and Planting Distance	Leaf Colour and Shape
coulteri	California	4' × 3'	Grey-green, smooth, divided.

ROSA

Content upon neutral soil rather than limy, medium light to heavy rather than clay, preferably in full sun. The roses listed below make complete cover and the higher ones are impenetrable. Apart from R. 'Macrantha' itself, there are two semi-double forms, 'Daisy Hill' and 'Scintillation', and rather taller is 'Lady Curzon'. Though there are many more roses of sprawling habit than those here listed they do not make dense cover. For further details see my book *Shrub Roses of Today*. R. *rugosa* and other species, see page 222. No pruning is required. R. *nitida* is noted for autumn colour.

	Country of Origin	Height and Planting Distance	Leaf Colour and Shape
'Macrantha'	Hybrid	5' × 8'	Dark green, rough.
'Max Graf'	Hybrid	3' × 8'	Dark green, glossy, sm:
nitida	E. N. America	18" × 2'	Shining green, small.
× paulii	Hybrid	5' × 15'	Dark green, rough.

Deciduous or Evergreen	Flower Colour and Fruits	Flowering Season	Habit	Propagation
D	Creamy-green, inconspicuous.	Spring	Hummock, rooting	CLS
D	Creamy-green, inconspicuous.	Spring	Hummock, rooting	CL
D	Creamy-green, inconspicuous.	Spring	Hummock, rooting	CL
D	5–7′. Large, white, silky, yellow stamens.	Summer onwards	Spreading	RS
D	Blush, large, fragrant, single, in clusters.	Midsummer	Hummock	CL
E	Bright pink, single, fragrant, in clusters.	Late summer	Carpet, rooting	CL
D	Small, single, pink; red heps.	Midsummer	Thicket	CD
D	White, in clusters, fragrant, single.	Midsummer	Hummock	CL

SHRUBS

	Country of Origin	Height and Planting Distance	Leaf Colour and Shape
ROSA *cont.*			
× paulii			
— 'Rosea'	Hybrid	3′ × 8′	Dark green, rough.
× polliniana	Hybrid	4′ × 9′	Dark green, rough.
'Raubritter'	Hybrid	3′ × 6′	Dark green, rough.
wichuraiana	Japan	18″ × 8	Dark green, smooth.
ROSMARINUS			
Well-drained soil, full sun. Often known as R. *officinalis prostratus*, R. *lavandulaceus* is only hardy in warm and maritime gardens. Rosemary.			
lavandulaceus (R. *officinalis prostratus*)		1′ × 6′	Dark green, smooth, beneath, fragrant.
officinalis		4′ × 5′	Dark green, smooth, beneath, fragrant.
RUBUS			
All thrive in sun or shade and are not particular as to soil. R. *tricolor* is one of the most rapid and satisfactory of covers. Rue.			
calycinoides (R. *fockeanus* of gardens)		2″ × 2′	Dark green, puckered.
tricolor	China	2′ × 10′	Dark green, shiny, stem covered red-brown h
RUTA			
Full sun, well-drained soil; hardy in all but the coldest gardens. Cutting back in spring helps to keep the plants bushy. Rue.			
graveolens	S. Europe	18″ × 18″	Grey-green filigree, fragrant.
— 'Jackman's Blue'		18″ × 18″	Blue-grey filigree, fragrant.
SALIX			
The many dwarf willows thrive on any soil that does not dry out, preferably in sun. They all bear catkins in spring. To make effective cover S. *caprea pendula* must be grown from cuttings.			
arbuscula (S. *formosa* in part)	Europe	1′ × 3′	The more prostrate fo make carpets of rich green.
caprea 'Pendula'		1′ × 5′	The 'weeping' form of Sallow.
× gillotii	Hybrid	1′ × 5′	Shining green, small, v vigorous.
× grahamii	Hybrid	1′ × 2′	Fairly prostrate, rich gre
lanata	N. Europe	3′ × 4′	Bluish grey-green, woo rounded, handsome. 'S artii' is a good form.
myrtilloides	N. Hemisphere	18″ × 2′	Similar to S. *arbuscula* S. × *grahamii*.

eciduous or vergreen	Flower Colour and Fruits	Flowering Season	Habit	Propagation
D	Clear pink, white centre, in clusters, fragrant.	Midsummer	Hummock	CL
D	Pale pink, single, fragrant, in clusters.	Midsummer	Hummock	CL
D	Bright pink, double, in clusters.	Midsummer	Hummock	CL
D	Small, white, single, fragrant, in clusters.	August onwards	Carpet, rooting	CL
E	Pale lavender, in clusters.	Late spring	Carpet, rooting	CL
E	Pale lavender, in clusters.	Late spring	Sprawler	CL
E	No floral beauty.		Carpet, rooting	CDL
E	White, small; occasional red fruits.	Summer	Carpet, rooting	CDL
E	Yellowish, small.	Summer onwards	Hummock	C
E	Yellowish; much superior in leaf.	Summer onwards	Hummock	C
D	Yellow catkins.	Spring	Carpet, rooting	CL
D	Grey-green catkins.	Spring	Sprawler	CL
D	Yellow catkins.	Spring	Carpet, rooting	CL
D	Yellow catkins.	Spring	Carpet, rooting	CL
D	Yellow catkins.	Spring	Hummock	CL
D	Yellow catkins.	Spring	Carpet, rooting	CL

SHRUBS

	Country of Origin	Height and Planting Distance	Leaf Colour and Shape

SALVIA
All need full sun, well-drained soil, preferably light. Apt to suffer in very severe winters in cold districts. Can be planted during growing season, but often fail from winter planting. If they become sparse they may be reduced in height in late spring to encourage basal growth.

officinalis. Sage.	S. Europe	18″ × 2′	Grey-green, soft, wool

— 'English Broad Leaf' — The handsome culinary form which does no flower.

— 'Purpurascens'
Closely resembles the 'English Broad Leaf', but sometimes flowers, and the leaves are a soft purplish-grey-green. A form with pink flecks on the leaves flowers freely.

More compact and less hardy varieties are *S. o. icterina*, leaves grey-green variegated yellow; and 'Variegata', grey-green marked white.

SANTOLINA
The Cotton Lavenders are all excellent for light, well-drained soils in full sun. If *S. chamaecyparissus* is clipped over every March it remains compact, but does not flower. By close planting all will join up and make dense cover. Not suitable for cold or very wet areas. They often need replanting after about five years, and the roots can be divided for this purpose in spring, and should be replanted deeply. See also *Addenda*.

chamaecyparissus (*S. incana*)	S. Europe	18″ × 2′	Whitish grey-green, wo dense filigree, fragra
— 'Nana' (*S. c. corsica*)		9″ × 1′	A compact, slow, dwa form.
neapolitana (*S. italica* 'Sulphurea' of gardens)		2′ × 2½′	Whiter than *S. chamaecyp sus*; feathery, fragrant
pectinata	SW. Europe	18″ × 2′	Greyish-green, woolly, dense filigree, fragrar
viridis (*S. virens*)	SW. Europe	18″ × 2′	Dark rich green, dense filigree, fragrant.

SARCOCOCCA
Shady places in any fertile soil suit these winter-flowering evergreens. The flowers are inconspicuous, but sweetly fragrant.

hookerana
Himalaya. Too tall for ground-cover, but the following variety is admirable, though slow, and has the most decorative flowers.

— digyna	China	2′ × 2′	Long, pointed, dark shi green.
humilis	China	15″ × 15″	Pointed, small, shining dark green.
ruscifolia	China	2′ × 2′	Oval, pointed, shining dark green.

SATUREIA
Full sun, well-drained, preferably light soil. These and the thymes assort well with heathers, etc.

montana	S. Europe, N. Africa	1′ × 18″	Small, dark green, fragr

eciduous or vergreen	Flower Colour and Fruits	Flowering Season	Habit	Propagation
E	Lavender-blue.	Midsummer	Hummock, rooting	CDLS
E			Hummock, rooting	CDL
E	Yellow buttons.	Summer	Hummock	CD
E	Bright lemon yellow.	Summer	Hummock	CD
E	Pale soft yellow buttons.	Summer	Hummock	CD
E	Yellow or lemon colour.	Summer	Hummock	CD
E	Tiny, pinky-white tassels; black fruits.	Late winter	Hummock, spreading	CD
E	Tiny, whitish tassels; black fruits.	Late winter	Hummock, spreading	CD
E	Tiny, whitish tassels; red fruits.	Late winter	Hummock, spreading	CD
E	Small, pale mauve, in small heads.	Late summer	Hummock	CDL

89

SHRUBS

	Country of Origin	Height and Planting Distance	Leaf Colour and Shape

SENECIO

Under *S. laxifolius* is described the well-known *S. greyi* of gardens. Flowers very brilliant; nipping out the ends of the strong shoots in spring prevents their flowering and is a useful tip where soft colour schemes are designed; it also keeps the plants bushy. *S. cineraria* is only for mild and maritime districts; much used as a bedding plant but a useful cover if allowed to expand. They both need full sun and well-drained soil.

	Country of Origin	Height and Planting Distance	Leaf Colour and Shape
cineraria	S. Europe	18″ × 2′	Greyish-white, downy, deeply divided.
laxifolius (of gardens)	New Zealand	3 × 4′	Oval, grey-green, woo white beneath.

SKIMMIA

Will thrive in any fertile soil if mixed with humus. All tolerate and thrive in shade, though they will also grow in sun, less luxuriantly. The flowers are small, creamy, in dense heads and the male forms are extremely fragrant. *S. j.* 'Rubella' is noted for the beauty of its winter buds. The leaves of *S. laureola* are fragrant and it is suitable for warm gardens and maritime districts.

	Country of Origin	Height and Planting Distance	Leaf Colour and Shape
japonica	Japan	3–5′ × 3–5′	Very variable species. D green, oval leaves.

Two noted female or hermaphrodite forms are 'Foremanii' and 'Rogersii'; a good male form is known as 'Bronze Knight'.

	Country of Origin	Height and Planting Distance	Leaf Colour and Shape
'Rubella' (*S. reevesiana* 'Rubella')		3′ × 3	Dark green, oval.
laureola	Himalaya	3–4′ × 3′	Rich green, fragrant w crushed.

SPIRAEA

Easily grown on any fertile soil, preferably in sun, though they grow and flower also in shade. Tiny flowers made conspicuous by their quantity. *S. hacquetii* is similar to *S. decumbens*.

	Country of Origin	Height and Planting Distance	Leaf Colour and Shape
× bumalda	Hybrid		

Forms of this species should have all weak thin wood cut out in winter, ensuring a longer flowering period. 'Walluffii' or 'Anthony Waterer Improved' is a form with richer colouring.

	Country of Origin	Height and Planting Distance	Leaf Colour and Shape
— 'Anthony Waterer'		3′ × 3′	Dark green, narrow, of flecked with pink.
decumbens	SE. Europe	8″ × 8″	Fresh green, small.
japonica			

One of the parents of *S.* × *bumalda* 'Anthony Waterer'. *S. j.* 'Froebellii' and *S. j.* 'Macrophylla' reach up to 4–5 ft, 3–4 ft apart, and make good cover; pink flowers; *S. j.* 'Macrophylla' has really splendid autumn colour. There is also a compact white form *S. j.* alba (*S. callosa alba*). Deciduous.

	Country of Origin	Height and Planting Distance	Leaf Colour and Shape
— 'Ruberrima' (*S. nana alpina*)		1′ × 18″	Dull green, small.

STEPHANANDRA

Culture as for spiraeas. Flowers inconspicuous; good autumn colour.

	Country of Origin	Height and Planting Distance	Leaf Colour and Shape
incisa (*S. flexuosa*)	Japan, Korea		

The dwarf form, *S. i.* 'Prostrata' or 'Crispa', is the only variety to describe as ground-cover.

	Country of Origin	Height and Planting Distance	Leaf Colour and Shape
— 'Prostrata'		3′ × 4′	Fresh green, deeply cut, small, arching branche

iduous or rgreen	Flower Colour and Fruits	Flowering Season	Habit	Propagation
E	Yellow daisies in branching heads.	Summer	Hummock	CS
E	Yellow daisies in branching heads.	Early summer	Hummock	CL
E	Female small flower-heads, creamy, red berries; male large flower-heads, fragrant, creamy.	Spring	Hummock	CL
E	Heads of red brown buds opening to creamy flowers.	Spring	Hummock	CL
E	Creamy; berries red.	Spring	Hummock	CL
D	Large flat heads of tiny crimson flowers.	Midsummer onwards	Hummock	CD
D	Small heads of tiny white flowers.	Midsummer onwards	Hummock	CD
D	Small heads of tiny pink flowers.	Midsummer onwards	Hummock	CD
D	Tiny, creamy.	Spring	Hummock, rooting	CDL

SHRUBS

	Country of Origin	Height and Planting Distance	Leaf Colour and Shape
SYMPHORICARPUS			
Easily grown in sun or shade in any fertile soil. Will bear most berries in sun. 'Hancock' i a new shrub of low habit and suckering from the root. Probably a seedling or hybrid o *S.* × *chenaultii* (*S. microphyllus* × *S. orbiculatus*). On trial. Flowers inconspicuous.			
'Hancock'	Hybrid	1'? × 3'?	Small, soft green.
THYMUS			
Labiatae. Full sun, light soil, acid or limy, well drained. The culinary thyme, *T. vulgaris*, i hardy and dense; its yellow-leaved form more so. *T. citriodorus* is suitable for sheltered sunny gardens.			
citriodorus	Hybrid		
Smaller than *T. vulgaris*; the creamy-white variegated 'Silver Queen' is highly attractive but not very hardy.			
nummularius	Asia Minor	8″ × 2′	Dark green, small.
vulgaris	S. Europe	10″ × 1′	Dark green, tiny, fra
— 'Aureus'		8″ × 1′	Yellowish-green, tin fragrant, very dens
— 'Variegatus'		8″ × 10″	Grey-green and whit fragrant.
VACCINIUM			
Lime-free somewhat moist soil with plenty of humus, sun or shade.			
macrocarpum	E. N. America, N. Asia	4″ × 3′	Tiny dark leaves, rapi carpeter when thri
oxycoccus	N. Hemisphere	3″ × 3′	Tiny leaves, rapid car dense when thrivin
vitis-idaea	NW. America	10″ × 1′	Box-like green leave burnished in winte
VIBURNUM			
All prefer full sun, though *V. davidii* and others will grow well in shade from a building also in open woodland. Any reasonable soil, heavy rather than light. Good on chalk. *V davidii* is slow, but worth waiting for and provides good 'line' and quality of leaf.			
davidii	China	2′ × 3′	Large, dark green, sm corrugated, handso
VINCA			
Periwinkle. Shade or partial shade, from buildings or trees; drained soil, good or poor limy or acid. Effective ground-cover when established, but they take two, three or fou years to become effective. *V. difformis* is only hardy in warmer counties. All produce lon; growths which root as they go; the flowers are borne on shorter shoots from centre o clump. *V. minor* and its green-leaved forms are the best for the average garden. Whe clumps get old and untidy, they may be cut over in winter, when the flowers will be more conspicuous. *V. major hirsuta* is the most rampant.			
difformis (*V. acutiflora*)	W. Mediterranean Region	15″ × 2′	Dark green, smooth, pointed.

Deciduous or Evergreen	Flower Colour and Fruits	Flowering Season	Habit	Propagation
D	Pink fruits in autumn.		Spreader	CL
E	Tiny, in small heads, lilac.	Summer	Carpet	CDS
E	Pale lilac, small, in small heads.	Summer	Hummock	CDL
E	Pale lilac, small, in small heads.	Summer	Hummock	CDL
E	Pale lilac, small, in small heads.	Summer	Hummock	CDL
E	Tiny pinkish-white bells; red fruits.	Summer	Carpet, rooting	CDL
E	Tiny dainty pink bells; red fruits.	Summer	Carpet, rooting	CDL
E	Tiny pinkish-white bells; red fruits.	Summer	Spreader	CDL
E	Flat heads of tiny white flowers. The female form has vivid blue berries.	Summer	Hummock	CLS
E	Palest blue.	Spring	Carpet, rooting	CD

SHRUBS

	Country of Origin	Height and Planting Distance	Leaf Colour and Shape
VINCA *cont.*			
major	Europe	15″ × 2′	Dark green, glossy.
— 'Elegantissima' (*V. m.* 'Variegata')		15″ × 18″	Dark green, splashed creamy-yellow, glos
— hirsuta (*V. m. pubescens* or *oxyloba*)		15″ × 2′	Dark green, dull.
minor	Europe	8″ × 2′	Dark green, small, sm pointed.

Many varieties: 'Argentea Variegata' and 'Variegata Aurea' have leaves marked cream and yellow respectively; 'Gertrude Jekyll' has white flowers and narrow foliage; these three are not so vigorous as the others. A more vigorous white variety is 'Alba'. 'Bowles' Variety' ('La Graveana') has large richly coloured flowers and broad foliage. 'Punicea' is red-purple; 'Multiplex' and 'Caerulea Plena' have double flowers, red-purple and lavender-blue respectively. These and others are all beautiful and useful.

XANTHORHIZA

Any reasonable soil; spreads fairly quickly by underground stolons in light soil. Sun or shade. Flowers inconspicuous before the leaves appear. Purplish-red autumn colour.

	Country of Origin	Height and Planting Distance	Leaf Colour and Shape
simplicissima (*X. apiifolia*)	China	3′ × 4′	Divided and lobed le ferny on erect stems.

ciduous or ergreen	Flower Colour and Fruits	Flowering Season	Habit	Propagation
E	Lavender-blue, large.	Spring	Carpet, rooting	CD
E	Lavender-blue, large.	Spring	Carpet, rooting	CD
E	Purple, narrow petals, poor.	Spring	Carpet, rooting	CD
E	Deep lavender-blue.	Spring	Carpet, rooting	CD
D	Maroon, tiny, in sprays.	Spring	Thicket	D

5

Climbing Plants

A CLIMBING plant, apart from a few annuals and those of herbaceous growth, may best be described as a shrub which will not
stand up without support. It is enabled to surmount obstacles by
means of twining round supports or attaching itself to them by
tendrils or prehensile leafstalks, or clambering over other plants
by means of hooked prickles, or with the aid of adventitious roots.
Climbers mostly achieve their object—to reach towards light and
air—rapidly and expertly, and are always the first choice we make
to cover an unsightly shed or to drape a wall or stump. Very
seldom are they considered for covering the ground, apart from
the ivies, and yet some of them would do the trick more quickly
than any other plant, and very beautifully.

Because *Rosa wichuraiana*, *Rubus tricolor*, *Forsythia suspensa
sieboldii* and *Jasminum nudiflorum* have none of the above aids they
have been included in the parts of this book devoted to shrubs,
though at first glance they might seem to be climbers. With
human aid they have generally been made to 'climb' fences, walls
and arches. Likewise some of the sprawlers mentioned in the last
chapter—*Euonymus fortunei radicans* and *Fatshedera lizei*, for instance
—could equally well be called climbers, but they are more shrubby
than climbing and so they also have received their due already.

How often we see, at the foot of a luxuriant climber such as a
Virginian creeper, a honeysuckle or clematis, a few shoots which
for lack of support lie flat on the ground and extend rapidly in
any direction until they encounter something over which they
can hoist themselves. This is just an example of how successful
they would be if they were deliberately encouraged to lie flat.
For they would need encouragement; they need to root as they
go, and for this reason need to be static, held in place by flat
brushwood to which they can cling, or by pegs, stones or logs.

There is no doubt that we should start our list with the ivies, among which *Hedera colchica* 'Dentata' (Fig. 21) has the largest leaves. It is handsome, distinctive, useful and of dark dull green. It reaches its highest achievement in the creamy-yellow variegated form, *H. c.* 'Dentato-variegata' (Pl. VIIIʙ) ('Variegata' or 'Aurea'), which is a most spectacular cover, somewhat less vigorous than the green. I remember a most beautiful winter example of it under big groups of *Rhododendron luteum* (*Azalea pontica*); its broad leaves contrasted vividly with the dense covering of fallen, brown azalea leaves. Of equal size but slightly tender is *Hedera canariensis*, which has the beautiful white and green variegated form known as 'Variegata' (Fig. 20) or 'Gloire de Marengo'; this should be given positions where icy winds cannot sere it.

Rather smaller but more glossy in leaf is the Irish Ivy, *H. helix hibernica* (Pl. XXIX). This is not only the finest ivy for ground-cover but is one of the most reliable and useful of all cover plants for large areas. Neither this nor the kinds mentioned above are as prone to ascend trees as the common ivy, but when fully estab-lished it will build up to the height of one foot in sun or shade. Some splendid large flats of it can be seen at Nymans, Sussex, Anglesey Abbey, Cambridgeshire, and at Kew; in the latter garden, coupled with big trees and lawns and great bulks of ever-green shrubs, it makes a remarkable contribution to the landscape both in its sombre colouring and its level sward—of considerable height compared with the mown lawn. It is ideal for large areas under trees.

Of the variation in colouring of the forms of *H. helix* there is, seemingly, no end. 'Silver Queen', 'Tricolor' and 'Marginata Major' are three good varieties with white variegation; 'Jubilee' ('Jubilee Goldheart' or 'Goldheart' of some nurseries) has a central tongue of yellow; 'Buttercup' (Pl. VIIIᴀ) is wholly yellow—or light green when growing in shade; 'Marmorata' is speckled with white, while a vigorous green form constantly breaking out into yellow-leaved shoots is called 'Angularis Aurea'. A luxuriant form with black-green, shining, long pointed leaves is 'Lobata Major'; it is handsome and efficient. *H. helix poetica* (*H. chrysocarpa*) 'Emerald Green' is a bright green small-leaved plant, coppery in winter. They are all excellent for the flat or on steep banks, and, if the young shoots are nipped at the ends and encouraged, they will speedily make good cover. So will the common ivy itself, but more often than not this is growing perforce in poor rooty soil under trees and is not an entire cover.

Taking the various vines and their relatives next I think the quickest-growing deciduous true climber is *Parthenocissus inserta* (*P.* or *Vitis vitacea*). Shoots will exceed ten feet in a season, and attach themselves to supports by twining tendrils. *P.* (*Vitis*) *quinquefolia* is the true Virginian creeper. It is similar, not quite so vigorous, and attaches itself by adhesive tendrils; the two therefore require different 'encouragement'. Both root as they go if secure, and both have brilliant autumn colour, thriving in sun or shade, with a preference for sun. *P. henryana*, with adhesive tendrils, has a preference for shade and is not so reliably hardy. The great leaves of *V. coignetiae* and *V. davidii* would be superb as ground-cover, creating a sheet of scarlet in autumn in sunny places; they both have twining tendrils. These twiners would certainly be best encouraged by brushwood laid flat and pegged in position; the twigs would eventually rot and the vine would assume complete and constant control.

For similar support we have the white *Clematis montana* and its selected pink forms, together with *C. rehderana*, *C. tangutica*, *C. glauca* and *C. orientalis*. They are arranged in decreasing vigour in this list, the last four having yellow bell-shaped flowers in late summer and autumn. All will thrive and flower in sun or shade. On hot sunny banks in warm counties the evergreen *C. armandii* would be magnificent, and lovely in flower in spring. A semi-herbaceous climber *C.* × *jouiniana*, for sun or shade, provides a froth of pearly blue flowers in autumn, while the still shorter *C. flammula* and *C. paniculata* have masses of tiny white flowers. *C. montana*, *C. rehderana* (*C. veitchiana* is very similar) and *C. flammula* are all fragrant. It is well known that *C.* × *jackmanii* and similar large-flowered garden hybrids can be trained on horizontal supports, but I do not feel justified to include them in my selection as they would need so much attention that they would not be work-free. Even *C.* × *jouiniana* would take some time to fill its allotted space; it dies back in cold winters in Surrey; on the other hand it will take root here and there along the stems, and fresh vigour will be given to the trails thereby.

A herbaceous climber for our quest is the perennial or ever-lasting pea, *Lathyrus latifolius*. On steep banks at The Weir, Herefordshire, and on the flat at Nymans, Sussex, both National Trust properties, this plant makes widespread masses of shoots and is covered with its magenta-pink flowers for weeks. I prefer the pale pink and the white forms, but all are equally vigorous.

I see that *Akebia quinata* and *Celastrus scandens* are recommended in the United States for cover; they are extremely vigorous twiners and such a mode of growth does not really lend itself to covering the ground, though those other twiners, the honey-suckles, will make excellent cover, being more bushy. One of the most rampant is *Lonicera japonica halliana*, and in all but exposed districts it is evergreen, and grows and flowers nearly as well in shade as it does in the sun. It has creamy flowers—turning to Chinese yellow as they wane—along the shoots, and appearing from July onwards. *L. henryi* is more handsome in leaf but has poor flowers. The common deciduous native honeysuckle has two good garden forms, *L. periclymenum belgica* ('Early Dutch') and *serotina* ('Late Dutch') (Pl. XXVIIb), both of which are heavily scented and flower in sequence at midsummer. They may frequently be seen making procumbent bushes two or three feet high and extending well. The richer pink *L.* × *americana* (*L.* × *grata* or *L.* × *italica*) and the very vigorous yellow *L. etrusca* 'Superba' are rather more bushy and wayward and would be less procumbent, though this might be no disadvantage on a big site. Both would grow to some six feet in height.

With adventitious roots like those on the stems of an ivy, enabling them to be self-clinging to a wall or pavement or rooting in the soil, are the Trumpet Creepers and the climbing hydrangeas. For the hottest of sunny banks the former would be useful. They are often known as *Bignonia* or *Tecoma* but their accepted name today is *Campsis*. *C. radicans* or *C. grandiflora*, or the superior hybrid between them both *C.* × *tagliabuana* 'Madame Galen', are all vigorous when established, with fresh green leaves and bunches of exotic orange-red trumpet-shaped flowers at the tip of every summer's shoot. Only a warm summer and autumn will encourage them to flower freely, when they make a superb display. The hydrangea is *H. petiolaris*, now known as *H. anomala petiolaris*; it is of similar habit and often recommended for north walls, though it flowers much more freely in full sun. As a ground-cover it will quickly colonize the ground, and bears fresh green leaves and great wide lace-cap heads of white flowers at mid-summer, borne on the strong side-shoots when established. Though the closely related *Schizophragma integrifolia* is a superior plant in flower and leaf I have never seen it covering the ground.

The heights and distances apart for planting given in the Table must be taken as more approximate than those in the rest of the book. The height will naturally depend on two factors: how high, if any, the initial support of twigs, wires, etc., is, and the tendency of the plant to mound itself into a shrubby mass. The widths might all be easily exceeded with good cultivation and patience, but with this type of cover, where long shoots will strike out in all directions and not thicken into weed-proof cover at least until the second year, cleaning the ground is not easy. The temporary lifting up of the long trails to apply a weedkiller would destroy their chance of rooting and so lessen their speed of covering.

A climbing plant used as ground-cover is the answer to those problems one occasionally meets where an unsightly flat area of concrete has to be disguised and beautified. Obviously the self-clinging kinds will be the most suitable, though others will succeed if kept in place by stones or bricks.

A last counsel is that climbers should only be used where there are no plants near by for them to cling to, otherwise they will take hold and smother small trees and large bushes.

CLIMBERS

	Country of Origin	Height and Planting Distance	Leaf Colour and Shape

ARISTOLOCHIA
Preferring sun, rather slow to start but all-conquering when established. It needs something to twine round. The flowers are intriguing, shaped like small tobacco pipes.

macrophylla (*A. durior, A. sipho*)	E. N. America	18″ × 5′	Large, rounded, soft green.

CAMPSIS
The commonest Trumpet Creeper (*Bignonia* or *Tecoma*) is *C. radicans*, and, when late summer and autumn are sufficiently sunny, it produces plenty of flowers; suitable for any fertile soil, preferably on a south-facing bank. *C. grandiflora* has wider more beautiful flowers. The most free-flowering is the hybrid *C.* × *tagliabuana* 'Madame Galen' (*C. radicans* × *C. grandiflora*). The annual flowering shoots are frequently damaged in a cold winter, and are best cut away in spring every year.

radicans	SE. U.S.A.	3′ × 8′	Fresh green, pinnate, elegant.

CISSUS
The species included is only likely to be hardy in full sun in our warmer counties; any fertile soil suits it. A rapid creeper when established.

striata (*Ampelopsis sempervirens*)	S. America	9″ × 3′	Dark glossy green, divided.

CLEMATIS
Best on retentive soils, neutral or limy; sun, or shade from buildings. *C. montana* and *rehderiana*, vigorous on acid soils. *C.* × *vedrariensis* and *C. chrysocoma* are similar, but superior, to most pink forms of *C. montana*. *C. veitchiana* resembles *C. rehderiana*. *C.* × *jouiniana* is a herbaceous plant in all but the warmest counties, but vigorous and effective. *C. tangutica* is usually known as *C. t. obtusiuscula*. All are fragrant except *C. tangutica*, *C. glauca* and *C. orientalis*.

armandii	China	18″ × 8′	Shining dark green.
flammula	S. Europe	2′ × 4′	Small, green.
glauca	W. China	2′ × 10′	Small, green.

The variety *C. g. akebioides* is usually considered the best.

× jouiniana	Hybrid	2′ × 8′	Dark green, handsome.
montana	Himalaya	2′ × 12′	Dark green.

Good forms of *C. montana* with pink flowers are 'Elizabeth' and 'Tetrarose'. *C. m. wilsonii* usually flowers in summer.

orientalis	N. Asia	2′ × 10′	Small, greyish-green.

Deciduous or Evergreen	Flower Colour and Fruits	Flowering Season	Habit	Propagation
D	Small, brown, hidden.		Creeper with twining stems	SL
D	Soft orange-red trumpets in clusters.		Creeper with rooting stems	DL
E	Inconspicuous; fruits small, purplish.		Creeper with adhesive tendrils	CLS
E	Pinky-white in clusters.	Spring	Creeper with twining leaf-stalks	LS
D	Small, white, in large clusters.	Late summer	Creeper with twining leaf-stalks	LS
D	Orange-yellow bells, borne singly.	Autumn	Creeper with twining leaf-stalks	LS
D	Pearly-blue, small, in clusters.	Autumn	Creeper with twining leaf-stalks	DL
D	White.	Spring	Creeper with twining leaf-stalks	LS
D	Small yellow bells, silvery seed heads.	Autumn	Creeper with twining leaf-stalks	LS

CLIMBERS

	Country of Origin	Height and Planting Distance	Leaf Colour and Shape
CLEMATIS *cont.*			
rehderana	China	2′ × 15′	Dark green, hairy.
tangutica	China	2′ × 10′	Small, green.

HEDERA

Thriving in any soil that is not a bog, the ivies will make admirable cover for dense shade or sun so long as the soil does not become too baked and dry. Most of them grow best in partial shade. The most effective rampageous cover is found in *H. helix hibernica*; it is far more effective than *H. helix*, though this in its many forms if well grown and encouraged to thicken by pinching out the growing tips becomes dense after a few years. Some good white variegated forms are 'Silver Queen', 'Tricolor' and 'Glacier'; 'Marmorata' is spotted; 'Jubilee' ('Gold Heart') streaked with yellow; 'Cristata', parsley-frilled, green; and 'Caenwoodiana' is dark green with narrow pointed leaves; 'Buttercup', soft yellow all over if grown in sun but not very vigorous; 'Angularis Aurea' becomes best splashed with yellow in full sun. *H. helix* 'Lobata Major' approaches *H. h. hibernica* in size, with very dark leaves. For the bright green 'Emerald Green' see *H. h. poetica*. *H. colchica* 'Dentata' and its primrose-yellow variegated form, together with *H. canariensis* and *H. c.* 'Variegata', are conspicuous by reason of their large leaves. The last species is not hardy in very cold districts. Some dwarf forms will be found in Chapter 4.

canariensis	Canary Islands	9″ × 5′	Broad, rounded, dark glossy green.

H. c. 'Variegata' ('Gloire de Marengo') is beautifully marked with green, grey and white.

colchica	Caucasus	9″ × 3′	Broad, rounded, dark gr

H. c. 'Dentata' and *H. c.* 'Dentato-variegata' are the most magnificent forms. 'Dentato-variegata' is handsomely marked with green, grey and primrose-yellow.

helix	Europe	6″ × 2′	Pointed, mottled in da and light green. Com Ivy.
— hibernica	Ireland, Scotland	1′ × 6	Dark green, large. Iris Ivy.
— poetica (*H. helix chrysocarpa*)	S. Europe, etc.	9″ × 3′	Bright green, rounded, coppery in winter.

HYDRANGEA

The climbing hydrangea, self-clinging on walls, makes good cover and will ascend stumps and tree trunks. Sun or shade. Not particular as to soil. Flowers most freely in sun. See also under *Schizophragma*.

anomala petiolaris (*H. petiolaris*)	Japan	2′ × 6′	Fresh green, rounded.

LATHYRUS

Easily pleased in any well-drained soil; excellent for dry slopes. Everlasting Pea. Herbaceous.

latifolius, Perennial Pea	Europe	2′ × 5′	Fresh green.

Deciduous or Evergreen	Flower Colour and Fruits	Flowering Season	Habit	Propagation
D	Small bells, yellow, in branching heads.	Autumn	Creeper with twining leaf-stalks	LS
D	Small yellow bells, silvery seed heads.	Autumn	Creeper with twining leaf-stalks	LS
E	Greenish; fruits blackish.	Autumn	Carpet, rooting	CL
E	Greenish; fruits yellowish.	Autumn	Carpet, rooting	CL
E	Greenish; fruits blackish.	Autumn	Carpet, rooting	CL
E	Greenish; fruits blackish.	Autumn	Carpet, rooting	CL
E	Greenish; fruits blackish.	Autumn	Carpet, rooting	CL
D	White florets around tiny greenish flowers.	Midsummer	High carpet, rooting	CLS
D	Magenta-pink, pale pink or white.	Summer	Creeper with twining tendrils	S

105

CLIMBERS

	Country of Origin	Height and Planting Distance	Leaf Colour and Shape
LONICERA			

The honeysuckles are content in any fertile soil. Cultivars of *Lonicera japonica* are not reliably evergreen in cold districts or cold winters. All are very fragrant. Flowers of all kinds turn to deep Chinese yellow with age.

	Country of Origin	Height and Planting Distance	Leaf Colour and Shape
japonica	Far East	1′ × 3	Broad, deep green, twining growth.

Well-known varieties are *halliana* (prolific, vigorous, cream flowers) and 'Aureo-Reticulata', foliage netted with yellow, non-flowering, more compact. *L. j. halliana* should be clipped severely in spring if it gets untidy. It responds well.

periclymenum	Europe, etc.	1′ × 4′	Broad, soft green; twining growths.

The names *belgica* ('Early Dutch') and *serotina* ('Late Dutch') refer to forms which have been selected to prolong the flowering season.

PARTHENOCISSUS			

(*Vitis*) Good growers in any well-drained soil; sun or shade. The leaves of *V. henryana* are most velvety and dark in shade. All have deeply lobed leaves and all have good autumn colour. *V. himalayana* has still larger leaves than those mentioned but is less hardy.

henryana	China	6″ × 8′	Velvety, dark green, pale veins.
himalayana	Himalaya	1′ × 10′	Large, deeply lobed, coarse.
inserta (*P. vitacea*)	N. America	1′ × 12	Large, deeply lobed.
quinquefolia (*Vitis hederacea*)	E. N. America	1′ × 10′	Large, deeply lobed, coarse.
tricuspidata (*Ampelopsis veitchii, Vitis inconstans*)	Japan, China	9″ × 8	Large, slightly lobed.

SCHIZOPHRAGMA			

S. hydrangeoides and the even more magnificent *S. integrifolia* should be nearly as successful for ground-cover as *Hydrangea petiolaris*, but they flower best in full sun. The outer flowers on the erect pyramids bear one large cream bract which lasts in beauty for three months. (*Hydrangea petiolaris* is of less duration, but is a commoner plant and more free-growing.)

VITIS			

Full sun and rich soil if they are to spread quickly. Brilliant autumn colour. For other species of *Vitis*, see *Parthenocissus*. Vine.

coignetiae	Japan	2′ × 12	Large, rounded, coarse.
davidii	China	2′ × 12′	Large, rounded, coarse.

ciduous or ergreen	Flower Colour and Fruits	Flowering Season	Habit	Propagation
E	Fragrant creamy honeysuckle.	Summer onwards	Twiner, rooting	CL
D	Fragrant honeysuckle; red berries.	Summer	Twiner, rooting	CL
D	Inconspicuous.		Creeper with adhesive tendrils	CL
D	Inconspicuous.		Creeper with adhesive tendrils	CL
D	Inconspicuous.		Creeper with twining tendrils	CL
D	Inconspicuous.		Creeper with adhesive tendrils	CL
D	Inconspicuous.		Creeper with adhesive tendrils	CL
D	Inconspicuous.		Creeper with twining tendrils	CL
D	Inconspicuous.		Creeper with twining tendrils	CL

6

Conifers

EVERYONE who picks up this book may be expected to know the difference between a shrub and a plant, and a grass, fern or climbing plant, but I think conifers may need a word of explanation. They are, to start with, all trees or shrubs and all the kinds suitable for ground-cover are evergreen. They embrace firs, pines, cypresses, yews, junipers and a few other genera, all of which have resinous wood, in fact the twigs and leaves are redolent of turpentine or other oily substances which are extracted from some of the species. The tiny, sharp or blunt, narrow, scale-like leaves sticking out from the twigs or appressed to them—or longer, like needles, in the pines and firs—are dark green or verging to blue or grey, sometimes flushed with yellow. The leaves are closely spaced and are smooth, but usually dull, and this surface and their dense array gives a special effect of uniform dusky velvetiness (though they are by no means velvety to the touch, even quite prickly in some firs and junipers) and of absorbing light rather than reflecting it. Heathers and their relatives have the same quality. It is this which makes the junipers so well worth studying when considering the contrast of different spreads of leaves, from which all interesting garden pictures are made. The title 'conifer' derives from 'bearing cones', but while many do bear these woody seed receptacles, a few have fleshy seeds, such as the sweet red fruits of the yew enclosing poisonous seeds, and the purple fruits of the juniper covered in a blue 'bloom' like those of a damson. An extract from the juniper berry is used to flavour gin, but I like to think that the value of their leaves in the garden is greater than that of their berries. . . .

From our present point of view ground-covering conifers may be divided simply into junipers and the rest. The junipers are extremely valuable to us both aesthetically and practically, and are useful in many ways. Their neat, level growth makes them just as suitable for formal as for informal covering, and a few discerning gardeners use them as informal edgings to the flower border, tidying the foreground as well as providing a dark foil for the colour above. They are of varied tints of green and the lie of their branches is equally varied, some prostrate and decurving, others prostrate with ascending tips, and yet others grow at an angle upwards and yet still make carpets of limitless width. A healthy juniper, advancing over the ground as the years go by, is as effective and all-conquering as any other cover.

Our native species, *Juniperus communis*, which may be seen growing on limy downland in Wiltshire and elsewhere, has several valuable prostrate cultivars. 'Hornibrookii' (Pl. Xa) is one of the best known and generally useful, and may be taken as an example. Like most of the varieties of common juniper its twigs, though rising from the ground, arch at the tip and give the impression of flowing like water over rocky ground. 'Silver Lining' and 'Prostrata' are still more prostrate, and in the former the whole plant is lighted by the grey-white undersurface of the leaves, many of which are tilted upwards, revealing this distinction. It assumes burnished tones in winter by way of contrast; the others mentioned retain their dark grey-green through the year. 'Repanda', whose growth is like 'Hornibrookii' but more vigorous and arching, becomes a soft brownish tint in winter.

Making considerably higher plants are the forms of *J. c. depressa*, the Canadian variant of the species. In this and its forms the leaves point to the ground and do not reveal whatever glaucous tint may be on their lower sides, and the growth is more arching. A well-known clone of *J. c. depressa* has been named 'Depressed Star'; there are gay yellowish varieties and one called 'Vase', which is considerably more erect and assumes deep brown or maroon tones in winter.

If the varieties of *J. communis* can be likened to flowing water, those of *J. horizontalis* (Pl. Xb) may perhaps be said to resemble water being forced out; particularly is this so when they are growing on a bank, with every tip held horizontally, eventually to lie down under the weight of the elongating shoot. There is, however, an extra prostrate form called 'Prostrata' which is the commonest in cultivation. Several forms are becoming popular in the United States, like 'Wiltonii', 'Bar Harbour', 'Glauca' and 'Douglasii', the Waukegan Juniper; they are all prostrate, grey-green in summer, turning to a light glaucous-violet in winter. A grouping of these and *Cyathodes colensoi* together with *Bergenia* 'Sunningdale' or 'Ballawley' and some of the orange-leafed callunas would provide a spectacle of great richness and interest throughout the year.

Completely in contrast to the subdued colouring of all of the above junipers except the yellow-tinted forms are some kinds of fresh green colouring. *J. procumbens* 'Bonin Island' is of a comparatively pale green, very dense and prostrate, following the contours of rocks or ground. It is an ideal foreground cover-plant, and is used with good effect at Tintinhull, a National Trust garden in Somerset. The other two species have much larger leaves than those already mentioned; they are the completely prostrate *J. taxifolia lutchuensis*, with blunt leaves, and *J. conferta* (*J. littoralis*), which achieves one foot in height, but speedily covers the ground with its prolific branchlets covered with long prickly leaves.

The last two are Japanese species while the Chinese Juniper, *J. chinensis*, has a stiffly semi-prostrate, clear green variety called 'Parsonsii' (or sometimes *J. davurica* 'Expansa'). This is a remarkable plant and must be the most horizontally growing shrub whose branches do not rest on the ground. I have seen plants six to seven feet across whose branches are rigidly held a few inches above the soil. Its foliage is mainly adult and it is rather slow-growing.

When we come to *J. sabina* and its hybrids we have before us plants which attain considerable height. *J. sabina* itself, if planted closely together, would make excellent cover up to four or five feet high, but its form *J. s.* 'Tamariscifolia' (Fig. 10) is low, compact, of deep blue-green. It is the best known of all these junipers, but the one I should choose last, because it is slow-growing, makes a mound rather than a carpet, and sometimes suffers from 'die-back' of the young branches. I am told that the more glaucous forms are not so prone to this trouble. Crossed with *J. chinensis*, *J. sabina* has given us *J.* × *media*, of which the clone known as 'Pfitzerana' or 'Knaphill Savin' is best known (Fig. 72). It is of soft grey-green; coupled with its yellowish form 'Aurea' and blue-green form 'Glauca' we have a trio of vigorous, feathery, graceful plants capable of achieving large proportions in time. These are suitable for the biggest areas, though often misguidedly planted in small gardens, where they have to be cut back eventually, completely spoiling their luxuriant and beautiful line. In addition to their general use in sunshine, they grow reasonably well under trees, even under cedars. A huge area of 'Pfitzerana' covers a chalky slope at Polesden Lacey, Surrey, to perfection and makes a lovely foil to the autumn-colouring berberis nearby. Care should be taken when planting these vigorous plants to ensure that the branches are in a horizontal position, or nearly so; if necessary they should be pegged down. The line of many plants is spoiled by the branches being left too upright at planting time.

The palest glaucous juniper for our purpose is *J. virginiana* 'Chamberlaynii', a prostrate variety of the so-called Pencil Cedar; this name is given—though it is not even closely related to a cedar—because its smooth fragrant wood is used for making pencils. 'Chamberlaynii' is a beautiful pale grey-green variety, lacy and flat-growing.

The remaining conifers are few. The prostrate spruce *Picea abies* 'Reflexa', sometimes labelled 'Pendula' (Pl. Xc), and the prostrate Hemlock Spruce *Tsuga canadensis* 'Pendula', are both delightful rather slow spreaders for preferably lime-free, sandy soil, and are often seen trained erect, like small weeping trees. Even so, the hemlock is a species that will tolerate some lime and it grows particularly well at Sizergh Castle, Westmorland, on a sunny and rather limy bank. Dark green *Podocarpus nivalis* forms a rich green low hummock, likewise the low-growing yew, *Taxus baccata* 'Repandens' in darkest green for any garden and any soil. Owing to its eventual very large size, in time achieving fifty feet across, I will leave *T. b.* 'Dovastonii' and its golden form for Chapter 10, though we may all be tempted to plant it in our small gardens for the horizontal poise of its branches, hung with drooping twigs. Three closely related forms of *Chamaecyparis lawsoniana*, 'Knowefieldensis', 'Nidiformis' and 'Tamariscifolia', slowly make great rounded bushes usually wider than high and densely clothed to the ground. They are useful for their heavy, bold effect.

There is no doubt that these plants, and the junipers in particular, fulfil all needs in ground-cover, and are the perfect adjuncts to the larger rock garden and heath garden, though they may be used, as mentioned above, in other positions, on flat or sloping ground, in formal or informal schemes. They are among the plants I recommend for planting graves, in Chapter 10.

All conifers transplant best when the soil is warm and moist, as it may well be in October; young stock can be moved safely through the winter if lifted with a ball of soil, or grown in a container; otherwise it is better to wait till warm moist weather in the spring—even as late as May in cold districts. All the conifers here mentioned grow best in well-drained soil, light rather than very heavy, and most attain their greatest luxuriance in full sunshine. The green varieties of *Taxus* will grow well in shade. *Taxus* and *Juniperus* grow well on lime and chalk soils. *Juniperus*, *Taxus* and *Picea* can be grown from cuttings or can be layered. All will achieve twice the width suggested for planting, in time. They must all be regarded as rather slow in growth, putting on three to six inches every year, but are dense and satisfactory.

CHAMAECYPARIS
lawsoniana. W. U.S.A. Lawson's Cypress. A tall tree of easy culture in any reasonably drained soil in sun or shade. The three following forms have drooping branchlets and create wide bun-shaped bushes, of rich lacy greenery. They are so full of character and solidity that they are best grown singly. They are closely related.
— 'Knowefieldensis'
— 'Nidiformis'
— 'Tamariscifolia'

JUNIPERUS. *J. sabina*, *J. conferta* and *J. × media* varieties will grow well in shade, but the rest are best in full sun, and exposure to winds keeps them compact. 'Juvenile' foliage refers to the leaves being at an angle to the branch (feathery); 'adult' indicates that the leaves are shorter and appressed to the twig (whipcord).
chinensis. Far East. Normally a fairly tall, erect tree, the Chinese Juniper has given some good varieties and hybrids of low or prostrate growth. 'Parsonsii' is a remarkably rigid, flat variety

with almost prostrate, long plumose branches, with clear green, mainly adult foliage. There is a variegated form. *J. c. sargentii* of bluish green with a still bluer form 'Glauca', together with 'San José', soft sage-green, all with juvenile and adult foliage. For linking together in a few years they may be planted about three feet apart and will probably grow to one to two feet in height.

communis. N. Hemisphere, including Britain. Of variable growth, thriving on chalk or any other well-drained soils. All varieties have comparatively long, sharply pointed leaves. The following are some of the more distinctive and prostrate cultivars.

— **depressa.** The Canadian variant, characterized by the leaves all pointing to the ground. Deep grey-green. A useful vigorous semi-prostrate plant. 1' x 3'. 'Depressed Star' is the name for a widely distributed clone of this variant. 'Depressa Aurea' has young growth of bright yellow, tarnishing as the year advances. 'Dumosa', 'Gimbornii' and 'Vase' are more upright forms, but still of spreading habit; the last named turns to a maroon tint in winter.

— 'Hornibrookii'. An Irish foundling, of dark grey-green. While remaining 9" high it will soon achieve 3' in diameter.

— 'Repanda'. Similar if not identical to *J. c.* 'Effusa'. A vigorous form, prostrate when young and quickly achieving 1' x 3' but gaining greater height later. Dark grey-green, burnished in winter.

— **saxatilis.** Dark grey-green, bushy and dense. 1' x 2'.

— 'Silver Lining'. Extremely prostrate, hugging the contours of the ground, leaves glaucous white beneath. Rather sparse when young. 6' x 2'.

conferta. Japan (*J. litoralis*). Prostrate stems giving rise to branchlets up to 1' high, clothed in long, bright green, sharp leaves. Not reliably hardy in the coldest districts but excellent at the seaside. 1' x 3'.

horizontalis. N. America. The Creeping Juniper lives well up to its name; its trailing stems are slightly upturned at the tips in the dark grey-green 'Prostrata'. 'Glauca' is somewhat higher than the following but all four make dense carpets of grey-green, which turn to glaucous violet in winter and are extremely effective in every way: 'Bar Harbor', 'Douglasii' (the Waukegan Juniper).

— 'Emerson' ('Black Hills Creeper') and 'Wiltonii' ('Wilton Carpet' or 'Blue Rug') are two which are popular in the United States, both with blue-grey foliage.

— 'Plumosa' is considerably taller than the others, more like the Pfitzer Juniper, and has mainly juvenile foliage.

— 'Viridis' is notably green. All of the above could be planted $2\frac{1}{2}$–3' apart.

× **media.** Hybrids between *J. chinensis* and *J. sabina*. Vigorous shrubs with ascending branches bearing drooping plumose branchlets; successful high ground-cover. Each plant will achieve about 6' x 20' in time, but can be planted at 4' apart for reasonably quick cover. Will grow under trees, even under cedars.

— 'Pfitzerana'. The best known: 'Knaphill Savin'. Perhaps the most vigorous, dense and successful. Soft green.

— 'Pfitzerana Aurea'. Slightly less vigorous. Young growths tinted with yellow, but the colour disappears as autumn approaches. 'Old Gold' is brighter but perhaps less prostrate.

— 'Pfitzerana Glauca'. Somewhat glaucous green.

procumbens. Japan. Bluish grey-green, carpet forming, dense and flowing over the ground. 'Nana' and the fresh light green 'Bonin Island' closely resemble each other, if they are not synonymous. 5" x $2\frac{1}{2}$'.

sabina. Europe and N. Asia. Savin Juniper. In its more normal forms it has branches ascending at an angle of about 45 degrees, but yet eventually forming high ground-cover of mainly adult, dark green leaves. Plant about 4' apart, though all forms will eventually achieve 8' or more across in time.

— 'Tamariscifolia'. Very popular, dense, blue-green, with mainly juvenile leaves; slow-growing, forming a flat-topped mound 1–2' x 2–4'.

— 'Arcadia', bright green, and 'Skandia', yellowish green, are comparatively compact, while 'Hicksii' is greyish-green and vigorous. All three are American selections from *J. s.* 'Tamariscifolia'.

scopulorum. Rocky Mountain Juniper. Deep green foliage. A prostrate form is *J. s.* 'Repens'.

taxifolia. Japan. A completely prostrate form is *J. t. lutchuensis*.

Ground-hugging, of fresh green like *J. conferta,* but with shorter, blunter leaves. 4″ x 2′.

virginiana. N. America. The 'Pencil Cedar' has a variety 'Tripartita' which bears considerable resemblance to the Pfitzer Juniper, but is more erect, of a darker bluish green, and more prickly in its juvenile foliage. 'Chamberlaynii' is an almost prostrate form of pronounced pale grey-green; perhaps 1′ x 3′.

PICEA. The Norway Spruce has one completely prostrate variety and one fairly flat-growing variety among the dwarf sports. Both make annual growth of about 5″.

abies 'Reflexa' ('Pendula' of gardens). 1′ x 3′. Rich green. Prostrate following the contours of the ground.

— 'Procumbens'. 1′ x 3′. Rich green. Stiff, nearly horizontal, forming a dense, low, flat-topped mound.

PODOCARPUS. The species listed is a pleasant though undistinguished mound of yew-like greenery.

nivalis. New Zealand. 2–3′ x 3–4′. Dark green, tiny; sprawling habit, rooting as it grows.

TAXUS. The English Yew thrives on any well-drained soil, including chalk, in sun or shade. Variegated forms need sun to give them good colour.

baccata. Europe, Asia. *T. baccata* 'Dovastonii' reaches an excessive size, but as a young plant both it and its golden variety are often chosen for creating a horizontal 'line' in planting design.

— 'Dovastonii'. Dark green leaves, borne on drooping twigs from almost horizontal branches. 'Dovastonii Aurea' is warmed with golden yellow. Limitless in spread, but it is long before it achieves 5′ in height. Plant about 5′ apart.

— 'Repandens'. 18″ x 3′. Very dark green, horizontal growth. Slow and dense.

TSUGA. Most of the Hemlock Spruces prefer sandy, lime-free soils, but *T. canadensis* will grow on lime provided there is plenty of humus present.

canadensis 'Pendula'. 18″ x 3′. A weeping form of the Eastern Hemlock, slowly making beautiful cover; bright green young foliage.

7

Herbaceous Plants

It MIGHT be claimed that *all* herbaceous plants such as phloxes, heleniums and Michaelmas daisies create ground-cover. So they do, but if they have few basal leaves or spread too slowly, or need staking, they have been omitted from this book.

We are not confronted in this chapter with so many qualifications as among the shrubs, but there are certain plants which create good ground-cover but which, for one reason or another, I have not seen fit to include in the Alphabetical Table. For instance, few of us garden in frost-free areas, but those who do so would no doubt consider the dignified *Beschorneria yuccoides* as a good cover-plant. Its basal rosettes of broad, grey-green, limp, yucca-like leaves make a splendid clump and, in early summer, everyone will stop to exclaim at the beauty of its long, arching sprays of exotic blooms. Likewise the Bromeliad *Fascicularia pitcairniifolia* should be used; its prickly grassy foliage rosettes turn scarlet around the stemless blue blooms at flowering time. We might even grow the Chatham Island forget-me-not *Myosotideum hortensia* (*M. nobile*)—like nothing so much as a blue bergenia—if we had a frost-free position by the sea and sufficient rotting seaweed to feed it on! But these are flights of fancy for a Surrey dweller and we must return to more practical things.

Just as ground-cover can be achieved by high dense shrubs, so can certain tall herbaceous plants be effective. In its full growth a really tall well-furnished plant possessing good leaves can be as dominant a partner in any scheme as a shrub to the uninitiated; it is only those of us who know that it will die down in winter that have to accord it second place in the majesty of things.

Certain *Ligularia* species (which used to be known as *Senecio*) provide some spectacular moisture-lovers with big heads of orange or yellow daisy-flowers in July. They make fairly good cover. The foliage of *L. dentata* (*L. clivorum*) is big and rounded on two-foot stalks and of a rich green, but I prefer the colour scheme afforded by 'Desdemona', whose leaf-backs and stems are mahogany-brown and contrast richly with the orange flowers. *L. veitchiana* has again great rounded basal leaves and statuesque spikes of yellow. With them can be grown *Telekia speciosa* (*Buphthalmum speciosum*), of similar attraction. One gets a bit tired of brassy yellow and hot orange by August and September when all the heleniums, solidagos and sunflowers have opened, but in July, on such dignified plants as these, it can be tolerated and even enjoyed.

Of delicate colouring, both in flower and leaf, is a rampant underground runner which is only safe in big areas which it will colonize effectively. It is *Macleaya microcarpa*, which has for many years been known as *M. cordata* (*Bocconia cordata*), the Plume Poppy. The big, lobed leaves, cool green above and grey beneath, carried on erect stems ending in a plume of biscuit-coloured small tassel-like flowers (coral tinted in 'Coral Plume') can be a focal point in the garden for many weeks. The genuine *M. cordata* is a less invasive plant with slightly larger flowers of ivory-white and equally handsome foliage and stance.

PLANTS IN THE ALPHABETICAL TABLE

Fortunately in spite of the term 'herbaceous' the leaves of many ground-cover plants are frost-proof and remain evergreen. Among them the bergenias (first and foremost), waldsteinia, tellima, *Helleborus foetidus*, heucheras and some epimediums will all thrive in sun or shade; on the other hand I suggest no hot sun for the saxifrages I have selected, the asarum, lamiums, pulmonarias and tiarella, while for full sun there is a choice between cerastium, pinks, thrift and arabis. A search through the Table will reveal more, particularly for the rock garden, but the above are the main evergreen plants for general use in the garden.

I realize more every year how valuable evergreens are during the winter, and, in a strange way, during the summer also, when their heavier greenery provides such a good foil to the plants that come and go during the growing season. A garden without evergreens during the winter is a forlorn sort of place and I like

especially to have rich greenery within sight of the windows so
that there is a good background for winter flowers.

It has been difficult to segregate the plants in the Table into
different groups according to their habit. Not a few are in reality
tiny dwarf shrubby plants; but I have put the bulk of these border-
line cases in the shrub chapter. Then there are clump-formers,
which are in reality slow spreaders or even increase by underground shoots; their proclivities in either respect might have
warranted relegating them to those groups. So that we must be
prepared both in the habit given against each plant in the Table,
and also in our discussion, to bear in mind that plants do not
necessarily conform to distinct groups, and every possible
variation occurs.

Colours and heights are easily picked out from the Table, so I
will arrange the plants in this introductory part of the chapter in
groups according to their habit and, roughly, to their leaf shapes;
this may help intending planters. Otherwise this chapter follows
more or less the procedure of Chapter 4 and is a selection from the
many kinds available. As I think it probable that many people may
look askance at the more vigorous spreaders and invasive plants
we will deal with the clump-formers first. These plants create
cover by their characterful basal leaves, no matter how tall or
how short their flower stems may be.

CLUMP-FORMING HERBACEOUS PLANTS—'SOCIAL
WORKERS'

Taking those with broad blades first, we can dispose of the
giant *Gunnera* species by saying that they are only suitable for
lakeside or riverside because their leaves are six feet across and
are borne on stalks six feet high. They are rough, coarse and
magnificent, and no other plant can add such majesty and contrast
to a big view as these South American relatives of the rhubarb.
Somewhat less in size and far more ornamental in flower are the
true rhubarbs, *Rheum officinale* and *R. palmatum*, with huge spikes
of cream or crimson flowers five feet or more high (Fig. 26). A
size down the scale still are the handsome *Rodgersia* species (Pl.
XXв, XXI; Fig. 25) and *Peltiphyllum peltatum*. All of these
delight in rich moist soil in full sun, while for a sopping wet bog

or ever-moist ditch *Lysichitum americanum* (Pl. XXA), and *L. camtschatcense* are producers of huge grass-green, paddle-shaped leaves of luxurious quality, quickly overshadowing the great arum flowers which arise in April. The former is yellow with a heavy odour and the latter is white, sweetly scented and of superior shape, but less easy to establish. They both seed themselves in the right conditions. Much smaller are the kingcups or marsh mari-golds (*Caltha*) and *Primula florindae* (Pl. XIXA). This Chinese cowslip is good-tempered, producing fragrant pale yellow bell-flowers in clusters from the tops of stout stems over fine rounded leaves, and it likes rich moist soil.

There can be few gardens in this country where *Aruncus dioicus* (*A. sylvester*) will not thrive, in wet or dry, acid or limy soils, in sun or shade. In June it throws out great creamy plumes seven feet or more in height, earning its name of 'goat's beard'; as soon as they fade they can be cut off and we are left with a handsome rounded clump up to five feet, of great ferny foliage so dense that no weed can grow around it. It is one of the best of the 'buffers' or clump-formers to be used to keep at bay the lower invasive covers. Often called *Spiraea* in error, on account of their marked resemblance, the species and varieties of Astilbe (Pl. XIXB) are not related, belonging as they do to the Saxifrage Family as opposed to the Rose Family of the spiraeas. But from our point of view they may well be likened to a short *Aruncus*, with every part reduced; the result is a feathery mass of beautiful foliage, green or mahogany-tinted, overtopped by plumes of flowers of any colour from white through pink to dark red and magenta-purple. Most of the darkest red varieties have also the dark foliage. They may have erect compact spikes or tall arching sprays, and they create a delightfully rich and colourful effect in moist ground in July and August, slowly increasing and smothering all weeds, besides being useful for holding firm the edge of pond or stream with their dense masses of roots.

There are several accommodating plants which will thrive in sun or shade. One of the best known is *Alchemilla mollis* (Fig. 40), lady's mantle, on whose velvety rounded leaves drops of moisture stay like quicksilver; the whole clump disappears under a cloud of greeny-yellow stars in summer, lasting for weeks. Both the flower and the foliage are invaluable for cutting. It can on occasions be a nuisance because it seeds itself freely (Pl. XV) if its flower stems are not cut off in good time, but it is always beautiful anywhere. Less well known is the meek little *A. conjuncta*, rather insignificant in flower but its leaves are like silk beneath. It is sometimes found in gardens under the name of *A. alpina*, which is a yet smaller species. *Anaphalis triplinervis* (Pl. XIVA) bears masses of white 'everlasting' flowers in late summer and autumn, over solid clumps of greyish foliage; it is one of the very few grey-toned plants which do not enjoy baking sunshine. I find it a satisfying contrast to the bigger sedums, bergenias and hardy fuchsias. The several larger *Sedum* species are first-rate for full sun, their big heads of soft pink or brownish coloured flowers appearing in August or September, and even as late as October, when 'Autumn Joy' opens to warm us with its rich colouring before autumn puts a stop to flowers. Healthy clumps make good cover. In similar conditions the two species of *Crambe*, *C. maritima*, the seakale, and *C. cordifolia*, should be used. There is no other glaucous foliage quite so splendid as that of the seakale; the leaves are broad, lying low round the clump but mounding up into a great mass, each one lobed and twisted in a variety of styles, and in limy soil and hot sun giving a grey-white tone only equalled by the bracts of *Eryngium giganteum*. While the seakale has quite large heads of white flowers growing from purplish shoots in early summer, *C. cordifolia* is one of the most striking of June-flowering plants, producing its vast, gypsophila-like, branching heads over huge, dark green leaves.

For shady places we can choose the species of *Pulmonaria* (Pl. XXIVA) or lungwort, with either green or spotted leaves, and the invaluable *Brunnera macrophylla* (Fig. 58), which is like a giant forget-me-not with large, rounded, hairy leaves. It used to be called *Anchusa myosotidiflora*. Both kinds of *Tellima* are splendid clump-formers and both these and the brunnera seed themselves here and there. Closely related to them are *Heuchera*, *Heucherella* and *Tiarella wherryi*; all are best in cool, partly or completely shady positions—though *Tellima* will also thrive in sun—and have dainty spires of small flowers in scarlet, pink or cream in spring and early summer.

The species of *Hosta* (*Funkia*) (Pls. XI–XIII; Figs. 27–35) are, without doubt, the best of all clump-forming, shade-bearing, static ground-cover plants, asking for nothing but to be left alone in good soil where their clumps can wax larger and denser as the years go by. Practically all have magnificent foliage, plain green, dark or light, vivid blue-green or glaucous, green with white edge or central splash, green with yellow edge or central splash; some are small and some are large; their flowers are pretty, small, lily-like bells borne on tall stems; they are mostly lilac, dark or light, but some are white. They flower in their different sorts from late June till October and several are flowering plants of value apart from the grandeur of their foliage. Though on the whole extremely easy to grow, they succeed best in somewhat moist, light or retentive soils with humus, and do not grow so luxuriantly in very limy soils. It is a pity to dig up an established clump to divide and distribute it; I find that if one or two sections are cut out with a spade (like portions out of a round cake), the holes can be filled in with good soil and the original clump is not disturbed or even spoiled for the following summer.

With this great family decorating our shady borders, we are fortunate to have the species and hybrids of *Bergenia* (*Megasea* or *Saxifrage*) (Pl. XIV), which can be used to balance the foliage of the hostas on opposite borders in sun. Or they will grow equally well in shade; indeed the bergenias may be counted upon to thrive anywhere except in a bog, and like the hostas they take kindly to town gardens. The large, evergreen, rounded, leathery leaves of the bergenias are invaluable for contrast to masonry or paths of any kind; they have a fine architectural quality that makes them firm favourites with anybody who likes their highly decorative flower-heads in spring, some of which err on the magenta side of pink and do it with a flagrant abandon, too, by having red stems! But for those who cannot stand Miss Jekyll's favourite *Bergenia cordifolia* 'Purpurea' (Fig. 44)—still the most luxuriant and satisfactory of the lot when it comes to ground-cover—there are delightful hybrids, some quite new, with clear pink, white or rich crimson-purple flowers. Some of these have leaves which in winter turn to mahogany-purple, and between them they cover a flowering period lasting at least two months.

With the above two invaluable genera in mind we can now turn to a third, equally valuable, the genus *Geranium*. Though the leaves are rounded in outline, they are more or less deeply divided, giving a much more dainty appearance. This does not prevent them from being effective and quick in covering the ground; they increase fast and can be divided and moved on to colonize fresh sites and are admirable for planting in areas where slow-growing shrubs are preparing to take over in due course. The fact that they increase quickly means that they are considerably cheaper to buy than hostas and bergenias, and if I had to choose one genus only for ground-cover it would be this. There are species for sun or shade and they are easily satisfied with any reasonable soil. In addition to their beautiful leaves they also provide a wealth of bloom, in some extending over a long period, but none are evergreen. In the Table I have mentioned some as carpeters and some as spreaders, but I think it would be best to deal with them all here together.

The chalk-pink *G. endressii* (Pl. XVIIA) and its more vigorous 'Wargrave Pink' in salmon-pink are excellent examples, flowering for weeks and giving a cover of delightful pale green foliage from early spring to late autumn. Even more vigorous is a comparatively new hybrid *G.* 'Claridge Druce', which can be relied upon to smother almost any weed, anywhere; it was found by its namesake and named in honour of him at Oxford University Botanic Garden by the then Curator, Mr G. W. Robinson, and myself, in 1960. All these prefer it a little cool rather than too hot; on the other hand the dense *G. renardii* (Fig. 38), a study in grey when in flower, and *G.* × *magnificum* (*G. ibericum* of gardens) (Pl. XVIIB) in vivid violet, can stand hot sun, likewise the carpeter 'Russell Prichard' (Pl. XVIB); this is a plant with one of the longest flowering periods I have met. The clear magenta-pink flowers appear over a mat of grey-green leaves for about three months from midsummer. It is not reliably hardy except in our warmer counties and should only be planted in spring. *G. wallichianum*, a trailer for sun or shade with white-eyed Spode-blue flowers, blooms for almost as long but seems perfectly hardy. 'Buxton's Variety' is a name given to the strain or type which is generally cultivated, named by A. T. Johnson after E. C. Buxton, who lived at Bettws-y-coed early in this century. *G. sylvaticum* in blue, pink or white, and *G. maculatum* in pale pink and 'Johnson's Blue' in clear Spode-blue, are spring flowers making good clumps.

The raiser of *G.* 'Johnson's Blue' was Mr Ruys of Dedemsvaart, Holland, to whom A. T. Johnson had sent seeds of *G. pratense.* Presumably a flower must have been crossed with *G. himalayense* and the result was duly named after the donor. It is particularly pretty when used in contrast to early yellow shrub roses. *G. himalayense* (Fig. 56) is an underground spreader with fine violet-blue flowers, while the double forms of *G. pratense* are most useful for a long display at midsummer. The most splendid is that flaming magenta species with black centres to its flowers, *G. psilostemon* (*G. armenum*) (Fig. 42), achieving three or four feet, with magnificent divided foliage often turning to vivid tones in autumn, which is an attribute also of *G. himalayense.* For part shade *G. macrorrhizum* is a rapid surface-carpeter (Pl. XVIA; Fig. 32), beautiful in flower in May in pink or blush; this I rank as one of the very finest and most beautiful of all ground-covers, though on account of its habit it should really be mentioned later. Of lesser calibre, equally efficient but with less vigour, are the forms of *G. sanguineum,* the native cranesbill in magenta; there are light pink (*lancastriense*) (Pl. XXVI), white (*album*) or rose-pink ('Glenluce') forms. This last was found by A. T. Johnson in Wigtownshire.

From January until April is the time of the hellebores. They are clump-formers, with big, divided, more or less evergreen leaves, and the many colour forms of *Helleborus orientalis,* by whatever name they may be called, are all excellent garden plants. Though shade is usually recommended for them, so long as their soil does not dry out they will be content and produce flowers faithfully every year if left alone and given old manure, or leaf-mould and bonemeal, after flowering. They grow just as well with lime as without and are much easier to cope with than the Christmas Rose, *H. niger,* and the other species. Their leaves lie more or less prostrate during the summer and do good work; the same may be said of all the other species listed. The semi-shrubby *H. foetidus* (Fig. 45) is of greater calibre.

The various catmints, nepeta, and *Calamintha grandiflora,* with their fragrant small leaves and dense growth, lead us into a few grey-leaved plants; all thrive in full sun and in well-drained soil. *Veronica incana* makes a really excellent dwarf grey tuft, *Scabiosa graminifolia,* silvery-grey with pale lilac blooms over a long period, and the pinks (*Dianthus*) of the 'Highland Hybrid' strain are not only lovely in flower but also useful the summer through on account of their hummocks of grey leaves. The more luxuriant pinks, such as 'White Ladies' and 'C. T. Musgrave', will also make wide tufts of good greyish leaves. *Ballota pseudodictamnus* is a good grey plant with intriguing palest mauve flowers poking out of what looks like an owl's face. These strange, woolly, grey-green flower sprays are borne above good, woolly, grey-green leaves.

While grey is always a useful tint to provide variety in a border, the grassy-leaved plants, of whatever colour, are needed to provide a light, uplifting line. Continuing with greyish-leaved plants we have the dwarf grass *Festuca glauca*, but this and the several other grasses are best left until we come to their own chapter; grassy-leaved plants we can mention here. There are several excellent clump-forming irises (Fig. 37), including the plum-tart (scented) *Iris graminea*; dainty-flowered and broad-leaved *I. japonica* and others; *Acorus gramineus*, which looks like a dwarf tufted grass but is really a close relative of the arums, and the autumn-flowering *Liriope muscari*. This bears spikes of mauve so perfect for contrasting with *Nerine bowdenii*, and it excels in dark green, grassy leaves. *Anthericum liliago*, the dainty white St Bernard's Lily, and the day lilies (*Hemerocallis*) are good flowering plants, whose tufts of arching leaves are sufficiently dense to make good cover.

There remain in this selection from the tabulated lists a few plants which, though in themselves good clump-formers, spread considerably by seeding. And with them I might have mentioned *Primula florindae* and *Alchemilla mollis*, both free-seeders. They range from the nine-foot-high cow-parsnip *Heracleum mantegaz-zianum* (Pl. XXXA) to the lowly *Corydalis lutea*. In between comes *Symphytum* × *uplandicum*. Neither this in its best flowering form of vivid blue, nor the heracleum, are to be trusted in the average garden unless the owner is prepared to remove the flower-heads before they seed. The heracleum is one of the noblest of plants, with magnificent divided leaves three to four feet across, and a stem as thick as a man's arm. The symphytum or comfrey has a most beautiful variegated form—at least, I attribute it to this hybrid plant, supposedly *S. asperum* × *S. officinale*, with pale mauve flowers—the large leaves are a foot or more in length, broadly margined with cream and grey. It is a rare plant, slowly increasing, of remarkable beauty.

Corydalis lutea is in flower from June until the frosts put an end to it and again is an exquisite plant, with fresh green, finely divided leaves and small heads of yellow fumitory-flowers, of which it is a close relative. It will seed itself in any cool spot and makes a close and beautiful cover. *C. ochroleuca* has white flowers. *C. lutea* is often looked upon as 'common'—but when did that epithet have any control over beauty?

The beautiful, almost circular, pleated leaves horizontally borne of *Pachyphragma macrophyllum* (Fig. 36) are a source of great enjoyment in any cool position throughout the summer. They do not develop to their fullest until May, but in early spring the heads of small white flowers are a cheering sight. It is closely related to our little dense-growing native, *Cardamine trifolia*. Its wads of dark green leaves slowly increase and are starred above with small white cuckoo-flowers in March. It is a perfect little plant where a dwarf and neat cover are needed and has the advantage of being evergreen.

CARPETING PLANTS, WHICH SPREAD BY SURFACE RUNNERS

On page 15 I have given a few suggestions for the covering of the verges of borders and beds. There is usually something of a gap between the actual verge of lawn or path and the first plants, where weeds are a persistent nuisance. There are many small plants which will fill this strip, covering it with a variety of verdure and in many cases obviating the necessity of using edging shears where the lawn runs alongside.

Among the smaller kinds there is not a wide variety of foliage to choose from. All have small leaves, but the various species of *Acaena* and *Cotula* have divided, ferny leaves, the former leaning towards bluish tones and the latter towards brownish-green. Only when they are really thriving are they truly weed-proof. All the antennarias are greyish-green; *A. plantaginifolia* is not well known but bears leaves three inches long; it promises to be one of the best covers. *Frankenia, Bellium minutum* and *Mentha pulegium* are some more of these little carpeters, often called 'paving' plants because of the excellent way they fill the interstices of paving, thus once again fighting the weeds for us. They all enjoy sunshine. For cooler verges there is the rampant 'Creeping Jenny', *Lysimachia nummularia*, with smooth leaves along the creeping stems which are studded at midsummer with little golden, cup-like flowers, and *Gunnera magellanica*, a Lilliputian relative of the giant lakeside plant; both of these have rounded leaves. Of moss-like effect for cool, well-drained spots, mainly on the rock gardens, are *Houstonia serpyllifolia* and *Selaginella helvetica*. The last two are hardy in the warmer counties of Britain in cool, shady positions that are fairly damp.

Where the border is both damp and sunny the dark-leafed bugle, *Ajuga reptans* 'Atropurpurea' (Fig 34), will give its best colouring. This is a plant that should be used more in design, as it provides a shining metallic purple carpet of leaves, rounded and flat. It is a wonderful contrast to anything with a soft feathery leaf such as geraniums or the grassy leaves of irises. On the other hand *A. r.* 'Variegata', in green and grey and white, needs partial shade to achieve its best variegation, and is the perfect contrast to ferns. *A. pyramidalis* is more vigorous than either, and all of them delight us in the spring with short spikes of pure blue flowers, most telling in the variegated form. The new very vigorous 'Jungle Beauty', 15 inches, has extra large green leaves. For hot sandy soil the chamomile, *Anthemis nobilis* (now known as *Chamaemelum nobile*) is sometimes used as a substitute for grass; the 'Treneague' variety produces none of the white daisies usual in the type, and is a very dwarf green carpet, though it is apt, like the prostrate thymes, to get bare in places. Thrift is another good, well-known plant whose dense green cushions (considerably more static than any of the above), in *Armeria maritima*, or 'Laucheana', may be covered in pink or white heads in spring, or brick red in the garden plant known as *A. corsica*. Unfortunately, unlike the others, *A. corsica* flowers freely only when frequently divided into young plants, though its green tussocks are as good, as long-lived and as dense as the others.

The thrifts bring us to the general run of what we may call large rock plants; plants often grown on the rock garden, but equally suitable for the fronts of borders, where the drainage is good. Several good grey kinds are available. *Arabis*, the double white and also the pretty variegated form, are greyish in hue, and the yellow *Alyssum saxatile* (Fig. 39)—whose name I gather is correctly *Aurinia saxatilis*—is one of the best. We are somewhat blinded to the excellent value of its luxuriant grey leaves by the brilliance of its 'gold-dust' flowers; those who prefer a more gentle yellow should choose 'Citrinum' ('Silver Queen'), which breeds more or less true from seed, and will not upset any colour scheme. Aubrietas, together with the prostrate *Gypsophila repens* (Fig. 55) and *G.* 'Rosy Veil', are also for full sun and good drainage, and are of greyish tint in leaf.

Saponaria ocymoides, a sheet of shocking pink in June, is a vigorous carpeter, with small dark leaves, and the many gay alpine phloxes (Fig. 54) and certain sedums, particularly forms of *Sedum spurium*, are all excellent for dry sunny positions, while for places where the shrubs in the border keep the ground cool the Mossy and London Pride groups of saxifrages, being evergreen, are unequalled. *Saxifraga hypnoides* and *S. trifurcata* are small and large mossy saxifrages with white flowers in spring, while I find *S.* × *geum* 'Monstrosa' is the perfect cover for the fronts of shady borders; its elegant, deep green, crisp rosettes are lovely through the year. Though its foliage is larger than, and superior to, *S. umbrosa*, the true London Pride (Pl. XIIIA; Fig. 46), its flowers are not quite so good. The above all make good thick rugs, rather than the dwarf carpets of their predecessors.

One of my favourite ground-covers is *Potentilla alba* (Fig. 57), a lowly grey-green carpeter whose white, orange-eyed, strawberry flowers appear in both summer and autumn. It is imperturbable and an efficient cover, and is an ideal plant. It will be obvious that among these small carpeters the leaves are neither large nor handsome, though in the mass they can make or mar a planting arrangement. The golden marjoram, *Origanum vulgare*, is first-rate for a brilliant spring effect of yellow foliage (Pl. XVIIIA).

All of the above are fairly manageable plants such as one would use for border verges, rose beds, rock garden ledges and the tops of retaining walls, and will not spread unduly. Let us now examine some of the more unruly.

The strawberries offer several cover-plants. The 'alpine' type, those delicious little morsels with red or white fruit, whose bouquet no less than whose flavour makes the tedium of filling a bowl so well worth while, are good covers and may be found under the name of *Fragaria vesca* 'Semperflorens', or just Alpine Strawberries. 'Baron Solemacher' is not a carpeter, but remains in a clump and so should have been mentioned earlier; planted at the required distance, it makes excellent cover nevertheless. Beware, however, of *Fragaria* or *Duchesnea indica*. Friends will offer it, for it grows ten feet in a season, with long runners, extending in every direction, rooting as they go. In late summer attractive, tiny red strawberries are borne erect on short stalks. They are tasteless and even the birds neglect them. It is a good cover for wide areas but should not be put into a mixed border. (A larger grower, but less invasive, is *F. chiloense*, a parent of our dessert strawberries; this is used in some parts of the U.S.A. for ornamental ground-cover. I think it would be very popular in public parks!) All of these strawberries prefer positions not too hot and dry, and are providers of rich green leaves. Liking the same cool conditions is one of the prettiest of spring-flowering rampers, the foam flower, so called because of its foamy masses of white flowers above its carpet of hairy heuchera-like leaves. It is *Tiarella cordifolia* (Pl. XXVA; Fig. 49). The most rampant surface-rooter is *Geranium procurrens*, a newcomer from Nepal; it is only suitable for large areas under trees, not shrubs. Flowers lilac with black eyes produced from July onwards. We should also give some coolness to the excellent colonizing *Prunella grandiflora*, the rich pink and also the 'Loveliness' forms; the only danger with them is that unless the flower spikes are cut off before the seeds set they are inclined to seed themselves, with the result that purplish forms arise.

Polygonum vacciniifolium is a rampant cover for the warmer counties, with tiny leaves and multitudes of small pink spikes in September; *P. affine* (Pl. XXIIIB) is a size larger, with a long flowering period. Apart from the value of its pink spikes of flower—superlative in the bright new form 'Superbum'—its mat of leaves turns to rich brown by December, lasting in beautiful colour through the winter, like those of a beech hedge. This is one of our most valuable cover-plants, nearly as good as the surface carpeting *Geranium macrorrhizum* which I mentioned out of its turn earlier. *Polygonum affine* grows best in partial shade, like

Lamium maculatum (Pl. XXIVb; Fig. 53), *Oxalis oregana* (Pl. XXIIA) and *Symphytum grandiflorum* (Pls. XXI, XXIII). These are the very cream of rapid covers for growing under large shrubs and trees, and save all work. The dense carpets of broad, hairy leaves of the symphytum, a small-growing comfrey, are covered with cream bells in spring. Two hybrids growing at Hidcote Manor, Gloucestershire, rather larger in growth, have been named 'Hidcote Pink' and 'Hidcote Blue'. These are partially evergreen, the oxalis is quite deciduous, whereas the lamium is evergreen. It is a relative of the dead-nettle, with dark green leaves each with a white stripe rather like that on a badger's forehead, producing a very thick carpet. For a very low green carpet I recommend most thoroughly *Oxalis oregana*, so like a larger version of *O. acetosella*, our native Wood Sorrel (Fig. 48); for cool freshness of greenery there is nothing to touch either of them; the first is bespangled with small deep pink flowers in early spring, and the latter may be white or pink in the variety 'Rosea'. To me they are not only valuable surface carpeters, but have the very greatest charm of leaf and flower.

In my light soil, I find *Viola cornuta* grows best and flowers longest in part shade; its prettiest form is 'Lilacina', although the ordinary purple and the white are both pretty. With a clip over in August they can usually be induced to flower freely again in autumn; they are the ideal contrast to *Hosta sieboldiana*.

There is not so much variety among carpeters for sunny places. Two good, well-known border plants have excellent basal leaves of soft hairy green, *Phlomis russeliana* (sometimes incorrectly grown as *P. samia* and *P. viscosa*, which are different species) and *Stachys macrantha* (*S. betonica* 'Superba') (Fig. 62). Both have erect stems bearing whorls of sage-flowers in summer, mauve-pink in the latter, soft yellow in the former, which is a most handsome plant. The most valuable stachys is *S. olympica* (*S. lanata*) 'Silver Carpet' (Pl. XVIIIb), a new non-flowering form of the ordinary Lambs' Ears, so good in hot, sunny positions. The dense pile of silvery woolly leaves is an asset in any scheme and a satisfying contrast against purplish leaves. The various dwarf species of *Thymus* are scarcely weed-proof, except when growing well on harsh limy soil such as one finds in the Cotswolds, where their fragrant mats of tiny leaves alone earn them a place.

There is no doubt that *Waldsteinia ternata* (Pl. XXIIB) is one
of the most valuable and beautiful of all carpeters. It grows
equally well in sun or shade, but produces more of its bright
yellow, strawberry-blooms in sun. It is the foliage, evergreen,
dark and glossy, broad and close to the ground which puts this
into so high a place, besides its easy nature. It is a perfect foil for
grassy leaves, and also for grey foliage.

SPREADERS, INCREASING BY MEANS OF UNDERGROUND SHOOTS

While surface-runners can be a nuisance at times, those which
spread underground can be a real danger in a garden, unless, as
I have written before, they are used with understanding and
circumspection. This cannot be stressed too often. Misuse—or
the generosity of donors—could well make a mockery of the
controlled vegetation of the garden, and has been known to
shake the confidence in plants as helpers in the minds of some
gardeners; so that they have eschewed all these spreaders and the
quick carpeters, thus depriving themselves of just those plants
which will save them most work if planted in the right place. It
is no use getting a collection of miscellaneous ground-cover
plants and putting them perhaps two feet apart in a border; the
effect will be muddled and the result will very likely be chaos.
That is why throughout these pages I have been at pains to stress
the choice that may be made between types of leaf and also suitable distances apart for planting, in addition to the different habits.

In our present category there are some very choice little plants
that might well have been put into the safe clump-formers, the
species of *Shortia*, *Schizocodon*, and *Soldanella villosa*. Where the
knowledgeable garden can provide the right conditions they will
give satisfaction, are never invasive and are almost too slow to
warrant inclusion. Likewise for part shade there are the exquisite
colour forms of *Dicentra formosa*—exquisite also in foliage—of
which the deep pink 'Bountiful' and the white seem to stay
. longest in flower. 'Bountiful' is prolific in self-sown seedlings
and I have yet to see an ugly one among them. Slowly spreading
too are the species of *Epimedium* (Pl. XXVA; Fig. 50) and
Vancouveria (Fig. 51); elegant in leaf, some are usefully evergreen,

and their flowers in spring are like tiny aquilegias. Though the foliage is the most important character, to enjoy to the full the flowers of *Epimedium* × *versicolor* and other deciduous species, the foliage should be cut away in January. They are imperturbable dense cover, slowly spreading into wide clumps.

I shall leave the petasites, physalis, *Salvia glutinosa* and certain polygonums for Chapter 10, as they are scarcely to be trusted nor are they really desirable in gardens; the possible exceptions being the variegated mint (*Mentha*), and also the Chinese Lantern (*Physalis*), which is so useful for picking for the winter. *Polygonum reynoutria* as known in gardens is a good plant up to two feet, for late summer and autumn display of its pink flowers and seed-pods. It is a female plant, the male being less conspicuous; it is correctly known as *Polygonum cuspidatum compactum*, but it is not such a fearsome spreader as *P. cuspidatum* itself.

A few strong plants that do the excellent composite job of providing first-class cover with handsome leaves and good flowers are the *Acanthus* species, the soft pink *Anemone tomentosa* (Fig. 71), *Euphorbia robbiae* and Solomon's Seal (*Polygonatum*). They all grow happily in part shade—or full shade for the last two—but acanthus flower best in full sun. None of these are very rapid spreaders, nor are they particular as to soil. The two best acanthus are *A. mollis latifolius*, with big, broad, lobed leaves, and *A. spinosus*, much more finely divided in leaf and more generous in flower. Both are undeniably handsome, making magnificent groups of arching, shining, dark green leaves. For best contrast they need grey, hairy leaves next to them, or some of the grassy blades. Both have equally fine, tall, prickly spikes of foxglove-like flowers in late summer, lasting into autumn. The anemone with handsome, vine-like, soft green leaves up to two feet, is, I find, a far better cover than the usual hybrid Japanese anemones, valuable though these are in the heavier soils. *A. tomentosa* flowers rather earlier too, in August. The *Euphorbia* bears the usual greenish-yellow heads of flowers in spring and is ornamental through the year, with rosettes of dark, glossy green leaves. Into this bigger category we must bring Bouncing Bet—*Saponaria officinalis*—an old cottage garden plant bearing white or pink flowers, single or double; *Coronilla varia* (Fig. 77), a mauve vetch, and the false maidenhair fern. The last is *Thalictrum minus*, a dwarf British native, usually encountered in gardens in the form of a two-foot plant called *T. adiantifolium*. Their leaves, so prettily divided into small fern-like segments, make them invaluable for cutting; the flowers are greenish and insignificant though dainty. On light soils they quickly colonize, but in heavier soils are inclined to be clump-forming. The most rampant of the above is *Coronilla varia*. A friend once wrote me that his 'Yellow Archangel' (*Lamium galeobdolon*) (Fig. 52) was 'spreading like the devil'; this is how the coronilla spreads also, only in a more dangerous fashion, below ground. It is only occasionally seen in gardens in England, thriving on neglect and originally misplaced interest, but has been used with tremendous effect as a bank-cover in the United States—tremendous not only on account of the speed with which it travels but also because of its long display of pinky-mauve flowers. Where a colonizer with broad, dark green leaves is required under trees or in full sun we cannot do better than *Trachystemon orientale* (Fig. 70), but this brooks no opposition and is better left for Chapter 10.

There are many lowly spreaders of first-class value. We can have a sheet of white stars in spring with pretty, small leaves in dense array for the rest of the season if we plant *Asperula odorata*, the Sweet Woodruff (Fig. 64); it will harm nothing over two feet in height, plant or shrub, and thrives in shade. The lily of the valley I have cited elsewhere as the type-plant for these spreaders. I can never have enough of the flowers and value the smooth green leaves highly. By planting some in sun and some in shade, and following them with the fine large variety *Convallaria majalis* 'Fortin's Giant', which flowers a fortnight later, one can have flowers to pick for a month or more. But it is no use making a special bed of leaf-mould and bonemeal or other choice ingredients in the hope that these plants will at once settle down and produce heartily for us; as likely as not the odd root which gets rolled into the gravel path will grow far better. They seem to spend a year or two getting established and then start pushing lustily in one direction where the conditions are most to their liking. A very charming close relative of less vigour is *Maianthemum bifolium* (Fig. 63), and I hear of a taller representative of this from Canada.

Asarum europaeum (Fig. 47) is a most worthy compact carpeter, covering the ground with shining, dark green, rounded leaves, while Blue-eyed Mary, *Omphalodes verna*, is a broad-leaved dwarf forget-me-not in effect; both love shade. The rare double form of *Houttuynia cordata*, with most intriguing white, cone-shaped inflorescences, revels in a moist, cool spot and bears good dark leaves with a strange orange-like fragrance.

Not particular as to sun or shade are some fairly rapidly spreading lilac-blue campanulas, *C. poscharskyana* and *C. portenschlagiana* 'Bavarica' ('Grandiflora'). Both may be relied upon to produce their masses of bright green leaves almost anywhere; they are usually classed as rock plants but thrive in the front of the border. *Geranium himalayense* and *G. sanguineum*, though included earlier in these notes, find their place here too because they are underground colonizers.

Spreaders for sunny places are found in some border plants, the dwarf, large-flowered and large-leafed form 'John Coutts' of *Centaurea hypoleuca* (Pl. XXVI), a perennial Sweet Sultan. I find this is infinitely more useful and beautiful than the ordinary type. For autumn effect in full sun the spreading, hardy plumbago, *Ceratostigma plumbaginoides*, is hard to beat; the foliage usually assumes gorgeous reds and purplish tints just when the dark blue flowers open in October; even later is the Japanese single pink *Chrysanthemum yezoense*, whose luxuriant fresh greenery delights us during the whole summer. *Zauschneria californica* will also, in well-drained, warm, sunny places, provide scarlet flowers in September and October, and if *Viola labradorica* is planted near by a good contrast will be obtained. Though like other violets this little plant will grow in sun or shade, the hot sun intensifies the metallic purple of its leaves. It is also ideal as a ground-cover around white colchicums, and sows itself freely as well as spreading by underground shoots.

Snow in Summer, really *Cerastium tomentosum*, is a plant of extraordinary beauty, avoided by many because it is so invasive and because it is common. For a hungry, hot, sunny bank there is nothing so effective and overpowering (for the weeds). Its questing roots throw up masses of small silvery-grey leaves— excellent against bergenias and other dark smooth greenery of hearty vigour—to disappear under a sheet of white flowers in June.

There are three good colonizers with narrow leaves, giving a grass-like effect in contrast to so many, dwarf, broad- or small-leaved plants, creating a dense array. The Day Lilies, *Hemerocallis*, offer a wonderful range of colouring today in the many new hybrids, but I find that the pale tones are the most telling in the garden, particularly the clear, light yellows. These are often fragrant. But strictly speaking they are clump-formers; it is *H. fulva*, with its brick-red flowers, that provides questing root-stocks, and *H. fulva* itself, the old double 'Kwanso Flore Pleno' (Fig. 61), 'Maculata' and other forms with this parentage are all capable of spreading widely. Apart from the beauty of the flowers, and the beauty of the narrow, arching leaves, most of the varieties and hybrids of *H. fulva* have the added value of growing very early in the spring, at which time their pale greenery is the most brilliant in the garden with the exception of *Milium effusum* 'Aureum', or Bowles' Golden Grass. This little grass seeds itself and also spreads quickly in cool positions.

The two lily relatives *Liriope spicata* and *Ophiopogon japonicus*, about ten inches high, are good value, on account of their dark, shining green, turf-like effect. While the former is quite hardy in Britain, the ophiopogon is tender, but would thrive in our warmest counties, and is a great favourite for replacing grass in the south-east states of America. They will take little traffic but on the other hand offer spikes of purple flowers in late summer and autumn.

Apart from the acanthus, anemone and trachystemon I have not been able to pick out many plants with noble foliage among these last two categories; the bulk are lowly and not strikingly noticeable, but do their work well. The greater leaves are found in the clump-formers, and their solidifying or steadying influence can be most useful in border design. They are in fact essential. I remember being asked to go and criticize a border in a friend's garden some years ago; though the owner had given it good width, with a wall behind on which were roses and climbing plants, and had gathered together a choice array of shrubs and plants, it did not please her, and she could not discover what was amiss. On examining it we found there was scarcely a leaf bigger than a privet's among all the plants, shrubs and climbers. It was a sunny border, so space was made for some bergenias, acanthus and crambe; also *Viburnum davidii*, with a *Vitis coignetiae* on the wall behind. These few additions made all the difference.

I (A) The heather garden at Ness, Cheshire, photographed in September. Dense little bushes of heath and heather – 'social shrubs' – link together, creating a picture which remains full of colour throughout the year.

(B) A small-scale heath garden in Cornwall, shewing varieties of *Erica carnea* in close association with *Genista hispanica* and other dwarf sun-loving shrubs.

II (A) The frosty blue-green foliage of *Hebe* (*Veronica*) *pinguifolia* 'Pagei', one of the several which assort well with heathers.

(B) 'Springwood White' and 'Springwood Pink', two of the most vigorous ground-covering forms of *Erica carnea*, in flower from January to April.

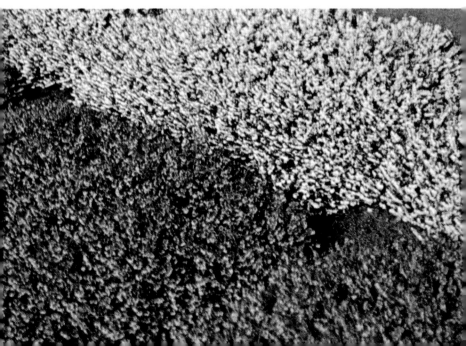

III   (A) A series of beds at Killerton, Devon, planted to give the maximum interest from flower and foliage through the year, with a minimum of upkeep. Santolinas, helianthemums, dwarf fuchsias, lavenders, *Hypericum* × *moseranum*, *Iris pallida dalmatica*, yuccas and others.

   (B) *Helianthemum* 'Rhodanthe Carneum' overspreading a sunny grass bank in Norfolk. The sun-roses are available in many colours, but this is probably the most vigorous.

IV (A) *Potentilla* 'Tangerine'. The forms and hybrids of *Potentilla fruticosa* are invaluable 'social' shrubs for limy or acid soil, and are in flower from June to October. They vary in colour from white to orange and in height from 1 ft to 5 ft.

(B) A sunny border in the author's garden, which requires no weeding at any time, being filled with skimmia, *Erica carnea* forms and hybrids, bergenias, with *Acanthus spinosus* and rhododendrons at the back.

V (A) The yellow-variegated form of the culinary sage, *Salvia officinalis* 'Icterina'; a gay, dwarf, shrubby plant for warm, dry positions.

(B) A sunny, sheltered bank covered with *Santolina chamaecyparissus* and the purplish-leafed form of the culinary sage, *Salvia officinalis* 'Purpurascens'.

VI (A) *Genista pilosa* 'Procumbens'.
  (B) *Genista sagittalis*. The dwarf brooms are admirable cover-plants for well-drained, sunny positions.

VII (A) *Rosa* 'Max Graf', a hybrid of *R. wichuraiana*. The latter is thorn-less, completely prostrate, and does not produce its flowers until August; its trails grow 10 ft a year. 'Max Graf' flowers in June, grows rather taller and is thorny. With R. × *paulii* and its pink variety (see pl. 18) they form a valuable quartet for ground-cover. (B) The evergreen *Lonicera pileata*, a rapid surface-spreader for shady places. It roots as it grows and has violet-blue berries.

VIII   (A) A variety of the common ivy, *Hedera helix* 'Buttercup'.
       (B) The large-leafed *Hedera colchica* 'Dentato-variegata'.
Two examples of ivies used as ground-cover.

IX (A) *Vaccinium oxycoccus*, a surface-creeper for lime-free soil.

(B) *Vinca major* 'Elegantissima' will brighten any corner.

(C) The varieties of *Vinca minor* make excellent dense cover for sun or shade; this is 'Bowles' Variety. They take root as they spread.

X (A) *Juniperus communis* 'Horni-brookii', successf on chalk soils; green.

(B) *Juniperus horizontalis*, soft bl green, ideal for exposed sunny positions. J. h. 'Douglasii' turns violet-blue in win

(C) *Picea abie* 'Reflexa', Fresh g young growths contrast with the ⟨ green of this prost spruce.

Three creeping c fers for ground co

XI (A) *Hosta fortunei* ' Albopicta '.

   (B) *Hosta fortunei* ' Aurea ' and the hybrid ' Thomas Hogg '. The hostas or funkias thrive in cool shady positions, in time making large dense clumps.

XII (A) The most sumptuous of hostas, *H. sieboldiana* 'Elegans'. The leaves achieve up to a foot across and the flowers are of so pale a tint of lilac that they are almost white. The surrounding *Vinca minor* is kept at bay.

(B) Wavy, dark green leaves edged with white are characteristic of the splendid *Hosta crispula*. The flowers are pale lilac.

XIII   (A) *Hosta crispula* surrounded by London Pride, *Saxifraga umbrosa*, in a shady border in May.

(B) The same border in September, with *Lilium tigrinum* 'Fortunei', *Rosa rubrifolia*, *Salvia officinalis* 'Purpurascens' and *Anaphalis triplinervis*.

XIV (A) Contrasting foliage in a position shaded by a wall for most of the day: *Anaphalis triplinervis*, whose flowers last for three months, and the evergreen *Bergenia schmidtii* 'Jan Schmidt' with *B. cordifolia* 'Purpurea' (left).

(B) *Bergenia* 'Sunningdale' photographed in January. It colours best in open positions, and has clean pink flowers.

(C) In gardens free from spring frosts *Bergenia ligulata* is a success, with flowers early in the year and large, hairy, crumpled leaves later.

(D) 'Silberlicht', a handsome white bergenia hybrid.

XV *Opposite page: Alchemilla m.* or lady's mantle, in comp control. It spreads freely by ; in sun or shade. *Rosa pollin* gives contrast and is a us< dense, low shrub.

XVI (A) *Geranium macrorrhizum*, a May-flowering surface-runner of the greatest value, growing in broken shade. It has fragrant leaves.

(B) *Geranium* 'Russell Prichard' flowers for three months. It dies back to a central root every winter and will annually cover a square yard. Suitable for full sun in drained soil in the warmer counties. Plant in spring.

XVII (A) *Geranium endressii*. A most useful, vigorous clump-forming plant for sun or shade. Long flowering period in summer.

  (B) *Geranium × magnificum* (*G. ibericum* or *platypetalum* of gardens) a vigorous clump for full sun, shewn with the invasive lyme grass, *Elymus arenarius*.

XVIII   (A) *Origanum vulgare* 'Aureum', the golden marjoram.
          (B) *Stachys olympica* (*S. lanata*) 'Silver Carpet'. This non-flowering form of the well-known lamb's ears and the golden form of the pot marjoram are useful plants for full sun on dry soils.

XIX (A) A fragrant Chinese cowslip, *Primula florindae*, with orange hybrids, which grows best in rich, moist soil and seeds itself freely.

(B) Astilbes are also moisture lovers, making dense clumps. Many of the darker flowered forms have coppery foliage. This is 'Rheinland' at Kew.

XX (A) Immense leaves follow the elegant flowers of *Lysichitum americanum*, smothering all weeds. For bog, wet ditch or stream-side. At Hidcote.

(B) By midsummer the noble leaves of *Rodgersia podophylla*, if exposed to the sun, take on coppery tints; it grows best in rich, moist soil.

XXI The stream
garden at Hidcote.
The steep bank on the
right is covered with
*Symphytum grandi-
florum*. The shuttle-
cock fern, *Matteuccia
struthiopteris*, *Brunnera
macrophylla* and the
bronzy young leaves
of *Rodgersia podophylla*
dominate the sloping
ground. All are
moisture-loving
plants.

XXII   (A) A wood sorrel, *Oxalis oregana*, which has deep pink flowers in early spring. The light green leaves last until autumn. Best in cool, shady places.

(B) The evergreen *Waldsteinia ternata*, which has brilliant yellow strawberry-flowers in spring. For sun or shade. Two dense, effective surface creepers.

XXIII   (A) For shady or moist borders *Symphytum grandiflorum* is a useful surface-creeper and effective cover. Two rather taller hybrids are 'Hidcote Pink' and 'Hidcote Blue'.

        (B) *Polygonum affine* also enjoys cool conditions. Though the species is good a finer form is 'Donald Lowndes', another excellent surface creeper. The leaves turn to rich brown in winter.

XXIV   (A) A shady border in July, shewing (left to right) the rapidly spreading fern *Onoclea sensibilis*, the spotted-leafed *Pulmonaria saccharata*, hostas and green *Pulmonaria rubra*, in the author's garden. All weeds are excluded.

(B) *Lamium maculatum* is an excellent surface-creeper for shady places. The white-flowered form has even more beautifully marked leaves.

XXV (A) Epimediums, slow dense colonizers, thrive in sun or shade, and provide pretty foliage tints in spring and autumn, besides the dainty spring flowers. Here they are growing with *Tiarella cordifolia* running around them.

   (B) *Glyceria maxima* (*G. aquatica*). One of the few ornamental grasses which grow densely enough to qualify as ground-cover. It is a rapid underground spreader for moist positions.

XXVII (A) In lime-free woodland soil *Cornus* (*Chamaepericlymenum*) *canadensis* will run yards a year by means of its threading roots. Some of the flowers are followed by red berries and the leaves turn to wine colour in winter.

(B) A climbing honeysuckle growing prostrate on the ground where it makes excellent cover: *Lonicera periclymenum serotina* or 'Late Dutch'.

XXVIII (A) The evergreen *Cotoneaster dammeri* (*C. humifusus*), gay in autumn with scarlet berries. It thrives in sun, or shade from buildings. A dense and lively cover.

(B) *Penstemon newberryi*, a dense prostrate little shrub for the sunny rock garden.

XXIX (A) Effective use of Irish ivy at Kew, providing contrast to the lawns and shrubs by reason of its height and glossy greenery. It will thrive under trees where grass will not grow, is completely weed-proof and seldom ascends the trunks.

(B) Irish ivy (*Hedera helix hibernica*) is a far better cover than the common *Hedera helix*, which is not reliably weed-proof.

XXX (A) *Heracleum mantegazzianum* at the beginning of its floral display. A deep-rooted, free-seeding giant plant best in rich moist soil.

(B) *Pachysandra terminalis*, quickly spreading by underground shoots. A neat, dense, glossy evergreen suitable for large shady areas. Invaluable in public places as well as under trees in the garden.

XXXI (A) High cover from *Rubus odoratus*. The running roots produce a dense thicket of stems, 6 ft high.

(B) Low cover from *Hypericum calycinum*. This, the Rose of Sharon, is one of the most popular ground-covers, but the running roots are very invasive.

XXXII *Geranium macrorrhizum*, completely excluding weeds, grows in between clumps of day lilies, *Curtonus paniculatus* and *Hosta sieboldiana* 'Elegans' in the author's garden.

HERBACEOUS PLANTS

	Country of Origin	Leaf Height and Planting Distance	Leaf Colour and Character
ACAENA			
Southern Hemisphere sun-lovers, thriving in well-drained soil. *A. anserinifolia* needs a warm position. *A. hirsutula* and *A. splendens* are further good species, occasionally seen.			
adscendens	S. America	9″ × 3′	Blue-grey, reddish ste
anserinifolia (*A. sanguisorbae*)	New Zealand	10″ × 3′	Grey hairy leaves and
buchananii	New Zealand	3″ × 2′	Pale jade green.
caesiglauca	New Zealand	2″ × 2′	Blue-grey, silky.
inermis	New Zealand	3″ × 2′	Glaucous bronze-gree
microphylla	New Zealand	2″ × 2′	Dark bronze-green.
novae-zelandiae	New Zealand	5″ × 18″	Rich green, larger tha others.
ACANTHOLIMON			
Full sun, well-drained soil, rock garden or tops of retaining walls.			
glumaceum	America	3″ × 9″	Dark green, needle-lik
ACANTHUS			
Deep rich soil, preferably sunny. Fleshy roots and crowns which when young sometimes suffer in cold districts but can be protected by mulching. Noble plants with handsome leaves and prickly spikes of flowers (somewhat resembling foxgloves) lasting long in beauty. Foliage does not last in water. *A. spinosus* is most free in flower; its variety, *A. s. spinosissimus*, has more spiny leaves.			
mollis latifolius	Portugal	3′ × 3′	Dark shining green, br lobed, arching.
spinosus	S. Europe	3′ × 3′	Dark shining green, d cut, arching.
ACHILLEA			
Sun lovers; well-drained soil; rock garden or tops of retaining walls, except *A. millefolium*, which is the common yarrow. It is an excellent plant for colonizing poor limy soil and is frequently found as a weed in lawns; the coloured forms are desirable. Many of the bigger achilleas, including some newer hybrids, are doubtfully perennial except in ideal conditions and form clumps rather than carpets.			
ageratifolia	Greece	3″ × 9″	Grey, prettily divided
chrysocoma	Greece	3″ × 15″	Grey-green, feathery.
× kellereri	Hybrid	3″ × 9″	Grey-green, divided.
millefolium	Europe	8″ × 2′	Dark green, feathery.
— 'Cerise Queen'		8″ × 2′	Dark green, feathery.
tomentosa	Europe	3″ × 1′	Dark green, feathery.

...uous / ...reen	Flower Height and Colour and Fruits (if any)	Flowering Season	Habit	Propagation
)	Flowers inconspicuous.	Summer	Carpet, rooting	D
)	Flowers inconspicuous.	Summer	Carpet, rooting	D
)	Flowers inconspicuous.	Summer	Carpet, rooting	D
)	Flowers inconspicuous.	Summer	Carpet, rooting	D
)	Flowers inconspicuous.	Summer	Carpet, rooting	D
)	Flowers inconspicuous, red spiny fruits.	Summer	Carpet, rooting	D
)	Flowers inconspicuous.	Summer	Carpet, rooting	D
?	6". Rose-pink, small, in sprays.	Midsummer	Hummock	CDL
)	4–5'. Mauve, in spikes.	Late summer	Spreader	DRS
)	4–5'. Mauve, in spikes.	Late summer	Spreader	DRS
E	8". White daisies in clusters.	Summer	Carpet, rooting	D
E	7". Flat heads of light yellow.	Summer	Carpet, rooting	D
E	6". Heads of white.	Summer	Carpet, rooting	D
D	2–2½'. White to pink, in flat heads.	Summer	Spreader	D
D	2–2½'. Cerise-crimson, in flat heads.	Summer	Spreader	D
E	7". Flat heads of yellow.	Summer	Carpet, rooting	D

137

HERBACEOUS PLANTS

	Country of Origin	Leaf Height and Planting Distance	Leaf Colour and Character

ACORUS
Tufted grassy-leaved aroid, for moist sunny positions. *A. gramineus* 'Variegatus' is les vigorous but highly ornamental.

gramineus	Japan	8″ × 1′	Narrow dark shining or variegated.

AJUGA
Bugle. Sun or partial shade; soil moist rather than dry. *A. reptans* 'Atropurpurea' colour best in sun; *A. r.* 'Variegata' colours best in shade. Successful ground-cover only when i ideal conditions. *A. reptans* 'Pink Spire' is a good pink form.

pyramidalis	Europe	3″ × 18″	Dark green, smooth, rounded.
reptans	Europe	2″ × 18″	Dark green, smooth, rounded.
— 'Atropurpurea'		2″ × 18″	Beetroot colour, shin
— 'Jungle Beauty'		8″ × 2′	Large, green, smoot rounded.
— 'Variegata'		2″ × 1′	White and grey-green variegated.

ALCHEMILLA
Sun or partial shade, easily satisfied regarding soil. The leaves of *A. conjuncta* are silver beneath. *A. mollis*, though clump-forming, increases freely by seed, and is known as Lady Mantle.

conjuncta	Europe	4″ × 1′	Green, divided, dens
mollis	Asia Minor	1′ × 2′	Green, velvety, roun handsome.

ALYSSUM
Sun; well drained, ideal on slopes, fronts of borders, large rock gardens, hanging over lo walls; and for carpeting rose beds where its grey leaves make a good foil for the brigh colours.

saxatile (*Aurinia saxatilis*)	Europe	10″ × 18″	Grey-green, long, n
— 'Citrinum' ('Silver Queen')		10″ × 18″	Grey-green, long, n
spinosum (see PTILOTRICHUM, Chapter 4).			

ANAPHALIS
Requires somewhat moist soil, sun or partial shade, but must be in an open position, other wise it becomes straggly. *A. margaritacea* and *A. yedoensis* are less dense and have less goo leaves.

triplinervis	Himalaya	9″ × 2′	Greyish, oval, large.

iduous or rgreen	Flower Height and Colour and Fruits (if any)	Flowering Season	Habit	Propagation
E	Flowers inconspicuous.		Clump	D
E	6″. Small, blue in spikes.	Spring	Carpet, rooting	D
E	5″. Small, blue in spikes.	Spring	Carpet, rooting	D
E	5″. Small, blue in spikes.	Spring	Carpet, rooting	D
E	15″. Blue, in spikes.	Spring	Carpet, rooting	D
E	4″. Small, blue in spikes.	Spring	Carpet, rooting	D
D	6″. Inconspicuous, greenish.	Summer	Clump	DS
D	2′. A cloud of greeny-yellow stars.	Summer	Clump	DS
E	1 . Masses of tiny yellow flowers.	Spring	Carpet	CLS
E	1′. Pale sulphur-yellow form.	Spring	Carpet	CLS
D	15″. Masses of white, starry, in broad heads.	Late summer	Clump	D

139

HERBACEOUS PLANTS

	Country of Origin	Leaf Height and Planting Distance	Leaf Colour and Character
ANDROSACE			

For screes and well-drained portions of rock gardens, tops of retaining walls; full sun.

lanuginosa	Himalaya	4″ × 1′	Grey, small, on trailing shoots.
— leichtlinii	Himalaya	4″ × 1′	Grey, small, on trailing shoots.

ANEMONE

Partial or full shade or sun, preferring a heavy soil rather than light; in light soil they tend to increase more but are less dense. *Anemone nemorosa*, the wood anemone, and *A. apennina* are pretty spring flowers and grow freely under shrubs, but, as their leaves die down by midsummer, can scarcely be considered as ground-cover.

× **elegans**, see *A.* × *hybrida*.

× **hybrida**		18″ × 2′	Dark green, deeply divided.

The race known as Japanese anemones are hybrids between *A. hupehensis* and *A. vitifolia*, known as *A.* × *hybrida*, sometimes *A.* × *elegans*. Good examples are 'September Charm', 'Queen Charlotte' (both pink), 'Honorine Jobert' and 'Louise Uhink' (white), 'Prince Henry' ('Profusion') (carmine-pink).

japonica, see *A.* × *hybrida*.

tomentosa	Tibet	2′ × 3′	Large, deeply divided.
(*A. vitifolia* of gardens)			

ANTENNARIA

Sun, light soil, mainly for rock garden or well-drained border verges. *A. aprica* promises to be a good vigorous plant but is not fully tested.

dioica	N. Hemisphere	1″ × 9″	Greyish, forming a close carpet.
— 'Hyperborea Rosea'		1″ × 8″	Greyish, forming a close carpet.
plantaginifolia	N. America	3″ × 1′	Dark green, broad, bare in winter.

ANTHEMIS

Sun and light soil. *A. cupaniana* is apt to die out in wet winters but small rooted pieces usually survive. *A. nobilis* (Chamomile) is useful for mowing as a substitute for grass in very sandy soil; fragrant when bruised; 'Plena', the double-flowered form, is more ornamental; the variety 'Treneague' is dwarf, non-flowering.

cupaniana	Italy	9″ × 3′	Silvery-grey, finely divided.
nobilis	Europe	5″ × 2′	Rich green, finely divided.
(*Chamaemelum nobile*)			
— 'Treneague'		2″ × 18″	Rich green, finely divided.

ANTHERICUM

Alpine meadow plant for sun, any reasonably drained soil. Apart from its beautiful flowers St Bernard's Lily gives a fine grassy effect, useful as a foil for the usual rounded foliage of most ground-cover plants.

liliago	S. Europe	1′ × 1′	Glaucous green, grassy, graceful.

Flower Height and Colour and Fruits (if any)	Flowering Season	Habit	Propagation
6". Small pink flowers in umbels.	Spring–autumn	Carpet	CDL
6". Small white, pink or yellow eyes.	Spring–autumn	Carpet	CDL
2½–4'. Large, from white to deep pink.	Late summer–autumn	Spreading	DR
3½'. Large, mauve-pink, on branching stems.	Late summer	Spreader	D
4". Small white heads.	Midsummer	Carpet, rooting	D
4". Small pink heads.	Midsummer	Carpet, rooting	D
7". White in small heads.	Midsummer	Carpet, rooting	D
15". White daisies.	Late spring	Hummock, rooting	CDS
9". White daisies.	Summer	Carpet, rooting	CDS
	Summer	Carpet, rooting	CD
3'. Small white lily-flowers in spires.	June	Clump	DS

HERBACEOUS PLANTS

	Country of Origin	Leaf Height and Planting Distance	Leaf Colour and Character
ARABIS			

Will thrive anywhere, preferably sunny, not clay or bog, preferring a rough limy soil. Th double form of *A. albida* is generally preferred.

albida	Europe	5″ × 18″	Greyish green, loose rosettes.
— 'Flore Pleno'		5″ × 18″	Greyish green, loose rosettes.
— 'Variegata'		4″ × 1′	Edged creamy-yellow

ARENARIA

A. balearica requires cool shady positions. *A. montana* and *A. ledebouriana* require sun open positions, on rock garden or top of retaining wall.

balearica	Balearic Isles	½″ × 18″	Bright green, minute
ledebouriana	America	3″ × 1′	Soft green, tiny.
montana	Europe	3″ × 1′	Dark green, soft, sm

ARISARUM

Woodland plant, thriving in any cool shady or partly shaded position, light to mediur heavy soil. Flowers hidden. The long tail of the flower earns it the name of 'mouse plant Leaves die down in late summer.

proboscideum	Apennines	4″ × 9″	Rich green, spear-sha smooth.

ARMERIA

Thrift; for sunny places, rock garden, border verges. Light soil preferred, well draine Ideal for planting between rocks to cover weedy clefts. *A. corsica* does not flower free unless divided every few years.

corsica (of gardens)	Corsica	5″ × 1′	Dark green, grass-li short.
maritima	Europe	5″ × 18″	Dark green, grass-li short.

A. m. 'Laucheana', more compact, flowers deeper colour; *A. m. alba*, pure white.

ARTEMISIA

Sun; for light, well-drained soils. Useful in maritime districts. Other well-known artemisia though spreading rapidly, do not make dense ground-cover.

stellerana	NE. Asia	1′ × 3′	Grey-white, downy, pinnate.

ARUNCUS

Sun or part shade; best growth on moist, even somewhat boggy soil, but will grow we in dry soil. The male form is the most ornamental. *A. sylvester* 'Kneiffii' has very daint foliage and is less than half the size.

dioicus (*A. sylvester* or *Spiraea aruncus*)	N. Hemisphere	5′ × 4′	Rich green, much d fernlike.

duous or green	Flower Height and Colour and Fruits (if any)	Flowering Season	Habit	Propagation
E	9″. Heads of white.	Spring	Carpet	CD
E	9″ Heads of white, double.	Spring	Carpet	CD
E	7″. Heads of white.	Spring	Carpet	CD
E	1½″. Tiny, white.	Spring	Carpet, rooting	CDS
D	5″. White. tiny.	Spring	Carpet	CDS
E	6″. White, small.	Spring	Carpet	CDS
D	3″. Hidden, brown and white.	Spring	Tuberous	D
E	10″. Coppery-pink in dense heads.	Early summer	Carpet	CDS
E	9″. Pink in dense heads.	Early summer	Carpet	CDS
E	2′. Downy grey-white stems of flower heads.	Summer	Sprawler	CDL
D	7′. Great plumes of cream.	Early summer	Clump	D

143

HERBACEOUS PLANTS

	Country of Origin	Leaf Height and Planting Distance	Leaf Colour and Character

ASARUM
Plants for cool, somewhat moist (not boggy) soil, in shady positions. *AA. canadense, caudatum* and *shuttleworthii* are also good ground-covers but lack the attractive glossy leaves of *A. europaeum*.

europaeum	Europe	8″ × 18″	Rounded, dark green, glossy.

ASPERULA
Sweet Woodruff. Cool, light or medium-heavy soil, in shady positions. Rampantly invasive. Good town plant.

odorata	Europe	5″ × 3′	Rich green, in whorls.

ASTER
The taller Michaelmas daisies are not usually to be regarded as ground-cover, but the more rampant varieties do make dense carpets and are good for holding verges of ponds, streams, etc. One of the best is the old 'Climax', lavender-blue, 5 ft, October. 'Lilac Time', 'Victor', 'Marjorie' are typical of a race of valuable dense growing dwarfs in various soft colours, 6 in. to 1 ft when in flower. All grow freely in any normal garden soil, and are easily increased by division in spring. *A. macrophyllus* grows well in shade but has not much quality.

macrophyllus	N. America	9″ × 2′	Dark green, rounded,

ASTILBE
Beautiful foliage and conspicuous flowers make these plants popular for moist ground and waterside; preferably in sun (especially for those with coppery foliage).

× arendsii		1′–18″ × 2–3′	Green or coppery, div. ferny.

This hybrid race is derived from E. Asiatic species, *AA. astilboides, davidii, japonica, thunbergii* and others. Short erect varieties are: 'Fanal', garnet red; 'Koblenz', deep pink; 'Rheinland', light pink; 'Bridal Veil', white; medium height: 'Red Sentinel', dark red; 'Peach Blossom', pink; 'King Albert', white; tall: 'Salland', rose red; 'Jo Ophorst', purplish; 'Erica', pink; all these have erect plumes. The following are tall with gracefully arching plumes: 'Professor van der Wielen', white; 'Betsy Cuperus', light pink; 'Ostrich Plume', deep pink. (Frequently and erroneously called *Spiraea*.)

rivularis	Nepal W. China	4′ × 4′	Green, boldly divided, ferny.
simplicifolia	Japan	4″ × 8″	Green, shining, divided
— **'Hybrida Rosea'**		9″ × 1′	Green, shining, divided

'Atrorosea' is a more colourful hybrid of the same charm. 'Bronze Elegance' adds coppery leaves to the rich pink flower colour.

sinensis	China	5″ × 10″	Green, divided, ferny, purplish.

Deciduous or Evergreen	Flower Height and Colour and Fruits (if any)	Flowering Season	Habit	Propagation
E	Flowers small, hidden.	Spring	Spreader	D
D	9". Starry, pure white, in heads; effective.	Late spring	Spreader	D
D	2–3'. Branching, pale lilac daisies.	August	Clump	D
D	2½–3'. Long plumes of tiny flowers.	Summer	Clump	D
D	6–7'. Long, arching plumes, greenish white.	Late summer	Clump and spreading underground	D
D	10". Arching plumes, cream, or pink (*A. s.* 'Rosea').	Summer	Clump	DS
D	18". Arching plumes, clear rose.	Summer	Clump	D
D	10". Feathery spikes.	Summer	Clump	D

HERBACEOUS PLANTS

	Country of Origin	Leaf Height and Planting Distance	Leaf Colour and Character

ASTILBE *cont.*
sinensis
   The species is seldom seen but has given rise to many dwarf forms and hybrids, usually classed under:
— pumila
   'Gnome', 'Kobald', and 'Perkeo' are compact with crinkled foliage.
taquetii 'Superba'   2′ × 4′   Bronzy green, divided.

ASTRANTIA
   Sun or partial shade, in any garden soil, not wet nor too dry.
major   Europe   9″ × 18″   Green, lobed, handsom
   'Sunningdale Variegated' has leaves strikingly marked cream and yellow, becoming less variegated from midsummer onwards.
maxima   E. Caucasus   9″ × 12″   Green, deeply lobed,
   (*A. helleborifolia*)   handsome.

AUBRIETA
   Sun, preferring rough limy soil rather than acid sands; good drainage. Border verges, rose beds, rock gardens, retaining walls.
deltoidea   Sicily to   5″ × 18″   Grey-green, soft, prof
   Asia Minor   small.
   There are many richly coloured named cultivars, such as 'Carnival', purple; 'Bressingham Red', carmine; 'Lilac Time', lilac; 'Maurice Prichard', pink. These are all vigorous.

BALLOTA
   Full sun, well-drained soil; impatient of winter damp. A perennial with a woody base and sprawling branchlets; these die back in winter or should be cut back.
pseudodictamnus   Crete, etc.   1′ × 2′   Small, grey-white, wo
   B. acetabulosa is similar.   rounded leaves.

BEGONIA
   Suitable for a sunny corner sheltered by shrubs, etc., in our warmest counties. Increases by means of bulblets.
evansiana   Malay, China,   1′ × 18″   Smooth, large lobed, g
   Japan   reddish beneath.

BELLIUM
   Compositae. Full sun, well-drained. rock garden. A tiny daisy.
minutum   Levant   1″ × 9″   Green, tiny, spoon-sha
   flat.

BERGENIA
   Megasea, Saxifrage. Sun or shade, but preferably not under low trees and shrubs; any soil that is not boggy. Most luxuriant on medium-heavy soil. Invaluable as ground-cover, and for permanent edgings. *B. ciliata* is only hardy in sheltered gardens in the south and west; *B. c. ligulata* is spring-tender. *B.* 'Ballawley' is less tough than others and this and the two previous species often lose their leaves in cold weather. *B. cordifolia* and its varieties and hybrids are the most reliable, particularly *B. c.* 'Purpurea', popularized by Gertrude Jekyll. The ideal foil for masonry and paved paths.
ciliata   Nepal, Kumaon   1′ × 18″   Dark green, large, roun
   hairy on both sides.

146

Deciduous or Evergreen	Flower Height and Colour and Fruits (if any)	Flowering Season	Habit	Propagation
D	4'. Long feathery spikes, magenta.	Late summer	Clump	D
D	2'. Erect, branching, whitish heads.	Summer–autumn	Spreader	DS
D	2'. Erect, branching, rose-pink heads.	Summer	Clump	DS
D	9". In heads.	Spring	Carpet	CDS
D	18". Pale mauve, inconspicuous.	Late summer	Clump	CD
D	18"–2'. Light pink.	Summer	Clump	D
E	2-3". White, pink tipped.	Spring	Carpet	D
D	1'. Clear pink, large heads.	Spring	Clump	D

HERBACEOUS PLANTS

	Country of Origin	Leaf Height and Planting Distance	Leaf Colour and Character
BERGENIA *cont.*			
ciliata			
— ligulata	Nepal	9″ × 1′	Dark green, ciliate edge.
cordifolia	Siberia	1′ × 2′	Dark green, large, round puckered.
— 'Purpurea'		1′ × 2½′	Dark green, large, round purplish in winter.
crassifolia	Siberia	1′ × 18″	Dark green, large, edge curved backwards.
delavayi (see *B. purpurascens*)			
ligulata (see *B. ciliata ligulata*)			
purpurascens (*B. delavayi*)	Himalaya	1′ × 1′	Dark green. Turns maro in winter with glossy reddish reverse.
HYBRIDS			
'Abendglut'	Hybrid	5″ × 1′	Dark green, maroon in winter, flat.
'Ballawley'	Hybrid	6″ × 2′	Shining dark green, la bronzy in winter.
'Morgenröte'	Hybrid	8″ × 1′	Dark green.
× schmidtii	Hybrid	1′ × 2′	Dark green, large, tooth edge, long stalk. 'E Schmidt' is the form usually found in cult tion.
'Silberlicht'	Hybrid	8″ × 18″	Dark green.
'Sunningdale'	Hybrid	9″ × 2′	Shining dark green; maroon, with red reve in winter.

BOLAX			
Full sun, well-drained slopes of rock garden; very dense.			
gummifera (*Bolax* or *Azorella glebaria*, *A. trifurcata*)	Chile, Magellan	3″ × 1′	Dark green, much divid mossy hummock.

BRUNNERA

Shade, full or partial; the leaves scorch in hot sun. Moist or dry soil. Seeds itself, easily satisfied. Looks like a giant forget-me-not, in flower for many weeks.

macrophylla (*Anchusa myosotidiflora*)	W. Caucasus	1′ × 2′	Dark green, large, round dull and hairy.

A rare and beautiful variegated form has large areas of creamy white on the leaves.

BUPHTHALMUM

Any reasonable border soil, sun. Very long flowering period.

salicifolium	Austria	10″ × 18″	Dark green, narrow, den

Deciduous or Evergreen	Flower Height and Colour and Fruits (if any)	Flowering Season	Habit	Propagation
E	9". Blush white, reddish calyces, in heads.	Early spring	Clump	D
E	1'. Light mauve-pink, red stalks, large heads.	Late spring	Clump	D
E	18"–2'. Mauve-carmine, red stalks, large heads.	Late spring	Clump	D
E	18". Light lilac-pink, large heads.	Spring	Clump	D
E	1'. Pink in heads, reddish stalks.	Spring	Clump	D
E	9". Brilliant magenta-purple, semi-double.	Spring	Clump	D
E	18". Rich carmine-pink, red stalks, large heads.	Spring	Clump	D
E	1'. Rich pink, large heads.	Spring and summer	Clump	D
E	18". Clear pink, large heads.	Early spring	Clump	D
E	12". Pure white fading pink, large heads.	Spring	Clump	D
E	18". Rich deep pink, reddish stalks, large heads.	Spring	Clump	D
E	3". Tiny, greenish-yellow.	Spring	Carpet	CD
D	2'. Tiny pure blue flowers.	Spring	Clump, spreader	DRS
D	2'. Yellow daisies.	Summer–autumn	Clump	DS

HERBACEOUS PLANTS

	Country of Origin	Leaf Height and Planting Distance	Leaf Colour and Character
CALAMINTHA			
Sun or partial shade, any soil, dry rather than moist; seeds itself. Of dwarf mint-like appearance.			
grandiflora	Europe	9″ × 18″	Light green, hairy, aroma
CALTHA			
Sun, boggy ground or streamside or deep moist border. *C. palustris* seeds itself.			
palustris	N. Hemisphere	9″ × 18″	Green, shining, rounded
— 'Plena'		6″ × 18″	Green, shining, rounded
polypetala	Caucasus, Asia Minor	15″ × 3′	Green, shining, rounded large.
CAMPANULA			
Bell-flower. Sun-loving, but will grow in partial shade. Well-drained soil, rock garden or borders. *C. poscharskyana* is an effective ground-cover, but is best kept away from small plants.			
alliariifolia	Caucasus, Asia Minor	1′ × 18″	Hairy, rounded, dull gre grey beneath.
carpatica	Carpathian Mountains	9″ × 1′	Light green, rounded, sm dense.
C. carpatica is available in numerous garden forms with flowers from white to purple; *C. c. turbinata* is a smaller geographical form.			
latiloba	Siberia	9″ × 18″	Light green, narrow, in large rosettes.
'Alba', white, and 'Highcliffe', violet-blue, are distinct and good variants. 'Percy Piper' is a newer richly coloured variant, and still newer is 'Hidcote Amethyst'.			
portenschlagiana 'Bavarica'	S. Europe	5″ × 1′	Deep green, small.
(*C. p.* 'Grandiflora', *C. muralis*)			
poscharskyana	Dalmatia	9″ × 2′	Mid green, dense.
There are various colour forms, white and lilac-pink, also 'Stella', clear bright blue.			
CARDAMINE			
C. trifolia for shade or part-shade; light to heavy soil. Cuckoo flower is the popular name for *C. pratensis*, of which the double form and also *C. raphanifolia* (*C. latifolia*) are fairly good carpeters for moist places. For *C. asarifolia*, see *Pachyphragma macrophyllum*, page 125.			
trifolia	S. Europe	3″ × 1′	Dark green, three-lobed, dense.
CENTAUREA			
The cornflowers and knapweeds are easy to grow in sun; light to heavy soil. *C. dealbata*, a Caucasian species, is not worth considering as a ground-cover plant and is very inferior to 'John Coutts', raised at Kew and named after the raiser by the writer. *C. simplicicaulis* is best on rock gardens.			
hypoleuca 'John Coutts'		9″ × 18″	Grey-green, grey beneath long, broadly toothed.

Deciduous or Evergreen	Flower Height and Colour and Fruits (if any)	Flowering Season	Habit	Propagation
D	18". Pink sage-like flowers.	Early summer	Clump	CDS
D	15". Large buttercup flowers, yellow.	Spring	Clump	DS
D	9". Large fully double flowers.	Spring	Clump	D
D	2'. Large buttercup flowers, yellow.	Spring	Carpet, rooting	D
D	2'. Branching stems, narrow white bells.	Midsummer	Clump	DS
D	15". Upturned wide bell-flowers.	Midsummer	Clump	CDS
E	3'. Cup-shaped flowers stud erect stems.	Midsummer	Clump	D
D	8". Small lilac-blue bells in clusters.	Midsummer	Spreader	CD
E	Trailing shoots, lavender-blue stars.	Midsummer and later	Spreader	CD
E	6". Pure white, in small heads.	Early spring	Spreader	D
D	18". Beautiful pink knapweed flowers.	Early summer	Spreader	D

HERBACEOUS PLANTS

	Country of Origin	Leaf Height and Planting Distance	Leaf Colour and Character
CENTAUREA *cont.*			
montana	Europe	10″ × 2′	Grey, woolly, narrow.

Various colour forms: 'Alba', white; 'Rosea', pink; 'Parham Variety', rich mauve.

simplicicaulis	Armenia	3″ × 9″	Dainty, toothed, grey beneath.

CERASTIUM
Snow in Summer is an invasive plant but admirable in rough conditions and where it cannot envelop other plants and small shrubs. Sun, drained soil.

tomentosum	S. and E. Europe	9″ × 2′	Silvery grey, dense mats.

CERATOSTIGMA
Sun, well-drained soil. The leaves take on bright autumn tints while the flowers are appearing.

plumbaginoides	China	10″ × 18″	Dark green, rounded, smooth.
(*Plumbago larpentae*)			

CHIASTOPHYLLUM
Any well-drained soil, sun or shade; more luxuriant in shade or part shade.

oppositifolium	Caucasus	4″ × 1′	Succulent, light green.
(*Cotyledon oppositifolia*; *C. simplicifolia* of gardens)			

CHRYSANTHEMUM
None of the normal chrysanthemums is admissible here, but the following are good covers, enjoying full sun on well-drained, preferably limy soil; *C. haradjanii* for the rock garden mainly.

haradjanii	N. Africa	4″ × 1′	Silvery grey, each leaf li a feather.
yezoense	Japan	1′ × 2′	Green, divided.

CLAYTONIA
Woodland plants for cool moist soil, probably thriving best in those which are lime-free. Apt to become a nuisance when suited. *C. perfoliata* is a prolific annual weed.

sibirica	Siberia	5″ × 9″	Fleshy, smooth, small.
(*C. alsinoides*)			

CONVALLARIA
Lily-of-the-valley takes some time to settle down. Will thrive in sun or shade, clay, sand, chalk; best in partial shade in well-drained soil; it is advisable to plant it here and there and wait to see which patch thrives best. Usually grows best where it has not been carefully planted!

majalis	N. Hemisphere	9″ × 1′	Smooth, rich green.
— 'Fortin's Giant'		10″ × 1′	Smooth, rich green.

The pink form *C. m.* 'Rosea' is less vigorous; a form with double white flowers, *C. m.* 'Prolificans', is sometimes seen. 'Fortin's Giant' flowers a fortnight later than the others and has larger flowers.

eciduous or vergreen	Flower Height and Colour and Fruits (if any)	Flowering Season	Habit	Propagation
D	18". Large blue corn-flowers.	Late Spring	Spreader	D
D	8". Pink cornflowers, small.	Early summer	Clump	DS
E	15". White, like small pinks.	Early summer	Spreader	CD
D	1'. Indigo-blue in heads.	Autumn	Spreader	CD
E	8". Tiny, yellow, in sprays.	Summer	Carpet	CDS
E	9". Yellow, small, in heads.	Spring	Carpet	CD
D	2'. Pinkish, usually white, in heads.	Autumn	Spreader	D
D	7". Tiny pinkish white, effective in mass.	Spring	Tuberous, spreader	DS
D	9". White bells, delicious scent.	Late spring	Spreader	D
D	10". White bells, delicious scent.	Late spring	Spreader	D

HERBACEOUS PLANTS

	Country of Origin	Leaf Height and Planting Distance	Leaf Colour and Character

CORONILLA
Sun, well-drained, spreading very freely, suitable for rough sunny banks; keep away from any plant or shrub under six feet in height.

varia	Europe	1' × 4'	Soft green, pinnate, sm

CORYDALIS
Will grow in sun but flowering period is much lengthened if growing in cool, somewhat moist, partly shaded, conditions. They seed themselves freely. Light or medium-heavy soils. *C. cheilanthifolia* is rather tender.

cheilanthifolia	China	9" × 18"	Smooth, bronzy-green, dainty, ferny.
lutea	Europe	9" × 1'	Smooth, light green, dai ferny.
ochroleuca	Italy	9" × 1'	Smooth, light green, dai ferny.
scouleri	NW. America	18" × 18"	Dainty, feathery, light green.

COTULA
Sun or shade, damp or dry soil. Dense mats of greenery; keep away from other low plants. Good carpeters for little bulbs. *C. potentillina* is similar.

reptans	Australia, Tasmania	2" × 2'	Dark green, ferny, tiny.
squalida	New Zealand	2" × 2'	Bronze, green, ferny, tin

CRAMBE
C. cordifolia is of largest dimensions, a gypsophila-like effect in flower. Full sun, well-drained soil. *C. maritima*, the culinary seakale, is one of the most ornamental of all foliage plants; thrives in rough limy soil in full sun.

cordifolia	Caucasus	3' × 4'	Dark green, broad, rou large.
maritima	Europe	1' × 2'	Broad, glaucous grey, lob twisted.

CROCOSMIA
The common montbretia will thrive in any light yet fertile soil, in sun or shade, and increases rapidly by means of its spreading corms. In some soils it increases so fast that it ceases to flower; it should then be thinned out and given a fertilizer, or moved into a fresh spot.

crocosmiiflora	Hybrid	18" × 2'	Long, grass-like, bright green.
masonorum	S. Africa	2' × 2'	Long, grass-like, bright green.

CYCLAMEN
The most prolific and dense-leaved species, seeding itself in the rather heavier limy soils, particularly under trees. Plant in summer, when dormant, from pot-grown seedlings, not

:iduous or ergreen	Flower Height and Colour and Fruits (if any)	Flowering Season	Habit	Propagation
D	18". Small, lilac-pink, in heads.	Spring to summer	Spreader	D
D	12". Small, yellow, in long heads.	Summer onwards	Clump	S
D	12". Small, yellow, in small heads.	Summer onwards	Clump	S
D	12". Small, creamy white, in small heads.	Summer onwards	Clump	S
D	20". Small, purplish, in branching spikes.	Spring	Spreader	D
E	2". Tiny buttons, inconspicuous.	Summer	Carpet, rooting	D
E	2". Small buttons, creamy yellow.	Summer	Carpet, rooting	D
D	6'. Branching stems and multitudes of tiny white flowers.	Early summer	Clump	DRS
D	2'. Small, white, in large heads.	Early summer	Clump	DRS
D	2½'. Nodding, orange, in sprays, graceful.	Late summer	Spreader	D
D	3'. Orange-red in sprays, graceful.	Late summer	Spreader	D

HERBACEOUS PLANTS

	Country of Origin	Leaf Height and Planting Distance	Leaf Colour and Character

CYCLAMEN *cont.*
from dried imported bulbs. A mulch of leaf-mould keeps weeds at bay after leaves have died down and benefits the plants.

hederifolium (*C. neapolitanum*)	S. Europe	5″ × 1′	Grey green, handsome mottled, lasting from October to May.

DIANTHUS
Pinks grow best in well-drained soil, preferably limy, in full sun. The small species listed (there are many others) are best on the rock garden. All very fragrant.

arenarius	N. Europe	2″ × 1′	Rich green, grassy.
deltoides	Europe	3″ × 1′	Rich green, small.

There are several richly coloured forms available, such as 'Superbus' with coppery leaves. They are not quite so vigorous as the green-leaved kinds.

fragrans	N. Caucasus	4″ × 1′	Grey-green, grassy.
gratianopolitanus (*D. caesius*)	Europe (Britain)	3″ × 10″	Grey, grassy, dwarf.

There are several good forms available, such as 'Flore Pleno' and 'Baker's Variety'.

Highland Hybrids		6″ × 18″	Grey, grassy, luxuriant.

Other garden hybrids such as 'Emperor,' 'C. T. Musgrave', 'Inchmery', 'Enid Anderson', 'White Ladies', 'Grenadier', are all valuable perennial carpeters with good foliage and flowers, white through pink to deep crimson. They thrive on well-drained soil in full sun, open position.

DICENTRA
Excellent for partial or full shade, but so long as the soil is not dry they will grow and flower well; less continuously in full sun. Best in light but good moist woodland soil, preferably not limy. *D. spectabilis* dies down too early in the summer to be an effective ground-cover. 'Bountiful' seeds itself prolifically, but is variable; 'Adrian Bloom' has flowers of even richer colouring.

ormosa	W. N. America	10″ × 2′	Fresh green, smooth, ferny.
— alba		10″ × 18″	Light green, smooth, dainty, ferny.
— 'Bountiful'		12″ × 2′	Fresh green, smooth, ferny.
oregana	Oregon	10″ × 18″	Glaucous, smooth, ferny.

DIMORPHOTHECA
Long-flowering plant for full sun in the warmer counties and gardens.

barberiae (of gardens) (*Osteospermum jucundum*)	E. S. Africa	9″ × 20″	Rich green, narrow, small.

DORONICUM
Sun, not particular regarding soil, light or heavy. Will also thrive in partial shade.

'Miss Mason'	C. Europe	10″ × 2′	Bright green, heart-shaped, broad.

duous / r / green	Flower Height and Colour and Fruits (if any)	Flowering Season	Habit	Propagation
E	7". Pink or white.	Late summer–autumn	Clump	S
E	9". Small, white, marked pink.	Midsummer	Carpet	CDS
E	9". Small, pink, various.	Midsummer	Clump	CDS
E	9". Small, white, deeply fringed petals.	Midsummer	Carpet	CDS
E	8". Small, pink, various.	Midsummer	Carpet	CDS
E	15". White to crimson, maroon eyes.	Midsummer	Carpet	CDS
D	15". Dull mauve pink, small, nodding sprays.	Spring	Spreader	DS
D	12". Pure white, small, nodding sprays.	Spring onwards	Spreader	D
D	18". Deep mauve-pink, small, nodding sprays.	Spring onwards	Spreader	D
D	12". Creamy-pink, small, nodding sprays.	Spring	Spreader	DS
D	18". Clear mauve-pink daisies.	Midsummer onwards	Clump	CDS
D	18". Large yellow daisies.	Spring	Clump	D

157

HERBACEOUS PLANTS

	Country of Origin	Leaf Height and Planting Distance	Leaf Colour and Character

DUCHESNEA
Similar to a wild strawberry. Sun or shade. Rampageous carpeter for any normal garden soil. Grows yards a year. Keep away from small plants. Fruit tasteless.

| indica | India, Japan | 3″ × 10′ | Dark green, lobed, eff |

EPIMEDIUM
Will grow well in sun or shade, in any fertile soil, sandy or heavy. Remove old leaves or deciduous species in winter to reveal flowers in spring. These plants are slow to settle down but once launched will continue their steady, dense growth. Leaves borne on wiry stems usually in three lobes, prettily tinted in spring and autumn. There are several smaller species and hybrids which scarcely come into the present scheme.

perralderanum	Algeria	15″ × 15″	Glossy, green, prickly
pinnatum colchicum	Transcaucasia, Georgia	1′ × 15″	Smooth, green.
pubigerum	Asia Minor, Balkans, etc.	1′ × 15″	Smooth, green.
× rubrum	Hybrid	1′ × 9″	Smooth, green.
× versicolor	Hybrid	1′ × 9″	Smooth, green, coppe spring.

There is a pretty pale yellow variety, 'Sulphureum', which is more vigorous.

| × warleyense | Hybrid | 1′ × 12″ | Smooth, light green. |

ERIGERON
Sun, light or heavy well-drained soil; specially for warm maritime districts. There are several floriferous garden forms: 'Elstead Rose' and 'Four Winds' being reliable and gay; their only detraction being the shortness of their ray-petals compared with the size of the central yellow disc. The popular varieties of *E. speciosus*, etc., scarcely qualify for inclusion here.

| glaucus | W. N. America | 9″ × 18″ | Greyish, broad. |

ERIOGONUM
Spreading over sunny well-drained rock-garden slopes or sandy soil; sub-shrubby, making dense carpets. Heads of tiny flowers freely produced.

| umbellatum | British Columbia | 3″ × 18″ | Soft green, bronzed i winter, small. |

E. umbellatum major is a recognizedly good form of a variable species.

ERIOPHYLLUM
Sun, extra well-drained soil. Apt to die out in damp soil.

| lanatum | N. America | 1′ × 2′ | Silver-grey, divided. |

(*Bahia lanata*, *E. caespitosum*)

ERODIUM
Sun loving, masses of leaves and a never-ending succession of flowers. Rather coarse. For other species see Chapter 4.

| manescavii | Pyrenees | 1′ × 2′ | Green, feathery, luxur |

Deciduous or Evergreen	Flower Height and Colour and Fruits (if any)	Flowering Season	Habit	Propagation
E	4". Yellow, red fruits.	Spring–autumn	Carpet, rooting	D
E	18". Yellow, in dainty sprays.	Spring	Spreader	D
E	15". Yellow, in dainty sprays.	Spring	Spreader	D
D	18". Creamy, small.	Spring	Spreader	D
D	15". Crimson, small.	Spring	Spreader	D
D	1'. Pale pink.	Spring	Spreader	D
D	1'. Orange-red and yellow.	Spring	Spreader	D
D/E	1'. Purplish-pink daisies, short rayed.	Summer	Carpet	DS
D/E	9". Creamy-yellow heads.	June–August	Carpet, rooting	CD
D	15". Bright yellow, in heads.	Summer	Spreader	DS
D	18". Magenta.	Summer	Clump	DS

HERBACEOUS PLANTS

	Country of Origin	Leaf Height and planting Distance	Leaf Colour and Character
EUPHORBIA			
Sun, but will thrive in part shade, particularly *E. robbiae*. Any fertile soil. *E. griffithii* makes effective cover in heavier soil. Spurge.			
polychroma	Europe	1′ × 18″	Fresh green, small, hairy, erect stems.
(*E. epithymoides* of gardens)			
griffithii 'Fireglow'	Himalaya	3′ × 2′	Rich green.
robbiae	Asia Minor	18″ × 2′	Dark green rosettes on erect stems.
FILIPENDULA			
(*Spiraea*)			
Sun; moist or boggy soil, streamside, except *F. hexapetala*, which thrives in dry ground. Tiny flowers conspicuous in the mass.			
hexapetala 'Flore Pleno'	Europe	6″ × 18″	Rich green, feathery, forming flat rosettes.
palmata	NE. Asia	18″ × 18″	Green, large lobes, handsome.
(*Spiraea digitata*)			
purpurea	Japan	3′ × 3′	Dark green, large lobes, handsome.
(*Spiraea palmata* of gardens)			
FRAGARIA			
The alpine strawberries are not only delicious to eat but make excellent dense cover. 'Baron Solemacher' is clump-forming, does not produce runners, but by its quick increase can provide a good carpet planted about 1′ apart. All like cool, partly shaded positions at least in the home counties. *F. chiloense* is an excellent glossy carpeter of same dimensions.			
vesca 'Semperflorens'		9″ × 2′	Rich green, divided.
FRANKENIA			
Sun, light soil, rock garden. Good in maritime districts.			
laevis	Europe	1″ × 1′	Dark green, minute.
thymifolia	Spain	1″ × 9″	Grey-green, minute.
GALAX			
Cool, partial or full shade, lime-free soil with humus. Choice plant; leaves 3″ across, beautifully burnished in winter.			
urceolata	E. N. America	10″ × 10″	Dark green, glossy, rounded, leathery.
(*G. aphylla*)			
GERANIUM			
G. sanguineum, endressii, himalayense, 'Johnson's Blue', × *magnificum* (*G. ibericum* or *platypetalum* of gardens), *pratense, psilostemon, renardii, wallichianum* grow perfectly well in full sun, but all are more luxuriant and last longer in flower when in part shade in cool soil. *G. macrorrhizum, nodosum, phaeum, punctatum*, thrive even in complete shade. They are all assets to any garden. *G. rectum album*, white, and *G. bergeranum* purple, are two newer kinds related to *G. pratense* which promise well. No soil difficulties apart from ill-drained clay. Indispensable ground-cover, with beauty of flower and leaf.			
'Claridge Druce'	Hybrid	2′ × 3′	Soft green, hairy, handsome.
endressii	Pyrenees	18″ × 2′	Cool green.

Deciduous or Evergreen	Flower Height and Colour and Fruits (if any)	Flowering Season	Habit	Propagation
D	18". Greenish-yellow, tall heads.	Spring	Clump	DS
D	3'. Brick-red.	Summer	Spreader	D
E	2½'. Greenish-yellow, tall heads.	Spring	Spreader	DS
D	18". Creamy masses in flat heads.	Summer	Spreader	DR
D	2'. Flat heads of pink.	Summer	Clump	D
D	4'. Flat heads of cerise.	Summer	Clump	D
E	Tiny, white; small, sweet fruits red or white.	May–November	Carpet, rooting	D
E	1". Pink, tiny.	Summer	Carpet, rooting	D
E	1". Pink, tiny.	Summer	Carpet, rooting	D
E	18". Tiny, white, in slender spikes.	Summer	Clump	DS
D	2'. Magenta.	Summer	Clump	D
D	18". Magenta-pink.	Midsummer	Clump	D

HERBACEOUS PLANTS

	Country of Origin	Leaf Height and Planting Distance	Leaf Colour and Character
GERANIUM *cont.*			
endressii			
— **'Wargrave Pink'**		2′ × 3′	Light clear green.
himalayense	Sikkim	12″ × 2′	Dark green, elegant.
(*G. grandiflorum*)			
The variety 'Gravetye' or 'Alpinum' is very similar with a reddish eye.			
ibericum, *see G. × magnificum.*			
'Johnson's Blue'	Hybrid	1′ × 2′	Light green, deeply cut.
macrorrhizum	S. Europe	1′ × 2′	Light green, hairy, fragr
— **album**		1′ × 2′	Light green, hairy, fragr
maculatum	N. America	2′ × 18″	Fresh green, handsome.
nodosum	Europe	1′ × 18″	Fresh green, glossy, see itself.
× **magnificum**	Georgia	18″ × 2′	Dark green, hairy, hand some.
(*G. ibericum* or *platypetalum* of gardens)			
phaeum	Europe	18″ × 18″	Dark green, hairy, hand some.
pratense	N. Europe	2′ × 2′	Green, long-fingered, ha some.

G. pratense spreads rapidly by seed and is only suitable for woodland or open spaces where trees and large shrubs are growing. The valuable double forms 'Violaceum Plenum', 'Caeruleum Plenum' and 'Album Plenum' do not set seed and are safe garden plants. Fine foliage results if stems are removed after flowering.

	Country of Origin	Leaf Height and Planting Distance	Leaf Colour and Character
procurrens	Nepal	18″ × 4′	Soft green.
psilostemon	Armenia	3′ × 4′	Bright green, long-fingered, handsome.
(*G. armenum*)			
renardii	Caucasus	10″ × 1′	Grey-green, velvety.
sanguineum	Europe	9″ × 18″	Dark green, hairy, deeply cut, pretty.
— **album**	Europe	1′ × 18″	Dark green, hairy, deeply cut, pretty.
— **'Glenluce'**		1′ × 2′	Dark green, hairy, deepl cut, pretty.
— **lancastriense**	Britain	9″ × 1′	Dark green, hairy, deepl cut, pretty.
sylvaticum	Europe	20″ × 2′	Green, hairy, handsome.
'Mayflower' is a good lavender-blue.			
vlassovianum	Siberia, Manchuria	1′ × 2′	Dark green, velvety, ha some.
wallichianum	Himalaya	1′ × 2′	Soft green, velvety, hand some.

'Buxton's Variety' is a name generally given to the Spode-blue form usually cultivated.

GEUM

Sun, normal drained soil, not boggy. *G. rivale* (the best is 'Leonard's Variety') grows well in moist soil, even in partial shade.

	Country of Origin	Leaf Height and Planting Distance	Leaf Colour and Character
× **borisii**	Hybrid	10″ × 1′	Rich green, rounded, hai
rivale	N. Hemisphere	9″ × 1′	Dark green, rounded, hai

ous een	Flower Height and Colour and Fruits (if any)	Flowering Season	Habit	Propagation
	2–3'. Salmon-pink.	Midsummer onwards	Clump	D
	12". Violet-blue, crimson eye.	Midsummer	Spreader	D
	2'. Lavender-blue.	Summer	Clump	D
	15". Pink to dark magenta.	Late spring	Carpet, rooting	D
	15". Blush, reddish calyces.	Late spring	Carpet, rooting	D
	2–3'. Pale lilac-pink.	Late spring	Clump	DS
	15". Lilac-pink, seeds itself.	Summer onwards	Clump	DS
	2'. Violet-blue, vivid.	Early summer	Clump	D
	2'. Maroon, mauve or white, seeds itself.	Late spring	Clump	DS
	3'. Lavender-blue to white.	Early summer	Clump	D
	18". Mauve.	Summer–autumn	Carpet, rooting	DS
	3'. Brilliant magenta-crimson, black eye.	Summer	Clump	D
	1'. White, maroon veins.	Late spring	Clump	D
	1'. Magenta-crimson.	Midsummer	Spreader	CDS
	15". White.	Midsummer	Spreader	CD
	15". Soft pink.	Midsummer	Spreader	CD
	1'. Pink veined crimson.	Midsummer	Spreader	CDS
	2½'. White or pink or lavender-blue forms.	Late spring	Clump	DS
	18". Lavender-blue, white eye.	Summer onwards	Carpet	DS
	18". Violet-purple.	Midsummer	Clump	DS
D/E	1½'. Vivid orange, branching stems.	Late spring	Clump	D
D/E	15". Coppery yellowish-pink, branching stem.	Late spring	Clump	D

163

HERBACEOUS PLANTS

	Country of Origin	Leaf Height and Planting Distance	Leaf Colour and Character

GUNNERA
> G. *manicata* is a giant bog plant for sun or shade; margins of lakes, etc. The big basal crown need winter protection in all but our mildest counties. Individual flowers inconspicuous, borne in immense spikes. G. *chilensis* (G. *scabra*) is similar. G. *magellanica* a carpeter of floral merit, for cool moist positions.

magellanica	S. America	3" × 18"	Rich green, rough.
manicata	Brazil	7' × 8'	Rich green, rough, 6'

GYPSOPHILA
> Sun, well-drained soil, with lime or without. Slopes of rock garden, border verges.

repens	European Alps	5" × 2'	Grey-green, smooth,
'Rosy Veil'	Hybrid	9" × 18"	Grey-green, smooth,

HELLEBORUS
> Long-lived perennials for deep rich soil, preferably in partial or full shade, with lime or without. They thrive on old manure and compost. Ideal for growing under deciduous shrubs. H. *niger* usually thrives best in limy well-drained soil.

cyclophyllus	Greece	10" × 2'	Rich green, deeply lo
foetidus	Europe	1' × 18"	Very dark green, nar fingered.
niger. Christmas Rose.	Europe	10" × 18"	Very dark green, dee lobed.

orientalis
> The Lenten Rose is a very variable species, usually separated in gardens into the following geographical or colour forms.

	SE. Europe, Caucasus, Asia Minor	1' × 2'	Rich green, deeply lo Their leaves freque tend to last into th winter and they are mainly evergreen.
abchasicus	Purplish, green within; nearly evergreen.		
antiquorum	Purplish, green at base; nearly evergreen.		
atrorubens	Reddish purple, deciduous		
guttatus	White to greenish pink, heavily spotted maroon.		
olympicus	White, green tinge, nearly evergreen.		
purpurascens	Purplish, green within, deciduous.		
kochii	Greenish yellow, deciduous.		
viridis	Europe	10" × 18"	Rich green, lobed.

iduous or ergreen	Flower Height and Colour and Fruits (if any)	Flowering Season	Habit	Propagation
D	Green, inconspicuous.	Summer	Carpet, rooting	D
D	Green, 3′ spikes.	Summer	Clump	D
D	8″. White (or pink variety, *rosea*), tiny, in clouds.	Midsummer	Carpet	CS
D	15″. Blush pink, tiny, in clouds.	Midsummer	Carpet	C
D	18″. Green, nodding in sprays.	Spring	Clump	DS
E	2′. Small green bells, maroon edged, nodding, in sprays.	Late winter	Clump	S
E	1′. White, large, often tinged pink externally.	Winter	Clump	DS
DE	Various.	Winter–spring	Clump	DS
		February–April		
		February–April		
		January February–April	Very variable from seed; careful division immediately after flowering is best.	
		February–April		
		February–April		
		January–March		
D	15″. Pure green, nodding, in sprays.	Late winter	Clump	DS

165

HERBACEOUS PLANTS

	Country of Origin	Leaf Height and Planting Distance	Leaf Colour and Character

HELICHRYSUM
Sun, good drainage or scree on rock gardens in mild counties.

bellidioides	New Zealand	3″ × 1′	Grey-green, tiny, silv beneath.

HELXINE
For cool shady places where the soil does not become dry. An ineradicable pest in a gree house or rock garden and it will choke small plants; safe and good under trees and shrub in areas free or nearly free from frost.

soleirolii	Corsica	1″ × 1′	Vivid green, tiny.

HEMEROCALLIS
Day Lily. Sun or partial shade, any fertile soil. Easily grown. An excellent example of hov a clump-forming plant, with long grassy leaves, can be an effective ground-cover an create a pleasant contrast to other greenery. By the end of March many kinds have produce sheafs of bright light green, welcome at daffodil time. Beautiful, fragrant lily-like flowers borne in clusters. The dead leaves should be left on the ground in winter for effective cover

dumortieri	Japan	18″ × 18″	Bright green, grassy, arching.
flava	China	18″ × 18″	Bright green, grassy, arching.
fulva		3′ × 3′	Bright green, grassy, arching.
— 'Kwanso Flore Pleno'		3′ × 3′	Bright green, grassy, arching.
middendorfiana		18″ × 18″	Bright green, grassy, arching.

GARDEN HYBRIDS
Available with flowers of lemon yellow (usually the most fragrant), deep yellow, apricot, coppery orange, apricot pink and maroon, with many intermediates and bicolors. Some good varieties are: 'Dorothy McDade', light yellow; 'Pink Damask', coppery pink; 'Bold Courtier', copper and cream; 'Spanish Gold', orange-yellow; 'Stafford', garnet-red; 'Dream Waltz', creamy apricot; 'Marion Vaughan', lemon; 'Maculata', apricot-pink.

HERACLEUM
The giant hog-weed is only suitable for rich moist soil in the wild garden, where its gigantic leaves and vast flower-heads create an unequalled picture. Seeds itself freely.

mantegazzianum	Caucasus	4′ × 8′	Rich green, deeply lob

HEUCHERA
Sun or partial shade; good soil, not dry in spring. Plant in early autumn. There are many fine garden hybrids of vigorous growth such as 'Carmen', 'Gloriana', 'Firebird', 'Pearl Drops' and 'Sunset'. The following make clumps, but if planted fairly closely together knit into a carpet. For *H. cylindrica* and hybrids, see *Addenda* page 258.

× **brizoides**
A name for Hybrids between *H. americana*, *H. sanguinea* and perhaps *H. micrantha*, covering numerous pretty cultivars.

micrantha	W. N. America	6″ × 18″	Greyish-green marbled flat, hairy.

ciduous or ergreen	Flower Height and Colour and Fruits (if any)	Flowering Season	Habit	Propagation
E	4″. Tiny, white, 'everlasting'.	Summer	Carpet, rooting	CD
E	Inconspicuous.		Carpet	D
D	18″. Rich yellow, brown without.	Early summer	Clump	D
D	3′. Clear yellow, very fragrant.	Early summer	Spreader	D
D	4½′. Soft brick red and apricot.	Summer	Spreader	D
D	4½′. Double form, effective.	Summer	Spreader	D
D	2′. Rich yellow.	Early summer	Clump	D
D	10′. Thousands of tiny white flowers in heads 4′ wide.	Midsummer	Clump	S
E	2½′. Tiny flesh-coloured in plumes.	Early summer	Clump	DS

167

HERBACEOUS PLANTS

	Country of Origin	Leaf Height and Planting Distance	Leaf Colour and Character
HEUCHERA *cont.*			
pilosissima	California	9″ × 18″	Green, hairy, flat, m
americana	W. U.S.A.	6″ × 15″	Glistening purplish-g
(*H. rubescens* of gardens)			flat, hairy.
sanguinea	S. N. America	6″ × 15″	Dull dark green, flat,

HEUCHERELLA

An intergeneric hybrid between *Heuchera* × *brizoides* and *Tiarella cordifolia*. Sun or par shade, cool soil that does not get dry in spring suits them best. 'Bridget Bloom' is a riche coloured counterpart to *H. tiarelloides*.

tiarelloides	Hybrid	8″ × 18″	Soft green, hairy.

HOSTA

Funkia or Plantain Lily. Partial or full shade, preferably from buildings rather than over hanging trees; in any case the plants if possible should be away from trees in towny areas as the leaves of some retain sooty deposits from drip in wet weather. *H.* 'Thomas Hogg is not prone to this disadvantage. Excellent for a north wall, or among shrubs. Deep ric soil containing humus is best, but they will grow in sand or clay; very limy soils inhibi their growth, but with abundant humus they can be made to thrive there also. Bogg positions are not desirable. It is easy to remove sections of an old clump for transplantin, with a spade, as if one were cutting a sandwich cake, without having to disturb the clump fill up the hole with good soil. They can be moved successfully at any time of the year. I time they grow high out of the soil and should be top-dressed or replanted. The flowers ar in the shape of lilies, hanging from one side of erect stems. Almost all are hybrids or garde clones.

albomarginata	Japan	9″ × 15″	Small, narrow, light with narrow white
— 'Alba'	Japan	9″ × 15″	Small, narrow, rich
(*H. minor alba*)			
crispula	Japan	1′ × 18″	Large, long pointed, edge, dark green, b white margin.
decorata	Japan	10″ × 12″	Broad, blunt, broad v margin.
elata	Japan	20″ × 2′	Large, broad, slightly glaucous, pale gree wavy edge.
fortunei	Hybrid	20″ × 2′	Large, broad, slightly glaucous green.
— 'Albopicta'		20″ × 2′	Large, vivid yellow, (green, becoming wh green later.
— 'Aurea'		1′ × 15″	Leaves wholly yellow, later.
— hyacinthina		20″ × 2′	Glaucous blue-green, broad, handsome.
— 'Marginato Alba'		18″ × 2′	Slightly glaucous gree white edge, broad, handsome.

ciduous or ergreen	Flower Height and Colour and Fruits (if any)	Flowering Season	Habit	Propagation
E	2'. White, hairy, tiny, in plumes.	Early summer	Clump	DS
E	18". Greenish, tiny, in plumes.	Early summer	Clump	DS
E	18". Scarlet, or similar, tiny, in plumes.	Early summer	Clump	DS
E	20". Tiny, pink, in erect sprays.	Late spring	Clump	D
D	20". Violet-mauve.	Summer	Spreader	D
D	20". Pure white.	Summer	Spreader	D
D	2¼'. Pale lavender.	Midsummer	Clump	D
D	2'. Rich violet.	Late summer	Clump	D
D	2¼'. Pale lilac.	Summer	Clump	D
D	2¼'. Pale lilac.	Summer	Clump	D
D	2¼'. Pale lilac.	Summer	Clump	D
D	2'. Pale lilac.	Summer	Clump	D
D	2¼'. Rich lilac.	Summer	Clump	D
D	2½'. Pale lilac.	Summer	Clump	D

HERBACEOUS PLANTS

	Country of Origin	Leaf Height and Planting Distance	Leaf Colour and Character
HOSTA *cont.*			
fortunei			
— 'Obscura'		20″ × 2′	Rich dark green, broa handsome.
— 'Obscura Marginata'		20″ × 2′	Green, edged bright yel
lancifolia	Japan	1′ × 1′	Dark green, glossy, nar small.
plantaginea	China	20″ × 2′	Bright green, glossy, br
(*H. subcordata*)			
— grandiflora		20″ × 2′	Narrower leaves.
rectifolia	Japan	20″ × 18″	Narrow green leaves, e
sieboldiana	Japan	20″ × 2′	Broad, corrugated, glau
(*H. glauca*)			green.
— 'Elegans'		20″ × 2′	Broad, rounded, corrug glaucous blue-grey.
— 'Frances Williams'		18″ × 18″	Similar, with broad ye
('Gold Edge')			edge.
tardiflora	Japan	6″ × 6″	Small, dark green, thic glossy, pointed.
'Thomas Hogg'		1′ × 20″	Rich green, broad whi edge, pointed, flat.
tokudama	Japan	1′ × 1′	Small edition of *H. s. elegans*; cupped, glau blue-grey.
— 'Variegata'		1′ × 1′	Cupped, glaucous blue-grey, striped green.
undulata	Japan	9″ × 10″	Rich green, glossy, twis broad creamy centre.
(*H. lancifolia medio-variegata*)			
— erromena	Japan	20″ × 2′	Rich green, glossy, lon;
(*H. lancifolia fortis*)			
— univattata	Japan	1′ × 1′	Rich green, broad slas cream in centre.
ventricosa	Japan	20″ × 2′	Rich dark green, broad, glossy beneath.
— 'Aureomaculata'		18″ × 20″	Rich dark green, yello central stripes.
— 'Variegata'		20″ × 2′	Broad, irregular cream; yellow margins.

HOUSTONIA
Cool, moist, shady positions on rock garden, with humus. Profusely flowering. *H. caerulea* is less spreading.

serpyllifolia	N. America	2″ × 18″	Tiny, fresh green.

HOUTTUYNIA
Part or full shade in moist, even boggy soil. Foliage has penetrating orange fragrance. The double form 'Flore Pleno' is more ornamental.

cordata	Far East	1′ × 18″	Dark green.

Deciduous or Evergreen	Flower Height and Colour and Fruits (if any)	Flowering Season	Habit	Propagation
D	2½'. Rich lilac.	Summer	Clump	D
D	2½'. Rich lilac.	Summer	Clump	D
D	2'. Lilac.	Late summer–autumn	Clump	D
D	2'. Pure white.	Autumn	Clump	D
D	2'. Flowers slightly larger.	Autumn	Clump	D
D	2½'. Lilac.	Late summer	Clump	D
D	2'. Palest lilac-white.	Summer	Clump	D
D	2'. Palest lilac-white.	Summer	Clump	D
D	2'. Palest lilac-white.	Summer	Clump	D
D	10". Lilac.	Autumn	Clump	D
D	20". Pale lilac.	Summer	Clump	D
D	15". Palest lilac-white.	Summer	Clump	D
D	15". Palest lilac-white.	Summer	Clump	D
D	18". Pale lilac.	Summer	Clump	D
D	4'. Lilac.	Summer	Clump	D
D	18". Pale lilac.	Summer	Clump	D
D	2½'. Rich violet-purple.	Late summer	Clump	DS
D	2½'. Rich violet-purple.	Late summer	Clump	D
D	2½'. Rich violet-purple.	Late summer	Clump	D
E	4". Violet blue to white, tiny.	Midsummer onwards	Carpet, rooting	CD
D	15". Pure white, cone-shaped.	Summer	Spreader	D

HERBACEOUS PLANTS

	Country of Origin	Leaf Height and Planting Distance	Leaf Colour and Character

HYPERICUM
St John's Wort. Mainly sun loving, but will also grow well in shade. Provided the soil is not boggy, they present no difficulties. For *H. calycinum* see Chapter 4. *H. reptans* is for sheltered rock-garden slopes.

reptans	Sikkim	1″ × 18″	Minute, green.
rhodopeum	Europe	3″ × 18″	Grey-green, downy, profuse.

— 'Sunspot'
American cultivar; reputedly bigger, brighter and longer in flower.

IRIS
All thrive in sunshine, but *I. foetidissima* will grow and flower in shade, from trees or buildings. It and the bearded irises prefer a rough limy soil with good drainage; some of the older bearded types such as *I. florentina*, *I. kochii*, *I. pallida* and *I. flavescens* have short rhizomes and create such a mass of roots and leaves that they are weed-proof. *I. innominata* and *I. douglasiana* and the garden strains bred from them thrive best in sandy soils. *I. unguicularis* (*I. stylosa*) is ideal for filling a narrow dry border at the foot of a south-facing wall; *I. japonica* is hardy in the warmer counties and 'Ledger's Variety' is usually grown. This and *I. pallida* have pretty variegated forms. The true *I. graminea* should be sought, not 'Hort's Variety' which, though more vigorous, is scentless.

douglasiana	California	1′ × 2′	Dark green, narrow, spreading.
foetidissima	W. Europe	18″ × 2′	Dark shining green, br[…] grassy.

A much more handsome plant, up to 2′, with longer broader leaves, larger pale yellow flowers and larger pods of handsome berries is known as *I. f. citrina* or 'Chinese Form'. The form with white variegated leaves is particularly handsome, more compact, but seldom flowers.

graminea	Europe	18″ × 9″	Dark green, narrow, er[…]
innominata	Oregon	9″ × 18″	Dark green, narrow, spreading.
japonica	Japan, China	10″ × 18″	Dark green, smooth.

LAMIUM
Partial or full shade, cool conditions, light or heavy soil. *L. galeobdolon* 'Variegatum' (*Galeobdolon luteum* 'Variegatum') is a rampageous plant and should only be planted under trees (where few things can equal its beauty and luxuriance) or under very large shrubs.

galeobdolon	Europe		

The wild Archangel or yellow dead-nettle is pretty enough in its way but lacks the beauty of its variety's marbled leaves.

— 'Variegatum'		1′ × 9′	Dark green, marbled wi[…] white.
maculatum	Europe	8″ × 3′	Dark green, white cent[…] stripe.

For those who dislike mauve-pink there are two varieties, 'Album' and 'Roseum', with white and clear pink flowers respectively.

— 'Aureum'		6″ × 18″	Brilliant yellow-green, white stripe.

...ciduous or ...ergreen	Flower Height and Colour and Fruits (if any)	Flowering Season	Habit	Propagation
D	1". Deep yellow.	Summer–autumn	Carpet	C
E	4". Deep yellow.	Early summer	Carpet	CD
E	1'. Various, exquisite.	Early summer	Clump	DS
E	18". Dirty lilac, veined; small red berries in pods.	Early summer	Clump, seeding	DS
D	9". Purple and crimson, fragrant.	Early summer	Clump	DS
E	6". Various, exquisite.	Early summer	Clump	DS
E	15". Marked white and yellow, pretty.	Spring	Carpet	D
E	1'. Yellow 'dead-nettle' flowers.	Early summer	Carpet, rooting	D
E	8". Mauve-pink 'dead-nettle' flowers.	Early summer	Carpet, rooting	D
D/E	6". Mauve pink; cool moist place.	Early summer	Carpet, rooting	D

173

HERBACEOUS PLANTS

	Country of Origin	Leaf Height and Planting Distance	Leaf Colour and Character
LIMONIUM *(Statice latifolia)* Sun, well-drained soil. The border statice or Sea Lavender; the flower sprays are useful for drying.			
latifolium	SE. Europe	1' × 18"	Long, broad, leathery, ᴅ green dull. 'Blue Cloud' is a fine fᴏ

LIRIOPE
L. muscari requires sun, well-drained soil; will grow in very dry positions, against south walls. Flowers lovely in association with *Nerine bowdenii*. Slow but steady increase. Purple to lavender and white forms. *L. spicata* ('Lily Turf' in U.S.A.) is invasive. As yet untested, *L. exiliflora* has been recommended for warmer counties, a good spreader.

muscari There is a good variegated form.	E. Asia	15" × 1'	Dark green, grass-like, glossy.
spicata	E. Asia	8" × 18"	Dark green, grass-like, glossy.

LITHOSPERMUM
Sun or part shade, well-drained soil with humus. Best in the damper, milder west. *Lithospermum diffusum*, see Chapter 4.

purpureo-caeruleum	Europe	9" × 3'	Dark green, small, hairʏ

LYSICHITUM
Sun or shade, sopping wet bog or streamside. Huge flowers appear before leaves. Self-seeding. Yellow is offensively, and white sweetly scented. (Often erroneously called Skunk Cabbage, which appplies to *Symplocarpus foetidus*.)

americanum	W. N. America	3' × 3'	Huge, rich green, broaᴅ blades.
camtschatcense	NE. Asia	4' × 4'	Huge, rich green, broadᴅ blades, glossy.

LYSIMACHIA
Partial shade and moist soil (especially in sun) enable Creeping Jenny to become a dense carpeter. The golden-leafed variety ('Aurea') should always be in partial shade and is less vigorous.

nummularia	Europe	1" × 2–3'	Bright green, small, rounded, smooth.

MAIANTHEMUM
Cool woodland conditions and humus-laden soil suit this relative of lily-of-the-valley. A taller form from N. America is recorded.

bifolium	N. Temperate Regions (Britain)	5" × 18"	Rich green, smooth, twᴏ per stem.

Deciduous or Evergreen	Flower Height and Colour and Fruits (if any)	Flowering Season	Habit	Propagation
D	18". Minute lavender-blue in clouds.	Late summer	Clump	RS
E	18". Spikes of tiny lavender flowers.	Autumn	Clump	D
E	10". Spikes of tiny lilac or white flowers.	Late summer	Spreader	D
D	12". Vivid purplish-blue, small in clusters.	Midsummer	Carpet, rooting	CLS
D	18". Bright yellow, scrolled.	Spring	Clump	S
D	1'. White, arum-like.	Spring	Clump	S
E	1½". Bright yellow, little cups.	Summer	Carpet, rooting	D
D	6–7". Creamy white, small spikes.	Late spring	Spreader	D

HERBACEOUS PLANTS

	Country of Origin	Leaf Height and Planting Distance	Leaf Colour and Character
MECONOPSIS			
Cool woodland conditions, partial or full shade, abundant humus, lime-free soil. *M. quintuplinervia*, when luxuriating in ideal conditions, is a good ground-cover.			
quintuplinervia	W. China, Tibet	8″ × 15″	Light green, hairy, narre
MENTHA			
The fragrant, culinary or medicinal mints (*Mentha rotundifolia*, *piperita*, *citrata* and others) are mostly very invasive plants spreading by long questing roots, and though they grow luxuriantly are not really satisfactory ground-cover except when growing freely in good soil. They are too tall to be tidy. *M. rotundifolia* 'Variegata' is pleasantly marked with white and is fairly dense and not so tall. *M. gentilis* 'Variegata' has leaves veined and blotted with yellow. *M. requienii* is almost too small to consider. *M. pulegium* is not reliably dense.			
MESEMBRYANTHEMUM			
Full sun, suitable for warm coastal districts on well-drained soils. Will stand full exposure and salt spray. The two following species are now usually classed in a separate genus, *Carpobrotus*. Daisy-like flowers of exceptional brilliance.			
acinaciformis	Cape Province	3″ × 2′	Succulent, greyish-green
edule	Cape Province	3″ × 2′	Succulent, greyish-green
MITELLA			
Cool woodland, or under shrubs and trees, moist soil with humus, spreading quickly by self-sown seeds.			
breweri	British Columbia	3″ × 8″	Rounded, rich green, small.
diphylla	E. N. America	2″ × 18″	Lobed, glossy, rich gre small.
NEPETA			
Sun, well-drained light soil for *N.* × *faassenii* (*N. mussinii* of gardens) and *N. gigantea*; shady for *N. hederacea* (Ground Ivy). *N. gigantea* is somewhat more hardy than *N.* × *faassenii*, which is unreliable in cold wet winters and dry cold springs. Do not cut down until spring. *N. hederacea* is a rampageous plant and may be called a weed. It is effective ground-cover; unfortunately its pretty variegated form is not so dense.			
× faassenii. Catmint (*N. mussinii*)	Hybrid	10″ × 18″	Grey-green, woolly, sma
hederacea (*Glechoma hederacea*)	Europe	5″ × 9′	Rounded, dark green.
— 'Variegata'		4″ × 5′	Rounded, green, matt, white splashes.
gigantea, of gardens ('Six Hills Giant')		18″ × 2′	Grey-green, woolly, sma

Deciduous or Evergreen	Flower Height and Colour and Fruits (if any)	Flowering Season	Habit	Propagation
D	18". Lavender-blue, singly, on arching stems.	Early summer	Clump	D
D	2–3'. Lilac, in small spikes.	Summer	Spreader	D
E	4". Orange, yellow and lilac.	Summer	Carpet	C
E	4". Mauve, large.	Summer	Carpet	C
E	10". Greenish, tiny.	Summer	Carpet	DS
E	6". Greenish-white, tiny.	Summer	Carpet	DS
D/E	18". Lavender-blue, small, in sprays.	Summer–autumn	Clump	CD
E	4". Lavender-blue, small clusters.	Spring	Carpet, rooting	D
E	3". Lavender-blue, small clusters.	Spring	Carpet, rooting	D
D/E	2½'. Lavender-blue, small, in sprays.	Summer–autumn	Clump	CD

177

HERBACEOUS PLANTS

	Country of Origin	Leaf Height and Planting Distance	Leaf Colour and Character
OMPHALODES			
Sun or part shade for *O. cappadocica*, part or full shade for *O. verna*. Both thrive in cool soil with humus. *O. cappadocica* also thrives in heavy soil in sun.			
cappadocica	Asia Minor	8″ × 18″	Rich green, broad.
verna	S. Europe	4″ × 2′	Rich green, broad.
OPHIOPOGON			
Sun or part shade, sandy soil; *O. japonicus* is used in S. Europe and in warmer parts of U.S.A. as a grass-like carpeter, where it is known as 'Lily Turf'. For the warm south-west.			
japonicus	Japan	9″ × 18″	Dark shining green, grass-like.
intermedius	China	9″ × 1′	Dark shining green, grass-like.
OTHONNOPSIS			
Sun, good drainage, light soil. For warmer counties. Unusual appearance.			
cheiriifolia (*Othonna cheiriifolia*)	N. Africa	8″ × 1′	Glaucous grey-green, narrow, erect.
OURISIA			
Mainly for the larger rock garden or border verges; cool shady conditions, lime-free soil.			
elegans (*O. coccinea* of gardens)	Chile	2″ × 9″	Light green.
macrophylla	New Zealand	5″ × 1′	Dark glossy green.
OXALIS			
Shade or part shade, cool moist woodland, or under shrubs and trees for *O. acetosella* (Wood Sorrel) and *O. oregana*. *O. rubra* warm sunny, well drained. *O. acetosella* seeds itself and runs and should be kept away from other small plants. *O. rubra* can be a problem on heavy soils, increasing by bulblets from the root. *O. oregana* is thoroughly recommended.			
acetosella	N. Temperate Zone	4″ × 18″	Pale green, smooth, like clover.
— 'Rosea'		4″ × 18″	Pale green, smooth, like clover.
oregana	W. N. America	7″ × 3′	Rich green, like large clover, smooth.
rubra	S. Brazil	10″ × 1′	Rich green, like large clover, smooth.
PARONYCHIA			
Full sun, well-drained, rock-garden slopes. Good cover for small bulbs. *P. capitata* (*P. nivea*) is similar.			
argentea	S. Europe	2″ × 1′	Dark green, tiny.
PATRINIA			
Sun or part shade, light to fairly heavy soil. Useful late-flowering plant for rock garden or border front.			
triloba (*P. palmata*)	Japan	9″ × 1′	Rich green, rounded, deep lobed.

178

Deciduous or Evergreen	Flower Height and Colour and Fruits (if any)	Flowering Season	Habit	Propagation
D	10". Clear blue in graceful sprays.	Early summer	Spreader	D
D	6". Clear blue, small.	Spring	Spreader	D
E	1'. White, small, in sprays.	Midsummer	Spreader	D
E	1'. White, small, in sprays.	Autumn	Spreader	D
E	10". Yellow in heads.	Midsummer	Carpet	CDS
E	9". Red, tubular, in spikes.	Summer	Carpet	DS
D	15". White in heads.	Early summer	Carpet	DS
E	4". Pearly white, charming.	Spring	Carpet, rooting	D
E	4". Soft pink, charming.	Spring	Carpet, rooting	D
D/E	3". Rich pink, before leaves develop fully.	Spring	Carpet, rooting	D
D	1'. Cerise-pink, in heads.	Summer	Clump. tuberous	D
E	2". Grey-white, tiny, papery bracts.	Spring	Carpet, rooting	D
D	1'. Yellow, tiny, in sprays.	Late summer	Clump	DS

HERBACEOUS PLANTS

	Country of Origin	Leaf Height and Planting Distance	Leaf Colour and Character

PELTIPHYLLUM
Sun or part shade, rich boggy soil, margins of streams and ponds. The roots are thick rhizomes on surface of ground. Flowers appear before leaves.

peltatum (*Saxifraga peltata*)	California	2′ × 2′	Green, rough, circular, lobed, one per stalk.

A dwarf variety, P. p. 'Nanum', growing to about 10″, promises to be useful.

PETASITES
Sun or shade. Rampageous spreaders in damp soil, preferably heavy. Not fit for use in gardens; ideal where large areas are to be covered and where a vigorous colonizer can be given an area to beautify and save all work. *P. fragrans* is the winter heliotrope, so called because of its scent.

albus	France, etc.	1′ × 4′	Large, light green, greyish below, rounded.
fragrans	Europe	1′ × 4	Large dark green, rounded.
hybridus. Butter Bur	Europe	3′ × 5′	Extra large (3–4′ across) rounded, light green, grey beneath.
japonicus	Sachalin Islands	3′ × 5′	Extra large (3–4′ across) rounded, light green.
— giganteus		5′ × 8′	Extremely large (4′ across) rounded, light green.

PHLOMIS
Sun, well-drained soil. Useful border plant; stems remain aloft and ornamental through winter.

russeliana (*P. samia* and *P. viscosa* of gardens)	Syria	7″ × 2′	Large, green, crinkled, hairy.

PHLOX
The rock-garden varieties require full sun (or will grow in part shade) on well-drained soil. There are many hybrid cultivars between *P. subulata* and *bifida*; and colours from deep magenta ('Temiscaming'); pink ('Margery', 'Sprite'); pale lavender ('Benita') are available. The hybrids of *P. douglasii*, 'May Snow' (white) and 'Boothman's Variety' (lilac), require perfect drainage.

amoena	S. E. U.S.A.	4″ × 18″	Dark green, small (also variegated).
douglasii	W. N. America	3″ × 1′	Green, tiny, narrow.
stolonifera	E. N. America	4″ × 18″	Green, small.
subulata	E. U.S.A.	4″ × 2′	Green, small, narrow.

PHYSALIS
Chinese lantern. Happy in sun or part shade in any fertile soil. Thick, white, questing roots cause it to spread rapidly. The stems are apt to flop over; large orange 'lanterns' persist through winter. *P. alkekengii* is not so ornamental nor so vigorous.

franchetii	Japan	1′ × 3′	Soft rich green, hairy.

Deciduous or Evergreen	Flower Height and Colour and Fruits (if any)	Flowering Season	Habit	Propagation
D	2'. Small, pink, in a large head.	Spring	Clump	DS
D	9". Small white daisies in heads.	Early spring	Spreader	D
D	9". Small, mauve, in heads.	Late winter– early spring	Spreader	D
D	8". Small mauve daisies in dense cone.	Early spring	Spreader	D
D	6". Small white daisies in dense cone.	Early spring	Spreader	D
D	8". Small white daisies in dense cone.	Early spring	Spreader	D
D	3'. Soft yellow sage-like flowers in whorls.	Midsummer	Carpet, rooting	D
E	9". Rich pink, or white, in heads.	Late spring	Carpet	CD
D	3". Various colours, singly borne.	Late spring	Carpet	CD
D	8". Lilac or violet, in heads.	Late spring	Carpet, rooting	CD
D	6". Various colours, in heads.	Late spring	Carpet	CD
D	2'. Fruits round, orange, in orange papery pods.		Spreader	D

HERBACEOUS PLANTS

	Country of Origin	Leaf Height and Planting Distance	Leaf Colour and Character

POLYGONATUM
Part or full shade, good soil containing humus, damp rather than dry but not boggy. When luxuriating *P.* × *hybridum* (*P. multiflorum* of gardens), Solomon's Seal (a hybrid between *P. multiflorum* and *P. odoratum*) is superior to its parents; a good form should be sought. The double and the variegated forms are interesting additions.

falcatum, of gardens	Japan	5″ × 9″	Light green, smooth, er stems.
multiflorum, of gardens		3′ × 12″	Light green, smooth, or arching stems.

POLYGONUM
Knotweed. Sun, part or full shade, most preferring damp soil that is not boggy; *P. campanulatum* is a superlative ground-cover and both this and *P. polystachyum* will cope with stream verges and the latter is rampageous. Even more rampageous are the two giant species *P. cuspidatum* and *P. sachalinense*; these are only suitable in a large wild garden where clumps twenty or thirty feet across can be tolerated. *P. equisetiforme*, sun, good drainage. *P. reynoutria* of gardens is correctly *P. cuspidatum compactum*, female form. *P. affine* is available in several varieties, the richest coloured being 'Darjeeling Red', and the most conspicuous in flower, 'Superbum'; all forms of this species are first-class cover.

affine	Nepal	2′ × 2′	Bright green, narrow, russet in winter.
amplexicaule	Himalaya	4′ × 4′	Dark green, large, poin
campanulatum	Himalaya	2½′ × 3′	Soft green, pointed, grooved.
cuspidatum	Japan	8′ × 6′	Rich green, rounded, la
— compactum, see *P. reynoutria.*			
equisetiforme	Mediterranean Region	2′ × 2′	Grey-green stems, like v no leaves.
polystachyum	Himalaya	4′ × 4′	Rich green, long, point
reynoutria, of gardens		2′ × 3′	Dark green, leathery, rounded.
rude	Himalaya	4′ × 4′	Rich green, long pointec
(*P. molle*)			
tenuicaule	Japan	2″ × 9″	Blue-green, small, pointe
vacciniifolium	Himalaya	3″ × 2′	Rich green, small, pointe

POTENTILLA
Sun; *P. alba* thrives also in shade and is the best ground-covering species. Well-drained soil. The tall, border varieties are clump-forming (like *P. argyrophylla*) and are scarcely ground-covers.

alba	Europe	4″ × 12″	Grey-green, deeply divid

Deciduous or Evergreen	Flower Height and Colour and Fruits (if any)	Flowering Season	Habit	Propagation
D	5″. Greenish-white bells, small.	Late spring	Spreader	D
D	3′. Flowers hanging, greenish-white bells.	Late spring	Spreader	D
D	1′. Tiny, pink, in dense erect spikes.		Carpet, rooting	D
D	5′. Crimson in 'Atro-sanguineum'. Bright red in 'Firetail'. There are white and pink forms also.	Summer onwards	Clump	D
D	3′. Pinkish, small, in dense branching heads.	Summer onwards	Clump	D
D	8′. Small white, feathery heads.	Autumn	Spreader	D
E	Minute, white, stemless.	Autumn	Clump	D
D	5′. Small, whitish to pink, large, feathery heads.	Autumn	Spreader	D
D	2′. Pink, small, in clusters; red seeds.	Late summer–autumn	Spreader	D
D	4″. Pinky white.	Summer–autumn	Spreader	D
D	3″. White, tiny, in spikes.	Early spring	Clump	D
D	6″. Pink, small, in erect spikes.	Late summer	Carpet, rooting	CD
D	4″. White, orange eye.	Spring and autumn	Carpet, rooting	D

HERBACEOUS PLANTS

	Country of Origin	Leaf Height and Planting Distance	Leaf Colour and Character
POTENTILLA *cont.*			
argyrophylla	Kashmir to Nepal	9″ × 18″	Grey, silky, deeply divided.
cuneata (P. *ambigua*, P. *cuneifolia*)	Himalaya	3″ × 1′	Dark green, tiny, grey beneath.
montana (P. *splendens*)	SW. Europe	3″ × 18″	Soft green, hairy, divid▮
verna	Europe	3″ × 1′	Bright green, downy, lo▮

PRIMULA

These all grow best in a rather heavy retentive soil that does not dry out, and appreciate shade during the hottest part of the day. All will grow in the cool of a north-facing wall. *P. auricula* should be well away from overhanging branches; when luxuriating in the right soil its prolific garden hybrids make good ground-cover, full of character. *P. florindae* will grow well in boggy conditions and seeds itself prolifically, making excellent cover. In some soils *P. vulgaris*, the common primrose, and its blue and other coloured strains, with *P.* × *pruhoniciana* (*P.* × *juliana*), 'Wanda' and 'Garryarde Guinevere', will increase fast, are easy to divide and large plantations can be made. *P. vulgaris* and its blue strains will seed themselves. They need to be moved on to fresh ground after a few years. In the cool of some Scottish gardens *P. edgeworthii* and others of the Petiolaris section are sufficiently permanent to be successful cover. *Candelabra* species and hybrids such as *P. beesiana, bulleyana,* × *bullesiana, helodoxa, poissonii, prolifera, pulverulenta* and strains, *japonica* and strains, when growing strongly will seed themselves. A good soil, preferably on the heavy side, neutral, suits them best, and they can stand full sun so long as the ground is permanently moist. Some thinning and hand-weeding are usually necessary, and occasional replanting in September or March.

auricula hybrids	Europe	6″ × 1′	Grey-green, powdery.
denticulata	Himalaya	9″ × 15″	Soft green, long, broad.
— cashmiriana (of gardens)	Kashmir	9″ × 15″	Soft green, long, broad.
florindae	SE. Tibet	1′ × 18″	Broad, rounded, rich gre▮
× pruhoniciana 'Wanda' (P. × *juliana*)		4″ × 18″	Dark green, smooth, primrose-like.
vulgaris sibthorpii	Middle East	3″ × 15″	Soft green, primrose-like.

PRUNELLA

Easy in any soil not sun-baked, preferring moist positions. Has several varieties, such as 'Loveliness', but if the seed-heads are not removed they sow themselves and other colours are likely to occur.

grandiflora	Europe	5″ × 18″	Hairy, dark green, small, pinnate.

PTEROCEPHALUS

(*Scabiosa pterocephalus*)

Sun, well-drained soil, on rock garden or top of retaining wall.

parnassi	Greece	2″ × 15″	Small, greyish-green, downy.

Deciduous or Evergreen	Flower Height and Colour and Fruits (if any)	Flowering Season	Habit	Propagation
D	18". Yellow in branching sprays.	Summer	Clump	DS
D	4". Yellow.	Summer onwards	Carpet	CDS
D	3". White.	Spring	Carpet, rooting	D
D	6". Yellow in branching sprays.	Spring	Carpet	DS
	9". Various, in branching heads.	Spring	Clump	DS
	1'. In small, lavender-blue, spherical heads.	Spring	Clump	DRS
D	1'. Similar; richly coloured forms; purple, crimson.	Spring	Clump	DRS
D	2½'. Sulphur-yellow bells in heads.	Late summer	Clump	S
D	5". Crimson-purple primrose.	Early spring	Clump	D
D	4". Lilac-pink primrose.	Early spring	Clump	D
E	9". Rich pink heads, like 'dead-nettle'.	Summer	Carpet, rooting	D
E	3". Flat heads, pale lilac-pink.	Midsummer onwards	Carpet	CDS

HERBACEOUS PLANTS

	Country of Origin	Leaf Height and Planting Distance	Leaf Colour and Character

PULMONARIA

Lungwort. Shade or partial shade, woodland or under shrubs, or against north walls. An soil that remains cool and moist in summer. Somewhat spreading by roots and seeds. The forms known as 'Mawson's Variety' and 'Munstead Variety' of *P. angustifolia* are almos identical to that usually called 'Azurea'. *P. picta* or *P. saccharata* (and 'Mrs Moon') is mor ornamental and vigorous than *P. officinalis*. There are white forms of most species.

angustifolia	Europe	5″ × 1′	Dark green, hairy, lo narrow.
officinalis	Europe	8″ × 20″	Dark green, hairy, he shaped, spotted wh
picta (*P. saccharata* of gardens)	Europe	8″ × 2′	Dark green blotched long.
rubra	Europe	8″ × 2′	Rich green, hairy, lor narrow.

saccharata, see *P. picta*.

PULSATILLA

(*Anemone pulsatilla*). Pasque Flower. Sun, well-drained soil, rock garden or border. By select ing colour forms and hybridizing with *P. montana*, strains today include pink, cherry-red wine-red, wine-purple, indigo-purple, white, etc.

vulgaris	Europe	6″ × 1′	Dark green, hairy, m divided.

PYROLA

Choice plants taking some time to settle down and only creating ground-cover when grow ing luxuriantly. Lime-free soil rich in humus, woodland conditions, or northern slopes o rock garden. *P. asarifolia incarnata* is pink, and there are several more species.

rotundifolia	Europe, N. America	3″ × 12″	Dark green, glossy, rounded, flat.

RANUNCULUS

Sun or partial shade, among shrubs or streamside, in rich moist soil. The double form i a valuable old garden plant.

aconitifolius	Europe	3′ × 3′	Rich green, fingered, smooth.
— 'Flore Pleno'		18″ × 18″	Rich green, fingered, smooth.

RAOULIA

Full sun, scree or extra well-drained soil; rock garden or troughs.

australis	New Zealand	¼″ × 9″	Silvery grey, minute.
glabra	New Zealand	¼″ × 1′	Green, minute.

RHEUM

R. rhaponticum is a parent of the culinary rhubarb which is one of the most productive, dense weed-smothering crops for untidy kitchen gardens. *R. officinale* is the medicinal rhubarb very ornamental. All enjoy full sun in rich, moist, or even boggy soil, with manure.

officinale	Tibet	3′ × 6′	Vast, rich green, lobe

iduous or ergreen	Flower Height and Colour and Fruits (if any)	Flowering Season	Habit	Propagation
D	8″. Vivid blue, small, in nodding heads.	Early spring	Clump	D
E	12″. Pink, turning blue, in nodding heads.	Early spring	Clump	D
E	12″. Pink, turning blue, in nodding heads.	Early spring	Clump	D
E	12″. Coral-red, in nodding heads.	Late winter–early spring	Clump	D
D	10″. Purple, hairy, nodding, solitary.	Spring	Clump	S
E	10″. Small white bells on erect stalk.	Early summer	Spreader	D
D	3′. Small white, single; wide-branching.	Early summer	Clump	DS
D	2′. Small white, double; wide-branching.	Early summer	Clump	D
E	Tiny heads of pale yellow; stemless.	Summer	Carpet, rooting	D
E	Tiny heads of white; stemless.	Summer	Carpet, rooting	D
D	9′. Tiny, white, in feathery spike.	Early summer	Clump	DS

HERBACEOUS PLANTS

	Country of Origin	Leaf Height and Planting Distance	Leaf Colour and Character
RHEUM *cont.*			
palmatum	China	3′ × 6′	Vast, dark green, de lobed.
— 'Atrosanguineum'		3′ × 6′	Vast, dark green, red beneath.

RODGERSIA
Sun or partial shade (or full shade from buildings), rich moist soil, even boggy. Gran plants for streamside, light woodland, big rock gardens. The circular leaves of *R. tabular.* are like those of *Peltiphyllum peltatum*, but larger.

aesculifolia	China	3′ × 3′	Large, five big divisic rich green, rough.
pinnata	China	3′ × 2′	Large, pinnate, rich rough.
— 'Superba'		3′ × 2′	Large, coppery when y
podophylla	Japan	3′ × 3′	Large, five big divisic rich green, smooth.
sambucifolia	China	3′ × 2′	Large, pinnate, rich
tabularis	China	3′ × 2′	Large, round; bright

SAGINA
Sun or partial shade, well-drained soil; also thrives in shade from buildings. Apt to ge damaged in patches by frost. Makes a spongy lawn.

pilifera (*S. glabra*)	Corsica, Sardinia	1″ × 1″	Rich green mossy turf.
— 'Aurea'		1″ × 9″	Greenish-yellow mossy turf.

SALVIA
Sun or part shade, drained soil. Coarse plant useful for colonizing large areas. Semi-woody at base.

glutinosa	Europe, Central Asia	2′ × 2½′	Large, hairy, pointed, aromatic.

SAMBUCUS
Herbaceous elder with leaves and flowers resembling common elder but smaller. Sun or part shade, drained soil. For wild garden and establishing in roadside verges, waste places. Makes a dense cover.

ebulus	Europe, N. Africa	2′ × 3′	Rich green, divided.

SAPONARIA
Sun, drained soil. *S. ocymoides* is best as a rock or edging plant or for hanging down retaining walls. Various colour forms are available, propagated by cuttings. *S. officinalis* (best in its double forms, white or pink), is a flopping plant of untidy appearance but effective as a cover; known as Bouncing Bet or Soapwort.

ocymoides	Europe, Alps	4″ × 2′	Dark green, downy, sr
officinalis	Europe, Asia	1½′ × 3′	Green, downy, medium

Deciduous or Evergreen	Flower Height and Colour and Fruits (if any)	Flowering Season	Habit	Propagation
D	6'. Tiny, crimson or pink, in feathery spike.	Early summer	Clump	DS
D	6'. Tiny, crimson, in feathery spike.	Early summer	Clump	D
D	4–5'. Tiny, creamy; elegant branching plume.	Midsummer	Clump	DS
D	4'. Tiny, pinkish; elegant branching plume.	Midsummer	Clump	DS
D	4'. Tiny, deep pink; elegant branching plume.	Midsummer	Clump	D
D	4'. Tiny, creamy; branching plume.	Midsummer	Clump	DS
D	3'. Tiny, white; dense head.	Midsummer	Clump	DS
D	4'. Tiny, white, dense head.	Midsummer	Clump	DS
D	1½". Tiny, white, singly borne.	Summer	Carpet, rooting	D
D	1½". Tiny, white, singly borne.	Summer	Carpet, rooting	D
D	3'. Pale yellow, sage-like, in spikes.	Late summer	Spreader	D
D	4'. Tiny elder flowers, creamy, tinged pink.	Summer	Clump	D
D	6". Tiny, pink, in heads.	Summer	Carpet	CS
D	2½'. Small white or pink, in heads.	Late summer	Spreader	D

HERBACEOUS PLANTS

	Country of Origin	Leaf Height and Planting Distance	Leaf Colour and Character

SAXIFRAGA

The 'mossy' saxifrages (Dactyloides section) (*SS. caespitosa, hypnoides, geranioides, trifurcata, muscoides,* etc.) make cushions of finely divided greenery and appreciate cool conditions in shade from buildings; good, drained soil. The London Pride saxifrages (Robertsonii section) like the same conditions and make handsome rosettes of rounded leathery leaves. The Mother of Thousands (*S. stolonifera*) for same conditions, in mild counties and districts thrives on heavy soil. There are numerous good garden hybrids of the 'mossy' section, of very mixed parentage with flowers from white to crimson; when luxuriating they make admirable ground-cover; some of the most vigorous are 'Letchworth Beauty' and 'Edie Campbell'. The light pink varieties are usually the most vigorous.

	Country of Origin	Leaf Height and Planting Distance	Leaf Colour and Character
× andrewsii	Hybrid	4″ × 9″	Dark green, toothed margins, in rosettes
cuneifolia	Alps	2″ × 1′	Dark green, small, in rosettes.
— subintegra (*S. c. infundibulum*)	Pyrenees	2″ × 1′	Dark green, small, in rosettes.
geranioides	Pyrenees	5″ × 9″	Mossy but rigid; green grey in winter.
× geum (*S. hirsuta* × *S. umbrosa*) — 'Monstrosa'		6″ × 20″	Dark green, rounded, rosettes.
— hirsuta	Yorks, Pyrenees	9″ × 2′	Dark green, rounded, large rosettes, hairy
hypnoides	Europe, N. America	3″ × 1′	Mossy, neat, rich green bronzed in winter.
stolonifera (*S. sarmentosa*)	China, Japan	5″ × 18″	Green, marbled grey, rounded.
trifurcata	Spain	6″ × 18″	Mossy, glossy, dark
umbrosa	Europe, etc.	4″ × 12″	Dark green, rounded rosettes.
— primuloides	Pyrenees	2″ × 10″	Dark green, rounded, rosettes.

SCABIOSA

Sun, well-drained soil. Rock garden or top of retaining wall.

	Country of Origin	Leaf Height and Planting Distance	Leaf Colour and Character
graminifolia	S. Europe	6″ × 15″	Silvery-grey, grassy.

SCHIZOCODON

Cool, somewhat moist, lime-free soil with humus; partial shade. The more exposure the better is the winter colour of the leaves, but plants will not stand baking by the sun. Choice and slow.

	Country of Origin	Leaf Height and Planting Distance	Leaf Colour and Character
soldanelloides	Japan	4″ × 9″	Rounded, dark shining green, bronzed in w

SEDUM

Stonecrop. Sun; drained soil of rough, limy quality, heavy rather than light, will suit them better than richness. All have fleshy, smooth leaves. *SS. spectabile, rosea, alboroseum,* 'Autumn Joy' are big hearty border plants; they are handsome through the growing season and link together into cover. *SS. ewersii, kamtschaticum, oreganum, spathulifolium* and 'Ruby Glow'

Deciduous or Evergreen	Flower Height and Colour and Fruits (if any)	Flowering Season	Habit	Propagation
E	8". Pinkish-white in small sprays.	Early summer	Clump	D
E	4". Creamy-white, tiny, in small sprays.	Early summer	Carpet	CDS
E	4". Creamy-white, tiny, in small sprays.	Early summer	Carpet	CD
E	1'. Small, white, in sprays.	Early summer	Hummock	CD
E	10". Pinkish-white in small sprays.	Early summer	Carpet	CD
E	15". Pinkish-white in small sprays.	Early summer	Carpet	CD
E	6". Small white in small sprays.	Early summer	Carpet	CD
E	6". Pinkish-white in small sprays.	Summer	Carpet, rooting	D
E	12". Small white in small sprays.	Early summer	Hummock	CD
E	1'. Pinkish-white in small sprays.	Early summer	Carpet	CDS
E	6". Pinkish-white in small sprays.	Early summer	Carpet	CDS
D/E	10". Pale mauve, in heads.	Summer–autumn	Hummock	CDS
E	8". Pink, fringed bells on stem.	Late spring	Spreader	DS

HERBACEOUS PLANTS

	Country of Origin	Leaf Height and Planting Distance	Leaf Colour and Character
SEDUM *cont.*			
are compact rock garden plants, making good clumps. *S. sieboldii* also, but tender. *S. album* roots where it touches the soil; *S. spurium* likewise but is a better carpeter.			
alboroseum	Far East		
— 'Variegatum'		6″ × 1′	Grey-green, broadly marked creamy-yellow
album	N. Hemisphere	2″ × 18″	Bright green, thick, like minute sausages.
— 'Murale'		2″ × 18″	Similar, but purplish.
anacampseros	Central Europe	4″ × 1′	Grey-green rosettes.
'Autumn Joy'		15″ × 2′	Bluish-green, large, flesh
ewersii	W. Himalaya, Mongolia.	3″ × 1′	Blue-green, making flat rosettes.
kamtschaticum	Kamchatka, E. Siberia	3″ × 1′	Rich green.
oreganum	W. N. America	3″ × 9″	Brownish-green.
populifolium	Siberia	8″ × 9″	Dull green, woody stems.
rosea (*S. rhodiola*)	N. Hemisphere	9″ × 1′	Green-grey, smooth.
'Ruby Glow'		3″ × 1′	Bluish-green, fleshy, rounded.
spathulifolium	W. N. America	2″ × 1	Grey, purplish tinged.
— purpureum is larger in all parts with rich purplish foliage; 'Capa Blanca' is whitish-grey, compact.			
spectabile	China	1′ × 1′	Grey-green, large, fleshy.
Various colour forms, such as 'Brilliant' and 'Meteor' of richer colouring.			
spurium	N. Persia, Caucasus	4″ × 2′	Green.
Various colour forms such as 'Album', white; 'Splendens', deep pink; 'Schorbuser Blut', beetroot-red.			
— 'Green Mantle'		3″ × 2′	Soft green, fleshy, rounde

SELAGINELLA

Many tender species of coarse moss-like growth; *S. helvetica* is hardy in our warmer counties. For cool woodland conditions.

helvetica	Old World	3″ × 2′	Bright green, moss-like.

SHORTIA

Cool, somewhat moist, lime-free soil with humus; partial shade. *S. uniflora* '*Grandiflora*' is a good plant flowering freely but is slow growing. Similar to *Schizocodon*.

galacifolia	N. Carolina	5″ × 1′	Rounded, dark shining green, burnished in winter.
uniflora	Japan	4″ × 1	Round, dark shining gree burnished in winter.

ciduous or ergreen	Flower Height and Colour and Fruits (if any)	Flowering Season	Habit	Propagation
D	9". Pink, starry, small, in large flat heads.	Late summer	Clump	CD
E	4". White, starry, tiny, in branching heads.	Midsummer	Carpet, rooting	CD
E	4". Pinkish, starry, tiny, in branching heads.	Midsummer	Carpet, rooting	CD
D/E	4". Tiny, in heads, purple.	Summer	Carpet, rooting	CD
D	2'. Coppery-pink, starry, small, in large flat heads.	Autumn	Clump	CD
D	5". Pink, starry, tiny, in dense heads.	Late summer	Clump	CD
E	5". Yellow, starry, tiny, in branching heads.	Summer–autumn	Clump	CD
E	4". Yellow, starry, tiny, in flat heads.	Late summer	Carpet, rooting	CD
D	1'. Pinkish, starry, tiny in flat heads.	Early summer	Clump	CD
D	1'. Greenish-yellow, starry, tiny, in flat heads.	Early summer	Clump	CD
D	8". Deep mauve-pink, small, in heads.	Autumn	Clump	CD
E	4". Yellow, starry, tiny, in branching heads.	Summer	Carpet, rooting	CD
D	15". Pink, starry, small, in large flat heads.	Late summer	Clump	CD
D/E	5". Pink, starry, small, in branching heads.	Summer	Carpet, rooting	CD
D/E	Non-flowering, a splendid carpeter.		Carpet, rooting	CD
E	No flowers.		Carpet, rooting	D
E	6". Pinkish-white fringed bells.	Late spring	Spreader, very slow	DS
E	5". Pink bells, fringed.	Late spring	Spreader, very slow	D

193

HERBACEOUS PLANTS

	Country of Origin	Leaf Height and Planting Distance	Leaf Colour and Character

SILENE
Full sun, slopes of rock garden. *S. acaulis saxatilis* is a free-flowering form.

acaulis	Arctic to Spain	1″ × 9″	Bright green, tiny.

SMILACINA
Cool, moist, lime-free soil with humus; shade or part shade. Handsome woodlanders taking a few years to develop. In flower, *S. stellata* is a poor edition of *S. racemosa*, and is terrible underground spreader and a less good cover.

racemosa	N. America	3′ × 18″	Rich green, broad, pe
stellata	NW. America	2′ × 2′	Rich green, broad, pe

SOLDANELLA
Cool conditions, with humus, shade from rocks or buildings, open position, rock garder *S. villosa* is the most vigorous species.

villosa	Pyrenees	2″ × 9″	Dark green, rounded,

STACHYS
Sun, well-drained soil. *S. olympica* (*S. lanata*) is known as Lambs' Ears. The non-flowerin; form 'Silver Carpet' is an ideal ground-cover for poor soil in full sun. *S. macrantha* is a goo flowering plant.

olympica (*S. lanata*)	Caucasus to Persia	4″ × 18″	Grey-white, woolly.
macrantha (*S. betonica* 'Superba')	Caucasus	6″ × 15″	Dark green, wrinkled,

SYMPHYTUM
Comfrey. Part or full shade, woodland, or under shrubs; cool moist soil, but not boggy Long flowering periods. *S. grandiflorum* and its near hybrids or forms, 'Hidcote Blue' an 'Hidcote Pink', make ideal ground-cover. *S. uplandicum* (*S. peregrinum* of gardens) is a bi; coarse plant for rough places.

grandiflorum	Caucasus	7″ × 2′	Rich green, broad, po hairy.
— 'Hidcote Pink' and 'Hidcoté Blue' are soft pinkish and pale soft bluish tint respectively about twice the height of *S. grandiflorum*.		2½′ apart	
× uplandicum	Hybrid	2′ × 4′	Dark green, long, bro hairy.
— 'Variegatum'		1′ × 2′	Long, broad, hairy, cr and grey-green.

TANAKAEA
Part shade, cool woodland conditions or humus-laden soil in shade of shrubs. Slow.

radicans	Japan	3″ × 9″	Leathery, dull green, pointed.

...luous / green	Flower Height and Colour and Fruits (if any)	Flowering Season	Habit	Propagation
E	1″. Stemless, starry, pink.	Summer	Carpet, rooting	CD
D	3′. Small, starry, cream, in terminal spike; fragrant.	Early summer	Clump	DS
D	2′. Small, starry, cream, in small terminal spike; fragrant.	Early summer	Spreader	DS
E	7″. Violet-blue fringed bells.	Spring	Carpet	DS
E	20″. Grey-white woolly stems, tiny mauve flowers.	Midsummer	Carpet	D
D	18″. Rosy-purple, sage-like flowers in whorls.	Early summer	Carpet	D
E	10″. Creamy tubes, nodding in heads.	Spring	Carpet, rooting	D
E	4–5′. Rich blue tubes, nodding, in heads.	Spring	Clump	DR
E	3′. Palest lilac-pink, nodding, in heads.	Spring	Clump	D
E	6″. White, tiny.	Early summer	Clump	D

HERBACEOUS PLANTS

	Country of Origin	Leaf Height and Planting Distance	Leaf Colour and Character
TELLIMA			
Part shade, or sun; best in cool woodland conditions, or under tall shrubs. Easily grow quickly spreading clumps, easily divided. Good town plants.			
grandiflora	Alaska to California	10″ × 2′	Bright green, round hairy, burnished in winter.
— 'Purpurea' ('Rubra')		10″ × 18″	Dark green, rounded purplish in winter.
TEUCRIUM			
Sun, drained soil. Wild Germander (*T. chamaedrys*) is often used as an edging. *T. pyrenaicu* for rock garden, scree, troughs.			
chamaedrys	Europe	9″ × 1′	Dark green, small, ha
pyrenaicum	S. Europe	2″ × 9″	Dark green, rounded,
THALICTRUM			
Sun or part shade, drained soil. Leaves like Maidenhair Fern. *T. adiantifolium* is a garde name for a large form of *T. minus*, and the description given fits this particular form. I light soil it is invasive, in heavy soil it does not travel so much.			
minus	Europe, N. Asia	18″ × 2′	Dark green, small, ro fern-like.
THYMUS			
Thyme. Sun, well-drained soil, open places on rock garden; sunnier counties. *T. serpyllu* varieties are apt to get bare in places, and are only satisfactory cover when young or growin luxuriantly. *T. pseudolanuginosus* is the most reliable. *T. herba-barona*, which smells of carawa seeds, is not reliable in cold districts. The better thymes for ground-cover are described i Chapter 4.			
herba-barona	Corsica, Sardinia	1″ × 1′	Dark green, minute,
hirsutus doerfleri	Balkans	2″ × 1′	Dark green, minute,
nummularius, see page 92			
pseudolanuginosus (*T. lanuginosus*)		1″ × 18″	Grey-green, minute, hairy.
serpyllum, of gardens (*T. drucei*)	Europe	1″ × 18″	Dark green, minute,
The crimson 'Coccineus' is not quite so vigorous; 'Pink Chintz', clear pale pink, an 'Albus', white, light green leaves, are good distinct forms.			
vulgaris, see Chapter 4.			
TIARELLA			
Cool, drained soil with humus; semi-woodland or in shade of shrubs. *T. cordifolia* (Foan Flower) is one of the most attractive and prolific of ground-covers.			
cordifolia	E. N. America	4″ × 2′	Rich green, lobed, l in winter, hairy.
wherryi	E. U.S.A.	5″ × 10″	Soft green, lobed, bur in winter, hairy.

~ciduous or ~ergreen	Flower Height and Colour and Fruits (if any)	Flowering Season	Habit	Propagation
E	2'. Small creamy bells on erect stem.	Late spring	Clump	D
E	2'. Small pinkish bells on erect stems.	Late spring	Clump	D
D	9". Soft pink, in terminal heads.	All summer	Clump	CDS
D	2". Cream and purple marked, small, in flat heads.	Midsummer	Carpet	CDS
D	3'. Yellowish tassels in branching spire.	Late summer	Spreader	D
E	1½". Tiny, in small heads, pink.	Midsummer	Carpet, rooting	CDS
E	2½". Tiny, in small heads, lilac-pink.	Midsummer	Carpet, rooting	CD
E	2". Tiny, in small heads, lilac-pink.	Midsummer	Carpet, rooting	CD
E	2". Tiny, in small heads, lilac-pink.	Midsummer	Carpet, rooting	CDS
E	9". Creamy-white, tiny, in feathery spikes.	Spring	Carpet, rooting	D
E	15". Pinkish-white, tiny, in feathery spikes.	Spring	Clump	DS

HERBACEOUS PLANTS

	Country of Origin	Leaf Height and Planting Distance	Leaf Colour and Character

TOLMIEA
Cool woodland conditions or under tall shrubs. Pick-a-back flower; young plants develop on older leaves. Excellent cover but rather weedy.

| menziesii | NW. America | 9″ × 2′ | Rich green, ivy-shaped, hairy. |

TRACHYSTEMON
Coarse, invasive, handsome, effective cover in full sun or dense shade; poor sand or heavy soil. Excellent under big shrubs and trees; keep away from small plants and small shrubs.

| orientale | Asia Minor, Caucasus, etc. | 1′ × 2′ | Rich, green, broad, large, hairy. |

TROLLIUS
The Globe Flowers are like double buttercups. Rich moist or boggy soil in sun or part shade. Many orange and yellow colour forms; 'Orange Princess' and 'Canary Bird' are two good clones of *T. × cultorum*.

| × cultorum (hybrids of *T. europaeus*) | Europe | 1′ × 18″ | Rich green, fingered, smooth. |
| ledebouri | E. Siberia, etc. | 1′ × 18″ | Rich green, fingered, smooth. |

VANCOUVERIA
Will grow well in sun or shade, in any normal garden soil, sandy or heavy. Slow to start. Similar to *Epimedium*.

| hexandra | U.S.A. | 1′ × 18″ | Divided into rounded leaflets. |
| planipetala | W. U.S.A. | 9″ × 12″ | Divided into rounded leaflets. |

VERBENA
Rampageous; moist soil, sunny open position. Keep away from small plants. Creates a tangle; shoots root as they spread, also roots run under ground. It is only effective as a cover when growing luxuriantly.

| corymbosa | S. America | 1′ × 6′ | Dark green, pointed, h |

VERONICA
Sun, open position, drained soil, border or rock garden. *V. incana* 'Wendy' is a more vigorous less grey form of the species. *V. gentianoides* 'Variegata' is less vigorous than the species with leaves broadly marked cream; *V. whittleyi* (of gardens) is a useful grey-leaved hybrid with clear blue flowers about 9″ high × 1′.

| gentianoides | Caucasus | 4″ × 15″ | Rich dark green, broad, glossy. |
| incana | Russia | 5″ × 15″ | Grey-green, downy, form-ing basal rosettes. |

Shrubby species, see under *Hebe* in Chapter 4.

Deciduous or Evergreen	Flower Height and Colour and Fruits (if any)	Flowering Season	Habit	Propagation
E	18". Brownish, inconspicuous.	Summer	Carpet, rooting	CDS
D	18". Blue, starry, in heads before leaves.	Early spring	Spreader	D
D	2½'. Lemon or orange semi-double, branching stems.	Late spring	Clump	DS
D	2½'. Orange-yellow, semi-double, branching stems.	Late spring	Clump	DS
D	18". White, tiny, in airy sprays.	Spring	Spreading	D
E	12". White, tiny, in airy sprays.	Spring	Spreading	D
D/E	18". Violet-blue, dense flat heads	Summer–autumn	Carpet, rooting	D
D	18". Tiny, powder-blue, in slender spikes.	Spring	Clump	D
D	1'. Tiny, violet-blue, in dense spikes.	Midsummer	Clump	D

HERBACEOUS PLANTS

	Country of Origin	Leaf Height and Planting Distance	Leaf Colour and Character

VIOLA

Well-drained soil, cool open conditions, for *Viola* species and garden hybrids (like 'Maggie Mott' and 'Jersey Gem', which do well in the north and cooler west of England). Reduce long shoots in July to encourage later flower crops. All are suitable cover for rose beds.

VIOLAS:

cornuta	Pyrenees	6″ × 2′	Light green, smooth, s:

— 'Lilacina' is a pleasing light colour, and also 'Alba', white; both equally vigorous.

'Huntercombe Purple'	Hybrid	5″ × 15″	Rich green, smooth, s:

VIOLETS:

V. septentrionalis, and the very similar *V. cucullata* and *V. papilionacea* seem to demand fairly heavy soil. Their handsome leaves make admirable cover for cool borders. *V. labradorica* colours its foliage best in full sun, but will grow equally happily in shade. The sweet violets (*V. odorata*) prefer cool shady positions. *V. riviniana* and *V. labradorica* seed themselves freely.

alba	Europe	2″ × 1′	Dark green, hairy.
labradorica	N. America, Greenland	4″ × 1′	Dark purplish green, ro
odorata	Europe, N. Africa, Asia	3″ × 1′	Dark green, hairy.

Many garden forms of larger proportions; some fragrant ('Princess of Wales'), some not ('Governor Herrick'). The big forms suffer from red spider unless in ideal rich soil in a cool place. There are several colour forms or hybrids of the species, yellowish apricot, pale mauve, etc.

riviniana, Dog Violet	Europe, N. Africa	4″ × 1′	Dark green, smooth.
septentrionalis	N. America	6″ × 1′	Dark, rich, shining gr large.

WALDSTEINIA

Drained soil. Will thrive in dry soil, or cool moist, or rich; full sun or in full or part shade. Creates thick mats, attractive through the year; ideal cover.

ternata (*W. trifolia, W. sibirica*)	E. Europe, N. and E. Asia	4″ × 2′	Dark green, lobed, smo

ZAUSCHNERIA

Sun, rock garden or border verges. Must have good drainage. Californian Fuchsia. For warmer counties.

californica	California	10″ × 1′	Grey-green, small, dow

Z. c. mexicana is not so free flowering. *Z. cana* has narrow extra grey leaves, but is not so dense.

~ciduous or ~ergreen	Flower Height and Colour and Fruits (if any)	Flowering Season	Habit	Propagation
E	9″. Lilac-purple, medium.	Spring–autumn	Carpet, rooting	CD
E	7″. Rich purple, large.	Spring–summer	Carpet, rooting	CD
D	2″. White; various colour forms; fragrant.	Spring	Carpet, rooting	DS
E	3″. Lavender-blue, scentless violets.	Spring	Carpet, rooting	DS
E	2–4″. Purple, fragrant, common violet.	Spring	Carpet, rooting	DS
D	4″. Lavender-blue (or white) scentless.	Spring	Spreader	DS
D	6″. Large, white, blue, scentless violets.	Spring	Clump	DS
E	4″. Bright yellow strawberry flowers.	Spring	Carpet, rooting	D
D	1′. Scarlet, fuchsia-like.	Late summer–autumn	Spreader	CD

8

Grasses and Rushes

ALTHOUGH grasses are simply narrow-leaved herbaceous plants,
I have accorded them a separate chapter because they are so outstanding in value for contrasting with broader leaves. Among
them are plants of widely differing habits.

There are clump-formers of several sizes. The giant oat, *Stipa
gigantea*, is six feet or more high when in flower; the flowers are
at first purplish, changing to harvest gold in late summer. The
tall stems do not need staking even in windy places, and arise
from a great basal tuft of grassy leaves. Quite distinct are the
extremely graceful plumose flower-heads of *S. calamagrostis*. One
of the rushes is *Carex pendula*, whose long, arching, green tails
resemble the green form of love-lies-bleeding, raised over the
broad, grassy, nearly evergreen, folded leaves and forming a
rounded tuft. While the oats prefer full sun the rush is content
with deep shade. Considerably smaller is *Pennisetum alopecuroides*;
the leaves, though not evergreen, remain aloft in a beautiful
arching tuft, parchment colour through the winter, or until snow
flattens them. If planted in a warm, sunny position to hasten the
flowers we shall be rewarded in a good autumn with spikes of
purple, white-tipped, like large, hairy caterpillars. This seems to
flower most freely when young; old clumps are not so prolific.
The smallest clump-forming grass I am going to recommend is
the dwarf blue-grey fescue often used in carpet bedding, *Festuca
glauca* (*F. ovina glauca*). Its flower spikes, not exceeding one foot, are
blue-grey also. It forms a slowly increasing tuft which can easily
be increased by division to decorate the border edge, and makes
a wonderful contrast with *Sedum maximum* 'Atropurpureum'.
It is equally attractive in the joints of paving or laid out in serried
array for formal plantings.

The closely allied *Festuca eskia* (*F. crinum-ursi*) (Fig. 60), unlike the blue species, creates wide creeping mats of dark green, rooting here and there, and is the smallest of our reliable grassy carpeters, and highly effective and useful. Also a colonizer above ground, the common wood rush *Luzula maxima* (Fig. 59) is a rampant and invaluable cover for moist woodland and cool banks. The variegated form is not quite so vigorous. In Devon and Cornwall, and equally in my dry Surrey garden, the species thrives and grows prodigiously, smothering everything in its path, rooting as it goes, and is always tidy and green. It is of inestimable value on steep banks where mowing is difficult or impossible, but is greedy-rooted and fit only for growing under trees and large established shrubs or holding firm the banks of a ditch. An excellent demonstration of its uses can be seen in the valley garden at Cotehele, a National Trust garden in Cornwall. Its presence saves all mowing and cleaning on the steep and difficult banks.

The two splendid variegated grasses, *Glyceria* (Pl. XXVb) and *Phalaris*, are suitable for soil that does not dry out, and add a great deal to the garden picture during the summer months, but they are highly invasive. For a brilliant patch of yellow-green in spring there is nothing so startling and beautiful as Bowles' golden grass, *Milium effusum* 'Aureum', which breeds true to colour and seeds itself gently here and there. This indispensable and long-lasting brightness begins to shew with the earliest daffodils, and is a glorious companion for the blue *Pulmonaria angustifolia*. The remaining grass, *Elymus arenarius*, is so invasive that I hesitate to recommend it for the average garden of today—though if I did I should have the good precedent of design by Gertrude Jekyll, who appreciated its glaucous grey colouring to the full. But I think it best to leave it for Chapter 10.

GRASSES AND RUSHES

	Country of Origin	Leaf Height and Planting Distance	Leaf Colour

ACORUS GRAMINEUS
Though so like a grass this is really a relative of the arum; see the Table for Herbaceous Plants.

CAREX
Large-size woodland rush, arching and graceful in leaf and flower. Preferably lime-free soil.

	Country of Origin	Leaf Height and Planting Distance	Leaf Colour
pendula	Old World	3′ × 2′	Green, broad.

ELYMUS
Like a giant couch grass, equally invasive and menacing, but useful for sandy open spaces. Sun. Frequently seen on sand dunes.

arenarius	N. Hemisphere	2′ × 3′	Blue-grey, broad.

FESTUCA
Fine leaved, for sunny, well-drained positions. *F. eskia* will cover wide areas densely.

eskia (*F. crinum-ursi*)	Pyrenees	6″ × 15″	Dark green, fine.
glauca (*F. ovina glauca*)	Temperate zones	6″ × 9″	Grey-blue, fine.

GLYCERIA
The variegated form of this invasive grass will grow in most soils, but is best in damp places in full sun.

maxima (*G. aquatica*)	N. Hemisphere	3′ × 2′	'Variegata' is evenly striped with ivory yellow

LUZULA
The common woodrush is exceedingly useful for cool, shady areas, particularly on steep banks where mowing is difficult. Greedy roots, keep away from choice shrubs. Preferably lime-free soil.

maxima (*L. sylvatica*)	C. and N. Europe	1′ × 3′	Green, broad, hairy.
— 'Variegata'		1′ × 2′	Leaves edged with cream yellow, more compact than the type.

MILIUM
The yellow-leaved form of the millet grass (Bowles' Golden Grass) is very gay in spring, succeeding in cool positions in part shade.

effusum 'Aureum'		10″ × 1′	Bright greenish-yellow.

PENNISETUM
Handsome spikes of flowers are only produced in sunny autumns. Plant in well-drained sunny position. Foliage remains ornamental in winter, palest buff.

alopecuroides	E. Asia to E. Australia	1′ × 18″	Green, narrow, long.

ciduous or ergreen	Flower Height and Colour	Flowering Season	Habit	Propagation
E	3–5′. Green, arching.	Summer	Clump	DS
D	4′. Long spikes of grey.	Summer	Spreader	D
E	10″. Light green, small.	Summer	Carpet	DS
E	10″. Grey-blue, small.	Summer	Clump	DS
D	3′. Greenish spikes.	Summer	Spreader	D
E	18″. Brownish.	Summer	Carpet, rooting	DS
D	2–3′. Bright greenish-yellow.	Spring	Clump	DS
D	2′. Dark purple.	Autumn	Clump	D

GRASSES AND RUSHES

	Country of Origin	Leaf Height and Planting Distance	Leaf Colour

PHALARIS

The variegated form is bold in its white striping. Best in soil that does not dry out in summer.

arundinacea	N. Hemisphere	3′ × 2′	'Picta' is white striped, graceful.

STIPA

These two are clump-formers, for sunny well-drained soil. Foliage not full of character but their flowers are highly ornamental, *S. calamagrostis* being feathery and dense; *S. gigantea* is in effect a giant oat.

calamagrostis	Spain	18″ × 2′	Green, long, narrow.
gigantea	Spain	18″ × 3′	Green, long, narrow.

Deciduous or Evergreen	Flower Height and Colour	Flowering Season	Habit	Propagation
D	3–5′. Creamy.	Summer	Spreader	D
D	2–3′. Green, turning fawn.	Summer, lasting	Clump	D
D	5–6′. Purplish, turning yellow.	Summer, lasting	Clump	D

9

Ferns

FERNS are out of fashion. A few devoted admirers, and particularly the members of the British Pteridological Society (to which fern enthusiasts belong), nurse and help to distribute some of the scarce, beautiful and rare species and varieties that have survived neglect and two wars, since the decline in their popularity after the Victorian era. The criticism I often hear levelled at them today is that 'they do not flower'. But if we are going to assess plants on their whole merit, rather than on the brief bit of colour provided by a few flowers, we shall have to accord them a high place in garden design.

Let us look at their good points, since their only possible detractions are that they do not flower and many are not evergreen. They provide exquisite beauty in the unfolding fronds (their leaves) in spring and early summer, not only in shape and delicacy, but also in their shuttlecock arrangement; once established in open soil with some humus they will increase and grow in elegance yearly; the bulk will thrive in limy soil, in fact they seem to prefer it, though perfectly at home in acid soils also; many are the most successful plants to grow in dry soil in shady positions—a combination of conditions which often defeats the gardener. Some delight us with autumn colour. Above all, their fronds provide a most perfect foil to the lumpy greenery of shrubs and plants; their dainty filigree is as valuable as the leaves of grasses, adding lightness to any scheme. And their only disadvantage is that they do not flower.

To the curious I should explain that what we look upon as the fern plant is analogous to the mushroom: it is the stage of life in a remarkable cycle that provides the spores from which the true fern plant (or the mushroom 'spawn') grows—which we do not normally see and which have a sex life all on their own. It is an easy matter to raise ferns from the dusty brown spores produced in countless millions from the backs of the fronds, or from special spore-bearing fronds; they should be sown very thinly on moist peat under a jam jar in a shaded garden frame or living-room. The tiny green, flat, moss-like plants will soon appear and should not be disturbed until they have produced their first real fronds, when they need careful handling. At all times they should be kept cool and shaded, and gradually hardened off until they are big enough to plant out.

From the ground-cover point of view ferns are invaluable. They love the shade; they thrive in rooty, well-drained soil under trees and shrubs, and against a north wall; the common male fern, *Dryopteris filix-mas*, will even thrive at the shady foot of a privet hedge if needed, or among rubble and brickbats in sunny positions —as long-suffering a plant as the bearded iris.

For really moist ground, the Royal fern, *Osmunda regalis*, is the largest and most handsome of hardy ferns, achieving six feet in ideal, wet, peaty conditions, and its broadly segmented fronds turn to yellow and bright brown in the autumn. It is a solid clump-former and may be relied upon to hold up the banks of a stream or pond with its matted roots. Two big ferns with broadly divided leaves for moist ground are the extremely handsome dark ever-green spreader, *Blechnum chilense*, and the fresh green, deciduous, equally handsome *Onoclea sensibilis* (Pl. XXIVA). The latter is a dense and rapid colonizer and will grow well in boggy soil. The ostrich plume fern, *Matteuccia struthiopteris* (*Struthiopteris germanica*) (Pl. XXI) colonizes slowly and may be seen on the streamside at Hidcote; its fronds make particularly handsome tall shuttlecocks from a short stem, but die off earlier than most ferns, especially in a dry summer.

It is unfortunate that a fern of tropical luxuriance, *Woodwardia virginica*, is only safe in the warmer west. Its great arching fronds develop small plantlets at their tips which take root and grow well, and it will quickly colonize a large area thereby.

The remainder of the hardy ferns normally encountered are clump-forming; the common male fern, *Dryopteris filix-mas*, together with the much more dainty lady fern, *Athyrium filix-femina* and its dense growing form 'Minor' (Fig. 69), which needs moister conditions, have many strange crested and bifurcated forms none of which are improvements on the original. (It was, I think, this strange obsession of the old fern 'fans' of the last century to name in verbose Latin terms every peculiar variant which helped to drive fern-lovers to distraction and cause them to forsake their loves.) Much the same may be said of *Polystichum aculeatum*, which is a fine semi-evergreen approaching in beauty the next.

Polystichum setiferum (*P. angulare*) excels in not only being happy in dry or moist soils but that its selected forms through increasing their feathery thickness are often among the most exquisite and coveted of all ferns today, and of days gone by. *P. setiferum* itself and the form known as 'Proliferum' (which has an easy means of increase in the little plantlets which form along the stem) are fairly readily available, but it will be many years before the superb 'Densum' and 'Divisilobum' forms appear on the general market again in any quantity.

As a complete contrast to these hardy, tough delicacies, we have the shorter evergreens with less lacy foliage: the drought-resisting *Polypodium vulgare* (Fig. 66)—which may sometimes be seen growing on tree branches, and makes a most admirably spreading carpet—and its lacy variant *P. v. cornubiense*; *Blechnum spicant* (a lime-hater), of distinctive neat rich greenery; and the hart's-tongue fern (*Phyllitis scolopendrium*), which will thrive anywhere in sun or shade, preferably shade, on chalk or peat, and enchant us with its broad, curved, tongue-like leaves in rich green, striped with brown spores at the back.

There are some miniatures too: the slowly increasing, very hardy maidenhair ferns *Adiantum venustum* and *pedatum*; clump-forming *Cystopteris fragilis* and bulbil-dropping *C. bulbifera*, and the rapid runners in the genera *Gymnocarpium* and *Thelypteris*, the oak fern and the beech fern, *G. dryopteris* (Fig. 68) and *T. phegopteris*. These are quite small but the prettiest light green colonizers I know for cool shady positions. For damp, shady places the ever-green *Blechnum penna-marina* (*Lomaria alpina*) (Fig. 67) is a slow but effective dwarf spreader.

The few species and varieties included in these pages are merely an introduction to a vast range of plants. In all, the ferns present us with great variety which we should treasure, and their dying fronds make a fine mulch around the clumps and should not be gathered up except on the score of tidiness.

Those close relatives of ferns, the mosses, are not without possibilities as ground-cover. In areas of constant rainfall they could be encouraged and even collected and cultivated. I know of one garden where a mossy sward is being created, and as a foil to the tree trunks, ferns and a few other plants it is ideal. This idea has been made easy to carry out of late years because the use of certain weedkillers such as amitrole and dalapon will kill grass and broad-leaved weeds but do no harm to mosses. Moss does not stand constant wear and tear of shoes well but will take light traffic, and as there are many species native to the British Isles the selection of species suitable to various districts should present little trouble.

FERNS

	Country of Origin	Leaf Height and Planting Distance	Leaf Colour
ADIANTUM			
Both are completely hardy; *A. venustum* is exactly like the tender *A. capillus veneris,* or greenhouse maidenhair fern.			
venustum	Himalaya	6″ × 9″	Soft green; dainty.
pedatum	N. Temperate Region	1′ × 1′	Soft green; dainty. Th 'Klondyke' variety young fronds tinged red.
ATHYRIUM			
The Lady Fern is a very beautiful, lacy, fresh green fern, preferring fairly moist positions.			
filix-femina	Cosmopolitan	2′ × 2″	Light green, very lacy.
— 'Minor'		9″ × 9″	Light green, very lacy.
BLECHNUM			
The most handsome of hardy evergreen ferns, *B. chilense,* thrives in moist ground in our warmer counties. It needs a good mulch in cold winters. *B. penna-marina* (*Lomaria alpina*) also needs moist ground; quite hardy. *B. spicant* quite hardy, fairly moist; all grow best in lime-free soils.			
chilense	S. Africa	3′ × 2′	Dark green, broad, leath
(*B. tabulare* and *Lomaria magellanica* of gardens)			
penna-marina	S. Temperate Region	6″ × 1′	Dark green, small, leath
spicant	N. Temperate Region	18″ × 1′	Dark green, ladder-like, leathery.
CYSTOPTERIS			
Easily satisfied, very daintily cut leaves. *C. bulbifera* increases by means of bulbils borne under the leaves.			
bulbifera	N. America	10″ × 1′	Bright green.
fragilis	Temperate Region	9″ × 6″	Dull green.
DRYOPTERIS			
Easily grown; *D. filix-mas* succeeds in dry and even sunny positions in poor soils.			
carthusiana	N. Temperate Region	2′ × 1′	Soft green, finely cut.
(*D. spinulosa*)			
dilatata	N. Temperate Region	2′ × 2′	Dull green.
filix-mas	Temperate Region	4′ × 2′	Dull green.
GYMNOCARPIUM			
Pretty little ferns, creeping rapidly.			
dryopteris	N. Temperate Region	6″ × 18″	Light green, smooth, dainty.
robertianum	N. Temperate Region	6″ × 18″	Light green, smooth, dainty.

Deciduous or Evergreen	Habit	Propagation
D	Carpet	D
D	Clump	D
D	Clump	DS
D	Clump, spreading	D
E	Spreader	D
E	Spreader	DS
E	Clump	DS
D	Clump	S
D	Clump	DS
D	Spreader	D
D	Clump	DS
D	Clump	DS
D	Spreader	D
D	Spreader	D

FERNS

	Country of Origin	Leaf Height and Planting Distance	Leaf Colour

MATTEUCCIA
Great shuttlecocks of lacy greenery. For moist positions. New crowns arise from spreading underground stolons. The fronds wilt by early autumn.

| **struthiopteris** | N. Hemisphere | 3′ × 2′ | Light green. |
| (*Struthiopteris germanica*) | | | |

ONOCLEA
Freely spreading by means of underground shoots, in moist or boggy soils.

| **sensibilis** | N. Temperate Region | 2′ × 3′ | Light green, bold. |

OSMUNDA
All species need moist peaty soil, and will grow at the edges of ponds and streams. Beautiful autumn colour, yellow and buff.

| **regalis** | Cosmopolitan | 4′ × 3′ | Fresh green, handsome, large. |

PHYLLITIS
The hart's tongue is excellent on chalk, and makes dense cover if closely planted.

| **scolopendrium** | N. Hemisphere | 18″ × 1′ | Rich green, broad, simp |

POLYPODIUM
Hardy and drought resisting. Often grows on tree trunks as an epiphyte. *P. interjectum* and *P. australe* are closely related.

| **vulgare** | Temperate Regions | 10″ × 1′ | Dull dark green. |
| — **cornubiense** | Cornwall | 10″ × 1′ | Bright green, lacy. |

POLISTICHUM
The many very lacy forms of *P. setiferum* such as 'Divisilobum' and 'Plumosum' are exquisitely fashioned and among the most beautiful of ferns. Best in a retentive soil, but will thrive in dry sandy soil. *P. s. proliferum* has plantlets on the fronds which form a quick means of increase.

aculeatum	Cosmopolitan	2′ × 2′	Lacy, dark green, leathe
munitum	W. N. America	3′ × 3′	Dark green, leathery, handsome.
setiferum	Cosmopolitan	3′ × 2′	Dull green, lacy.

THELYPTERIS
| **phegopteris** | N. Temperate Region | 6″ × 18″ | Light green, downy, daint |

WOODWARDIA
Only hardy in our warmest counties. Plantlets are formed at the apices of the large arching fronds and form a ready means of increase.

| **radicans** | N. Temperate Region | 3′ × 3′ | Light green, large, elegan |

For *Hypolepsis* and *Dennstaedtia*, see *Addenda*, page 260.

214

iduous or rgreen	Habit	Propagation
D	Spreader	D
D	Spreader	D
D	Clump	DS
E	Clump	DS
E	Spreader	DS
E	Spreader	D
E	Clump	DS
E	Clump	DS
E	Clump	DS
D	Spreader	D
E	Clump	Tips

10

Ground-Cover Plants for Large Areas

WITH PARTICULAR REFERENCE TO FACTORY SITES,
SCHOOLS, HOSPITALS AND AREAS UNDER MUNICIPAL
CONTROL

THE chapters of this book so far have dealt with ground-cover for private gardens, with a passing reference now and again to the uses of the more vigorous kinds for large areas, particularly those under public control. Much depends on the scale of the design, of course, and all the plants I have mentioned could be used in public gardens and parks; even the smallest are as suitable for public as for private gardening.

But gardening is not confined to small schemes. At risk of repeating a few paragraphs in the Introduction I want to call attention again to the really large gardens still in private hands—many of them open to the public—together with outlying areas approaching the parkland, which are crying out for tidying and bringing under control by labour-saving methods. In addition there are the ever-increasing big buildings, the factory sites, huge blocks of offices and flats, and other major works many of which, unless on a narrow town site, need suitable embellishment and softening greenery around them. The grounds around our big hospitals, schools and institutions are a necessary adjunct and need to be controlled and beautified in the most economical way. Further, there are our fine public parks and municipal gardens, the amenity areas of new towns and villages, and spare areas and embankments alongside the mown verges of trunk roads and other highways; all have grass as the main surface unless it be concrete or tar. Though I have admitted earlier that I know of no plant that will stand the regular wear and tear of pedestrians except grass, there are places off the beaten track where suitable ground-cover would not only provide a welcome change from mown grass but would also involve far less maintenance.

It seems to me a confession of ignorance and weakness when I see gangs of men mowing steep banks along our new trunk roads—ignorance because of the vast assembly of plants there is to choose from and weakness because those in authority either have not the courage or the enterprise to try them. Of course the initial cost might well be greater than for grass, but to do away with practically all maintenance for ever or at least for many years seems to me a compelling factor in the favour of ground-cover plants. Neither hot sun, dense shade, sand, chalk nor bog need defeat us if we select carefully.

First let me briefly review certain vigorous cover-plants which have already been described in the Tables, and then look further into more rampageous plants.

To take herbaceous plants first this time, I have already described *Cerastium tomentosum*, *Acanthus mollis* and *A. spinosus* (Pl. IVB), *Anemone tomentosa* (Fig. 71) and *Trachystemon orientale* (Fig. 70). There is no doubt that the last is one of the answers to a need for big permanent cover for sun or shade. A British native herbaceous elder, *Sambucus ebulus*, if planted three feet apart, will provide excellent cover and also will not strike a horticultural note where a natural planting is desired. *Salvia glutinosa* is semi-shrubby, spreading and making dense thickets to about two feet, bearing soft yellow flowers through the summer, in sun or partial shade. For really high cover, up to six or seven feet, *Macleaya microcarpa* is dignified and elegant, and there is no doubt that in the wider landscape those two giant polygonums, *P. cuspidatum* and *P. sachalinense*, are completely trouble free, except, as for most of these deciduous plants, that the stems must be cut off and burnt in late winter, after their red-brown thicket has added beauty to the scene for many weeks. They burn with resounding explosions, reminiscent of bonfire night. Of lesser size are the beautiful *P. campanulatum*—an invaluable plant for flower and densely covering the ground—and *P. polystachyum*, both enjoying moist conditions, and the plant grown in gardens as *P. reynoutria*. All flower well into the autumn.

Petasites deserve a paragraph to themselves. Of very large size is *P. japonicus giganteus*; it should only be used on rough river banks, and in boggy stretches, where its huge leaves, sometimes four feet across, will smother anything. Like the others it has a vigorous underground root system. *P. hybridus*, the Butter Bur (Fig. 74), is slightly smaller and is better known. *P. albus* (Fig. 75) and *P. fragrans* are considerably smaller, with foliage about eighteen inches high, rounded and handsome. The flowers of all appear before the leaves; they are like dense heads of daisies, *P. hybridus* having a ruff of broad pale green bracts around the posy of white flowers, while *P. fragrans* is the notorious winter heliotrope, so often planted for the fragrance of its mauve flowers in February, with later regret. Wide roadside colonies of this may be seen in many western counties of Britain, though it will grow luxuriously almost anywhere. The leaves of *P. albus* are beautifully grey beneath, revealed when the wind blows. They are all colonizers of greatest vigour, most at home in retentive soil, in sun or part shade.

On the other hand, for large areas of dry sandy soil around our coasts and inland few things are more beautiful than the lyme grass, *Elymus arenarius*; in effect it is a giant couch grass, with broad, steely blue leaves and five-foot flower spikes (Pl. XVIIB). Able colonizers among other grasses are phalaris and glyceria (Pl. XXVB), both needing damp positions.

I have mentioned *Coronilla varia* (Fig. 77) in an earlier chapter, calling attention to its highly invasive qualities. That this quality has been put to good use in the United States is amply proved by photographs shewing it covering banks densely with a carpet of finely divided leaves more or less smothered with its mauve-pink vetch-flowers in summer. In Pennsylvania it is known as the 'Penngift Crownvetch'.

In some of the States *Aegopodium podagraria* is recommended as a rampant ground-cover, particularly in its beautiful, rather less vigorous, variegated form. Lest the unwary should be sold this plant by some unscrupulous vendor in need of quick returns, I must warn them that this is the notorious ground elder, gout weed or bishop's weed. It is normally a plant which one is at particular pains to destroy because it is so invasive. These three popular names for this pestilential weed owe their origin to the resemblance of the leaf to that of an elder, to once being used as a cure for gout, and to the fact that its persistence in the garden, despite careful cultivation, is enough to make a bishop swear . . . or so I have been told. As seeds are seldom borne even on the green type, the variegated form might be a safe garden plant; it is certainly very beautiful.

There are some fine, rapid, surface covers among herbaceous plants. The most rampageous and useful for cooler parts of the country, under trees, is the wood rush, *Luzula maxima* (*L. sylvatica*) (Fig. 59), spreading by stems and seeds. I am certain that savings in labour could be made by the use of this almost evergreen native rush on steep banks where mowing is difficult, and also on the level. It will even take some wear and tear from traffic, though its appearance would be spoiled thereby. A big coarse plant for rough areas is found in *Symphytum* × *uplandicum* (*S. peregrinum* of gardens), with vivid blue flowers; it is a clump-former, but seeds itself prolifically. *Lamium galeobdolon* 'Variegatum' is an excellent plant for growing under trees (Fig. 52). Of less size but beautiful, thoroughly weed-proof, and vigorous are *Symphytum grandiflorum* and its Hidcote hybrids, *Lamium maculatum* (Fig. 53). *Geranium macrorrhizum* (Pl. XVIA), *Sedum spurium* 'Green Mantle', *Mesembryanthemum*, *Waldsteinia ternata* (Pl. XXIIB), *Oxalis oregana* (Pl. XXIIA) and *Saxifraga* × *geum* 'Monstrosa' (Fig. 46); all are lowly spreaders and carpeters of vigour and reliability.

Of grass-like effect in the level swards achieved are *Sagina glabra* and *Helxine soleirolii*. I have included sagina in the Table for Herbaceous Plants, but, though making a dense, moss-like sward, it is apt to bunch itself up and these higher portions are inclined to die in dry, cold periods in winter and spring. On retentive ground and in mild climates it is the nearest and best substitute for grass on the slopes of the rock garden, and in this way is used admirably and neatly in the garden of the École d'Horticulture near Paris (Fig. 78). *Helxine* has a popular name, 'Mind your own business', which prepares us for its way of growing into clumps of plants and between stones. It is the rock gardener's curse. But in mild climates it will give a close, bright green sward on retentive soils, only two inches or so high like the sagina, and is admirable for carpeting a woodland area. *Selaginella helvetica* can be used likewise in warmer districts, and all three propagate so readily that vast stocks can be raised in a short time. They are included here because this propensity makes them possible substitutes for grass over large areas. They will all take a little traffic and are completely weed-proof when luxuriant. None of these needs mowing, whereas camomile does to keep it dense.

Whether I can recommend the so-called 'ground ivy' for cover I am not sure. It is used extensively in the United States—and botanically is *Nepeta* (*Glechoma*) *hederacea*. The pretty variegated form is far less vigorous and cannot be counted a good cover except in favourable circumstances, but the green-leaved species will cover tracts quickly in cool woodland conditions. It is, however, more of a weed than a garden plant and can scarcely be chosen in the face of the numerous more ornamental 'weeds' from other countries mentioned in this book.

Among the clump-formers are several stalwarts. The seven-foot goat's beard *Aruncus sylvester* (*Spiraea aruncus*), the day lilies, the hostas, astilbes, bergenias, *Brunnera macrophylla* (Fig. 58), *Geranium endressii* (Pl. XVIIA) and *G.* 'Claridge Druce', *Tellima grandiflora* and *Alchemilla mollis* (Pl. XV; Figs. 40, 41) are good examples of useful, dense, clump-formers of considerable vigour. Though they take long to establish, the epimediums are first rate and seem to last for ever, and are completely weed-proof.

In areas where the soil is deep and rich and something statuesque is wanted, the giant cow parsnip, *Heracleum mantegazzianum* (Pl. XXXA), will achieve nine feet or so, and produce superb leaves annually. It will also seed itself with abandon.

So much for a few of the stronger herbaceous plants. Many can be used in their own right, so to speak, or as complementary planting to shrubs. An ideal evergreen shrub would be the great, slow-growing *Taxus baccata* 'Dovastonii Aurea' (Fig. 73), and its golden variety, casting out long horizontal branches hung with drooping twigs, together with the larger junipers—*J.* × *media* 'Pfitzerana' (Fig. 72) and its yellow and blue variants. All are only suitable in maturity for really large gardens or areas, though often planted and enjoyed in small gardens for a few years, after which they have to be cut back, which destroys their beauty for ever. Though these are slow in growth their ground could be covered with one of the vigorous dwarf plants or shrubs, which they would eventually smother when fully grown, and thus the whole area would be weed-free from the start, and beautiful as well.

For cooler positions in part shade or at least sloping away from the sun I should choose *Cotoneaster conspicuus* 'Decorus', the flat-growing forms of *Euonymus fortunei* (Fig 17), *Fatshedera lizei* and *Rubus tricolor* (Fig. 13), the more vigorous ivies such as *Hedera colchica* 'Dentata' (Fig. 21), or just Irish Ivy. The last is the best long-term policy, and it is low and flat; but some of the others would be more ornamental and less 'wild' looking. The arbores-cent form of *Hedera helix* is a useful, sprawling, glossy evergreen for sun or shade. The rubus together with *Rosa wichuraiana* are the quickest evergreen covers I have come across. For a low, dark green carpet one could choose *Actostaphylos nevadensis* (Fig. 12) on suitable lime-free soils, or the underground spreaders *Hypericum calycinum* (Pl. XXXIb) and *Pachysandra terminalis* (Pl. XXXb); all are evergreen, rampant and efficient.

Rampers of lesser calibre but of considerable speed are *Vinca major hirsuta* (Fig. 14) and *Lamium galeobdolon* 'Variegatum' (Fig. 52), but both prefer part shade. Their counterpart for sun is *Verbena corymbosa*. These are midway between sprawling shrubs and evergreen herbaceous plants. Among deciduous rapid car-peters are *Lonicera pileata* (Pl. VIIb), *Rosa* × *paulii*, R. 'Max Graf' (Pl. VIIa), *Salix* × *gillotii*, the winter jasmine, *Jasminum nudiflorum*, and the climbing plants in Chapter 5. I have already mentioned some big shrubs, at the beginning of Chapter 4, which do noble work in covering, while of lesser size are *Senecio laxifolius* (Fig. 8), various hebes, *Ephedra gerardiana* (Fig. 9), and, planted closely together, *Chaenomeles japonica* (*Cydonia maulei*) and *C*. 'Crimson and Gold'. *Lonicera nitida* itself makes an unsurpassed high evergreen cover in good soil, but unless well nourished tends to grow bare in places. It has the advantage of rooting freely from pieces stuck in the ground and so can be a cheap and rapid means of colonizing a large area.

It is among the larger thicket-forming shrubs that I think the greatest bulk of material may be found apart from the numerous plants already mentioned. I need hardly call attention to the weed-suppressing uses and high pictorial value of large groups of *Cornus alba*, the red-stemmed dogwood. Thriving best in moist soil, rooting as it goes, it is seen to its greatest advantage on the north bank of a lake or river, where the winter sun warms and lights its rich colouring, which is nearer to plum-crimson than actual red in spite of its name. Like *Lonicera nitida*, it may be taken as a good example of high, shrubby ground-cover, forming a dense weed-proof thicket. Its brighter counterpart, *C. alba* 'Sibirica' ('Atrosanguinea') the 'Westonbirt' dogwood, and the greenish-yellow twigged *C. stolonifera* 'Flaviramea' are not so vigorous but are equally good colonizers in time. *Salix alba* 'Vitellina' (*S. vitellina* 'Britzensis') and *S. alba* 'Chrysostella' are excellent when coppiced annually or biennially and if planted some four feet apart make thick cover with their orange-red twigs, though they are not so reliable as *Cornus alba* and do not of course colonize. *S. gracilistyla* is a very bushy, early-flowering 'pussy' willow and all of these can be increased by inserting cuttings direct into the open ground, as for *Lonicera nitida*, though the Westonbirt dogwood and 'Flaviramea' are not so responsive as the others.

Rosa rugosa itself, and its closely allied forms such as 'Alba', 'Scabrosa', 'Blanc Double de Coubert', 'Roseraie de l'Haÿ' and 'Fru Dagmar Hastrup', if established on their own roots, will soon spread into thickets on light, well-drained soil in full sun. *R. rugosa* is established like a native on the sands at West Wittering, Sussex, and also in Breckland, Norfolk and Suffolk. It is weed-, dog- and hooligan-proof. Where something even more prickly and inhospitable is needed, growing to seven feet in height, the freely suckering *R. woodsii fendleri* would be my choice, while *R. virginiana* and *R. foliolosa* are two excellent American species of thicket-making habit, rather less prickly than *R. rugosa*, but equally determined to settle down in any light or heavy fertile soil. It is the custom in the United States to cut these over from time to time to keep them bushy. These two roses have single pink flowers, red heps and brilliant autumn colour. *R. virginiana* indeed can hold its own with any shrub in this respect. Fuller details of all these roses will be found in my book *Shrub Roses of Today*.

Spiraea douglasii, or a close relative of it with white flowers, forms roadside hedges by the mile near Lake Bala in North Wales, and I have seen it as dense elsewhere. This is a shrub that thrives in acid or limy soils, thriving best where the rainfall is fairly high, and its stems arise very thickly from the questing roots. The flower spikes, not very distinguished, are normally mauve-pink; a superior hybrid with greater vigour is *S. menziesii* 'Triumphans', in darker pink. Taking a while to get established but eventually making a great and wide thicket is the bush chestnut *Aesculus parviflora*, whose long plumes of scented white flowers appear in August. With them flower the species of *Sorbaria*, which used to be called *Spiraea*. *S. tomentosa* (*S. lindleyi*), *arborea*, *aitchisonii*, *assurgens* and *sorbifolia* are all big shrubs of suckering habit for sunny positions, particularly the last, which rapidly makes thickets. All of them produce handsome pinnate leaves and panicles of creamy white flowers, which can be large and impressive on good soil, if the stems are occasionally thinned out. *Rubus odoratus* (Pl. XXXIA) in strawberry-ice pink, and R. *nutkanus* with white flowers, are two closely related, handsome, thornless, suckering shrubs of great elegance and of raspberry-like growth. They bear large palmate leaves on their erect stems and are, like the sorbarias, easy to please in the way of soil, and thrive in sun or shade.

Likewise for sunny places—where it will fruit best, though it will live in shade—*Symphoricarpus albus* (*S. racemosus*) is useful. It is eclipsed in beauty by the equally vigorous *S. albus laevigatus* (*S. rivularis*), whose ropes of white berries are familiar in the late autumn scene. The variety 'Constance Spry' bids fair to beat all others in length of fruiting sprays. It thrives on chalk, as well as on acid soils. For lime-free soil in shade we need not look further for dense high cover than *Gaultheria shallon* (Fig. 24); or if in sun the equally dense evergreen *Pernettya mucronata*. Both are evergreen and impenetrable up to four or five feet. There is also *Clethra alnifolia*, with its several garden forms; they form large shrubs, freely suckering at the base so that there are always roots to give to one's friends. And welcome they are, for few shrubs give such a wealth of scent from their creamy or pinky spikes of bloom in August, freely produced. *C. tomentosa* is useful because it flowers much later. They all grow up to six feet or more, bearing fresh green leaves turning yellow in autumn. They are, however, rather large to be called ground-cover except in big areas.

For extra large areas where a high permanent cover is required some shrubs or trees with a spread of some twenty feet across might be considered. Grown as bushes certain trees of semi-weeping habit would be invaluable, so long as their flowers are borne more or less above the branches. For example, *Malus flori-bunda, Crataegus oxyacantha* 'Punicea', *C. prunifolia,* and *Pyrus salicifolia* 'Pendula', would all make great mounds of growth, dense to the ground, and would be very inspiring and suitable alike for parks and for roadsides. In more horticultural areas *Clematis viticella* varieties could be planted among them here and there to give a great splash of colour in August, particularly against the silvery leaves of the weeping pear. As these clematises are best pruned to one foot off the ground every January they do not get into a tangle or spoil their living supports.

Lastly there are the bamboos. On previous occasions when I have written about these graceful evergreens it has been to pick out the static, choice shrubs such as *Phyllostachys flexuosus, P. aureus* and *Sinarundinaria nitida,* but these are the reverse of what we want for our present purpose. Running like couch grass and making a beautiful light green cover up to about $2\frac{1}{2}$ feet is *P. viridi-striatus vagans,* which was formerly called *Bambusa pygmaea.* With *Luzula maxima (L. sylvatica)* (Fig. 59), Irish Ivy and *Rubus tricolor* (Fig. 13), it is one of the plants which give a labourless cover on any reasonably retentive soils, or sandy soils which do not entirely dry out in the summer. Its fresh colour is a contrast to other evergreens and mown grass. It gives the effect of coarse grass.

Quite a different matter are the three broad-leafed bamboos, *Sasa senanensis (Arundinaria palmata), S. tessellata (A. ragamowskii)* and *S. veitchii (A. veitchii).* These are all tremendous colonizers, creeping through the ground by several feet a year, and making dense cover; they are ideal for big areas on wet or dry soils. In the landscape they are nothing less than magnificent, their leaves varying from one to two feet in length, several inches broad, while *S. veitchii* has the added distinction of developing greyish-white margins to the leaves in autumn and winter.

S. senanensis has been flowering now for some years and it remains to be seen what the result will be. Though some species have recovered splendidly after flowering, the well-known *Pseudosasa (Bambusa) japonica* is not reviving everywhere. At those

remote intervals when different species of bamboo flower sometimes the stock dies. If this is going to happen to *Pseudosasa
japonica*, which has been used so frequently for screening purposes,
there will be some unfortunate gaps to fill. Like most others this
bamboo grows as well on dry sand as it does on heavier soils, but
I should seldom choose it for ornament, for it falls into neither
of the genera of bamboos which I esteem most—the graceful,
dainty Phyllostachys and the great solid Sasa. But like all bamboos
it wins approbation when the wind blows and the leaves rustle
so delightfully.

There is one bamboo which combines the all-out colonizing
drive of the above species with the dainty grace of the phyllostachys, and that is *Arundinaria anceps*. One of the quickest growers
both horizontally and vertically, it is of extreme grace, its ten-foot
canes arching sometimes to the ground. This is possibly the most
beautiful of all thicket-forming shrubs throughout the year, and
it and all of them can be kept in check simply by keeping a shallow
trench dug round them; the extruding roots can then be cut off
easily. When established, the underground stems of bamboos are
like iron wire, and more than a match for a blunt spade.

We have good examples of cover around our coasts. Municipal
gardens frequently show dense colonies of shrubs for two reasons,
partly because they are planted thickly—the hebes, senecios,
fuchsias, escallonias and olearias—for their own protection, also
because the wind keeps them dwarf and compact; in addition the
maritime climate and the wind restrict the number of species that
can be selected, with the result that 'thickets' are planted of each,
which is surely an indication of how ground-cover plants and
shrubs should be used.

The whole subject of ground-cover plants is so wrapped up
with nature and naturalness that one is apt to forget their uses in
formal design. As a whole their uses are more to the fore in the
United States than in Britain. The Americans are more apt to
consider plants in the light of furnishings; we incline to think of
them as 'plants'! There is no doubt that a neat, formal effect can
be achieved with many of them. Apart from private terraced
gardens and formal parks there are cemeteries and old churchyards
to be considered. There is usually sufficient labour for the larger
cemeteries, since they are part of an urban scheme, but going

about the country one finds dilapidated churchyards simply crying out for the grass and weeds to be cut. As a saving in labour certain ground-cover could be of immense benefit—we all know how difficult it is to mow among gravestones and other obstacles. The most efficient ground-cover plants—*Pachysandra terminalis* (Pl. XXXB), flat junipers, *Arctostaphylos nevadensis* (Fig. 12), ivies, *Hypericum calycinum* (Pl. XXXIB)—could be planted in large formal areas and provide the answer beautifully. In the outlying areas *Symphytum grandiflorum* (Pl. XXIIIA), *Trachystemon orientale* (Fig. 70) and *Geranium macrorrhizum* (Pl. XVIA; Fig. 32) would be more suitable. As an adjunct to paved paths or other features of a formal design few things are more telling than the dense greenery of bergenias, junipers and pachysandra.

GROUND-COVER FOR GRAVES

In cemeteries there are usually too many tarred paths and too many graves covered with white marble chippings for my liking. I should prefer to see shorter headstones and more greenery other than the ubiquitous grass.

Graves can be of three types—covered with a slab of stone, or other masonry or pebbles, surrounded by a stone or brick kerb, or just grass. Having spent hours in the past trying to clip with hand-shears old grassy graves I know how tedious this can be, and how unrewarding: unless done monthly there is no resemblance to a good lawn. It would be so much simpler to cover each grave with a carefully selected ground-cover plant, and indeed *Rosa wichuraiana* in the United States is called the 'Memorial Rose' because of its frequent use as an evergreen cover for this purpose. But it is not one I should recommend, for I consider it far too rampant. To my mind one wants something evergreen if possible, which will fill the area in a compact way. Because the turf in a cemetery or churchyard is not likely to be of perfect quality one has to choose plants which will defeat grass and weeds for a grave that has no kerb, and at the same time something pretty static which will not spread unduly from the narrow area. Possible plants and shrubs that come to mind are *Epimedium perralderanum*, *Erica carnea* (Pl. IIB) of the more compact kinds such as 'Vivellii' or 'Ruby Glow', *Galax aphylla*, *Saxifraga* × *geum* 'Monstrosa',

Armeria maritima 'Laucheana', *Asarum europaeum* (Fig. 47), *Sarcococca humilis* and *Aucuba japonica* 'Nana Rotundifolia'.

Graves with a kerb can take a much wider choice. The kerb will keep at bay plants which run underground such as *Gaultheria procumbens*, *Pachysandra terminalis* (Pl. XXXB), and the excellent deciduous *Asperula odorata* (Fig. 64), the little oak fern *Gymnocarpium dryopteris* (Fig. 68), *Polypodium vulgare* (Fig. 66) and *Cornus (Chamaepericlymenum) canadensis* (Pl. XXVIIA). After a time these would exhaust the fertility of the soil and would need top dressing or taking up, manuring and replanting. Some flat trailers could also be used, the more compact ivies like 'Silver Queen', 'Feastii', 'Marmorata', 'Sagittaefolia' and its variegated form (Fig. 20); *Waldsteinia ternata* (Pl. XXIIB), *Dryas* × *suendermanii*, *Hypericum rhodopeum*, *Juniperus procumbens* and others and *Cotoneaster microphyllus cochleatus*. These are all evergreen; if deciduous plants can be tolerated I should choose *Oxalis oregana* (Pl. XXIIA), *O. acetosella* 'Rosea' (Fig. 48), *Potentilla alba* (Fig. 57), *Tiarella cordifolia* (Pl. XXVA; Fig. 49), *Sedum spurium* 'Green Mantle' and *Campanula portenschlagiana* 'Bavarica'. Rather higher cover is provided by the long-flowering, exquisite *Dicentra formosa* varieties, *Hosta lancifolia* (Fig. 28) and *H. undulata univittata* (Fig. 27), all deciduous. Through or around some of these deciduous kinds could be planted snowdrops (*Galanthus* 'Atkinsii' followed by 'Sam Arnott'), winter aconite, *Crocus tomasinianus* and the big later kinds, erythroniums and miniature daffodils, all to flower during the first three months of the year, with *Leucojum autumnale*, *Crocus kotchyanus* and *Galanthus olgae* for the end of the year.

Teucrium chamaedrys would be a nice bushy little plant, needing an annual clip over in spring; it can be used like box edging. The most appropriate plant for graves is rosemary. The common is an untidy flopper, but 'Miss Jessop's Upright' can be kept compact by a little pruning after flowering. Neither are suitable for covering graves, and unfortunately the prostrate species *Rosmarinus lavandulaceus* (*R. officinalis prostratus*) (Fig. 16) is suitable only for warm climates.

II

Annuals and Biennials

I THINK there is a case to be considered for annuals and biennials in our ground-cover schemes so long as they will sow themselves freely. Like the rampant colonizers in the last chapter they can be quelled with an application of weedkiller if they get out of hand, or if they are only needed temporarily.

One of the most interesting examples of annual ground-cover that I have met was under a dense cedar tree at Hidcote, where the needles were weekly swept away and the grass, despite fertilizers, top dressing, re-seeding and re-turfing, simply would not grow. Rather than have a muddy area in wet weather it was decided not to sweep up the needles, and within a twelvemonth the area became self-sown with a close and permanent sward of *Poa annua*. This little grass regenerates itself constantly so that it makes a lawn, though each plant has only a short life.

What can be done with *Poa annua* can also be done with *Oxalis rosea*, a dainty, tiny-leafed, pink-flowered annual (occasionally living longer) growing to about ten inches high, and flowering from July onwards; this also is highly successful in the shade of cedars or any other tree. So is *Cyclamen hederifolium*, but as this is a perennial, though sowing itself freely when suited, it is mentioned in the Table; the only excuse for its inclusion here is because plants to grow under cedars and yews, somewhat away from the trunks, are very few.

For a cover of temporary duration I know of nothing so showy and easy as a sheet of 'Gleam' nasturtiums (*Tropaeolum*) or eschscholtzia; both are free-flowering and brilliant and easily pulled up, though like all annuals it may be a year or two later before all dispersed seeds have germinated. *Silene armeria* is another annual, in vivid carmine-pink, and candytuft, *Iberis amara*, is equally successful in a wide range of colours. A dwarf cover is

228

the Sweet Alyssum, *Lobularia maritima*, a fragrant carpet in late summer.

At Arlington Court, a National Trust property in North Devon, at high altitude and with high rainfall, *Claytonia sibirica* (*Montia sibirica*) is a very beautiful sight in spring, growing under trees where the grass is thin. It has a tuberous root and so does not really qualify for inclusion here. It covers the area—interspersed with primroses and *Oxalis acetosella*—with a mass of pinky-white stars a few inches above the ground. *C.* (*Montia*) *perfoliata* is annual; it is usually classed as a weed but is excellent cover in cool, acid soil, but far less conspicuous in flower.

For the more retentive soils, particularly streamsides and river banks and the fringes of boggy ground, the annual balsam, *Impatiens glandulifera* (*I. roylei*), is frequently seen about the country seeding with great abandon and growing to six feet or more; its many, intriguing pink flowers make a great show. It is a rapid colonizer because its seeds are ejected with some force from the ripe pods.

For full sun and rather drier soils there is the biennial *Angelica archangelica*, very quickly producing great green heads in spring, ripening quickly, with the result that the ground is thickly covered with seedlings again in late summer. The evening primrose, too, *Oenothera biennis*, will colonize any sunny waste place and produce its lovely lemon-yellow blooms for weeks in summer; it is also a biennial. *Lychnis coronaria* is another prolific seeder, in gorgeous magenta-crimson or white, two to three feet high, with large rosettes of silvery basal leaves, while an equally ardent sun-lover is *Erysimum linifolium*, a soft lilac wallflower of approximately biennial duration like the lychnis.

Though they are mostly perennials, the remaining few plants seed about with such abandon that they may well be mentioned here: *Phytolacca americana* (*P. decandra*), a statuesque plant with great spikes of shining black seeds, earning its name of poke weed; *Geranium pratense*, a soft blue, three feet high, with a fine basal clump of elegant divided leaves; *Myrrhis odorata*, a charming old garden herb known as Sweet Cicely, a relative of the cow-parsley, and the pale blue *Borago laxiflora*. In some places, on neutral, well-drained soil preferably, the lupins are useful, both annuals like *Lupinus hartwegii* and the usual border species *L.*

polyphyllus, while the yellow tree lupin, *L. arboreus*, is nearly as prolific. Nor should we forget the value as a temporary ground-cover of *L. angustifolius* and *L. luteus*, which are used agriculturally to enrich the land as a 'green manure'. *Verbascum nigrum*, producing yellow or white three-foot spikes in summer, makes good basal rosettes and sows itself freely.

These few suggestions may be found useful for large areas outside our gardens where a 'show' for a summer or two is needed, while shrubs and perennial ground-covers are being increased for later permanent planting. They are all easy to control if one studies the life-cycle with a view to allowing seed to develop if required or to remove it before it is shed.

On looking through all the preceding pages I have come to the conclusion that it has been nearly as difficult to know what to leave out as it has been to decide what to include. For instance, foxgloves (*Digitalis*) and honesty (*Lunaria*) seed themselves freely and in a way will act as a ground-cover on account of their large basal leaves; they might have been included. But nobody is likely to approve of my choice whole-heartedly; it must be regarded as a start towards a reliable guide to the uses and abuses of ground-cover plants, to save labour and increase the beauty of our gardens and controlled areas.

66 The polypody fern, *Polypodium vulgare*, will thrive in shade even in dry soil.

67 *Blechnum penna-marina* is an excellent dwarf fern for cool, moist places in woodland. Two evergreen creeping ferns.

68 *Gymnocarpium dryopteris*, the rapidly spreading oak fern. Deciduous.

69 *Athyrium filix-femina* 'Minor', a dense, spreading clump of fresh green. Deciduous.

70 In early spring blue borage-like flowers are produced by *Trachystemon orientale* and for the rest of the season its large leaves make perfect cover in sun or shade, moist or dry soil. Rampant spreading roots.

71 High ground-cover from *Anemone tomentosa* (*A. vitifolia* of gardens), with soft pink flowers in late summer. It is more vigorous and dense-growing than the usual Japanese anemones. Rampant spreading roots.

72 Perfect high cover (25 ft by 6 ft high) achieved on chalky soil with a plant or two of *Juniperus* × *media* 'Pfitzerana'.

73. The golden form of the drooping yew, *Taxus baccata* 'Dovastonii', with a foreground of astilbes; rodgersias and ligularias behind. A grouping which provides perfect cover.

74 A mass of leaves, each 3 ft wide, of *Petasites hybridus*. High ground-cover only for vast moist areas. Photographed by the roadside in Derbyshire.

75 Less vigorous than the above is *Petasites albus*, whose leaves are grey beneath. Both have attractive flowers before the leaves appear.

76 A cool bank in Northern Ireland, completely covered with a mixture of *Lithospermum diffusum* 'Heavenly Blue' and *Erigeron mucronatus*.

77 *Coronilla varia* used as a floriferous and dense cover at Easton High School, Easton, Pa., U.S.A. It is highly invasive, known in the U.S.A. as 'Penngift Crownvetch'. *Courtesy H. J. Brusca Nursery, Inc., Philadelphia.*

78 *Sagina glabra* used as a lawn in a French rock garden.

79 *Helxine soleirolii* providing a fresh green cover in the Jardins Kalm, near Paris. *Courtesy M. Littledale, Esq.* These two carpeting plants are not suitable for much frequented paths.

Appendix I

WEEDS, WEEDKILLERS, FERTILIZERS AND SOILS

A BOOK on ground-cover plants would not be complete without some notes about those arch-enemies the weeds themselves. As explained earlier, ground-cover plants should be set in well-nourished ground, free from perennial weeds, in order to gain the best results and to avoid trouble in the future.

Weeds of annual or biennial duration are not difficult to control. It is important not to let any of them set seeds, though this cannot cure the trouble completely because seeds of some species lie dormant in the soil for a considerable time; moreover many kinds of seeds are distributed by wind or by animal agency. Obviously the best way of preventing weeds from sowing themselves is to study the life-cycles of the different species and to destroy them before they are full grown, and certainly before they seed. Some species, like groundsel, will regenerate several times during the year; others like dead-nettle may germinate in the autumn and not flower until the following summer; others, true biennials, will seldom produce flowers and seeds except in the year following germination. All annual and biennial weeds, including annual grass, can be controlled easily on light soil by hoeing or cultivating the soil in the summer. A very wet summer, or heavy soil, can upset this programme and in any case disturbing the soil results in further seeds germinating.

On the contrary an application of a paraquat-diquat mixture will kill all these short-lived weeds effectively and few fresh ones will germinate unless the soil is disturbed. One can of course simply repeat-spray with paraquat-diquat if they do. While the application of this weedkiller is straightforward on fallow ground awaiting planting, it is not generally realized that paraquat-diquat can be safely applied around newly planted shrubs and plants, before they have linked together to make effective cover, so long as the liquid does not touch the plants, their stems, or leaves. For immediate post-planting control of germinating annual weed seeds in shrubby species the safest and most reliable approach is to use a combination of propachlor and chlorthal-dimethyl, which gives a wide spectrum of control. Simazine can be applied, in very diluted strength, safely around many *established* shrubs, but some shrubs and many herbaceous plants are intolerant of it. (An instance of its use can be clearly seen in Plate XA.). Although less effective against certain weeds, lenacil is safer than simazine for established mixed shrubby plantings. Also for herbaceous and mixed shrub/herbaceous groupings – although one may possibly encounter occasional signs of intolerance if using it with a wide range of herbaceous species.

It is when we have to consider ground infested with perennial weeds that we are sometimes nearly defeated. It will be obvious that whatever sort of planting is envisaged – trees, shrubs, plants or bulbs – these persistent nuisances must be completely removed. To leave one small piece of ground elder root where it can re-establish itself in the roots of a hedge or shrub will result in a ceaseless battle, with only the tedious remedies of lifting the shrub and washing off the soil and then picking out every thread of weed root, or carefully spot-treating weeds with glyphosate, using a small brush, or where the situation allows, a roller or wick-type applicator. It is equally fatal to leave such weeds in the matted roots of hostas, astilbes, geraniums and others. Couch grass can give similar problems but is easily controlled by means of an overall spray with alloxydim-sodium, which is harmless to non-grassy plants. As I explained in Chapter 2 it is a mistake to be in a hurry with perennial weeds; it is wisest to allow a full growing season to pass after apparently ridding the soil of the weed before doing any planting. The problems of site clearance before planting (and subsequent control of any surviving perennial weeds) have however been greatly simplified with the introduction in the early 1980s of the weedkillers glyphosate and alloxydim-sodium; the former killing non-selectively a very wide range of weeds; the latter being specific to perennial grasses. In the meanwhile it is sometimes a good idea to beautify the area with a temporary annual flower crop.

NEGLECTED GROUND: VARIOUS WEEDS

1. To kill *most* kinds of weeds use the foliage-acting glyphosate or a strong soil-acting or soil-acting/foliage-absorbed weedkiller (i.e. aminotriazole, ammonium sulphamate, atrazine, simazine, sodium chlorate) when weeds are in active growth. A few kinds

of very persistent weeds may survive. If so, dig out carefully or, if a heavy infestation, identify and then use appropriate chemical control measures. Control any weed seedlings emerging in later stages of treatment with paraquat or paraquat/diquat mixtures.

2. Mainly grass weeds with a few clumps or patches of broad-leaved weeds. Use glyphosate, aminotriazole; alternatively dalapon or alloxydim-sodium for grasses, such as couch-grass, identifying and applying weedkillers appropriate for the control of broad-leaved weeds present, e.g. dock, brambles, etc. (or digging them out).

3. Shrubby weeds, e.g. brambles, elder, ivy, etc., use ammonium sulphamate, 2, 4, 5-T or 2, 4, 5-T/2, 4-D mixtures.

Note: Some persistent weeds may require treatment over two growing seasons, or longer, to bring under control.

TROUBLESOME PERENNIAL WEEDS

The following list embraces most of the more common perennial weeds, with notes on their means of increase, their removal by cultivation and their destruction by weedkillers where this is possible.

BRACKEN (*Pteridium aquilinum*)

Spreads by means of underground roots and by spores. Removal of growing shoots when about 9 inches high for three summers will sometimes control it.

Chemical control: very difficult. In agriculture asulam, dicamba, aminotriazole with picloram are used to control bracken in grassland. Gardeners will find that repeated paraquat with diquat, glyphosate or dichlobenil applications may check and eventually eliminate it.

BRAMBLE (*Rubus fruticosus*)

The long arching shoots root where they touch the soil; seedlings abound. Removal by digging is effective, but care should be taken to leave no stout roots exposed to the light and air since they often produce green shoots.

Chemical control: 2, 4, 5-T or 2, 4, 5-T with 2, 4-D applied to foliage in summer.

Large thickets are best cut to the ground in winter, encouraging fresh basal growth which can easily be sprayed in late summer.

BINDWEED OR BELLVINE

The small, pink-flowered species (*Convolvulus arvensis*) spreads by increasing roots from deep tap-roots. The large, white-flowered species (*Calystegia sepium*) spreads by mainly horizontal growth of thick white roots in the upper layer of soil. Both seed freely. Both can be eradicated by careful forking, though the first is very persistent.

Chemical control: 2, 4-D, glyphosate or MCPA applied at, or just before, flowering time kills the shoots and some of the root system. Applied earlier, it is much less effective. Applications over two or three seasons may be necessary. If it is growing among established plants the solution may be applied by brush to the foliage, with great care, or with a weed-glove. Can be checked or progressively controlled with dichlobenil, dependent on situation.

DOCK (*Rumex obtusifolius* and other species)

Similar characters to Dandelion.

Chemical control: 2, 4-D, glyphosate and MCPA control seedling docks effectively, but treatment over two seasons or longer may be needed for established plants. Mecoprop has given good control, also aminotriazole. For old-established docks use dichlobenil.

DANDELION (*Taraxacum officinale*)

Spreads freely by seed and by roots severed by digging or cultivating. Deep-rooting, should be dug out.

Chemical control: 2, 4-D, MCPA, dichlobenil, glyphosate.

BUTTERCUP, Bulbous and fibrous rooted species (*Ranunculus acris*, *R. bulbosus*). Creeping species (*Ranunculus repens*)

All spread freely by seeds. The creeping species is difficult to eradicate on moist soils. The other species can be killed by deep digging or forking out.

Chemical control: 2, 4-D and MCPA applied before flowering. Also glyphosate. *R. bulbosus* is the most resistant.

GRASS. Perennial tufted and surface-creeping species of grass seed freely and can be removed by forking out or deep digging. (*Dactylis* and *Agrostis* species.)

Chemical control: glyphosate or alloxydim-sodium applied when in active growth; also, but less effective, dalapon. Paraquat with diquat is eventually successful if repeatedly applied.

Species which in addition to seeding spread by running roots such as Couch grass, Squitch, etc. (*Agropyron repens*). Every portion of root left in the soil will start life afresh. In light soil can be eradicated by constant forking out. In heavy soil it is difficult to be thorough and weedkillers are recommended.

Chemical control: glyphosate, alloxydim-sodium or dalapon.

GROUND ELDER, GOUT WEED, BISHOP'S WEED (*Aegopodium podagraria*)

Spreads mainly by running roots. Every portion of root left in the soil will start life afresh. In light soil can be eradicated by constant forking out. In heavy soil it is difficult to be thorough and a weedkiller is the answer.

Chemical control: glyphosate, aminotriazole applied when in vigorous growth is very effective; 2, 4, 5-T with 2, 4-D; dichlobenil.

RAMSONS (wild onion) (*Allium ursinum*)

Spreads by seed and by small bulbs being distributed by cultivation or animal agency. Some impression can be made by forking out in early summer.

Chemical control: glyphosate, aminotriazole or paraquat with diquat repeatedly used, with cultural help, will usually be successful.

WILLOW HERB (*Chamaenerion angustifolium*—Rosebay Willowherb)

Spreads freely by seed, and also by running roots. In light soil can be eradicated by forking out, but in heavy soils a weedkiller should be used.

Chemical control: glyphosate, paraquat with diquat repeatedly used; dichlobenil; 2, 4-D repeated.

THISTLE, CREEPING or FIELD (*Cirsium arvense*)

Spreads by seed and also by deep, running roots. Very persistent but can be controlled by not allowing it to grow above ground.

Chemical control: repeated treatments with glyphosate, 2, 4-D, MCPA, mecoprop, dichlobenil or paraquat with diquat will progressively weaken this troublesome weed.

HORSETAIL (MARE'S TAIL) (*Equisetum arvense*)

Spreads by spores from the short cones which appear before

the green stems, but also (mainly) by running roots, which may be as much as fourteen feet deep in the soil. Digging out and constant cultivation have no effect, but digging and cutting up the roots·increase it.

Chemical control: glyphosate or aminotriazole in late summer will give partial kill. Dichlobenil, 2, 4-D and ammonium sulphamate will give some degree of check but a thorough and persistent approach is essential.

NETTLES. Red Dead-nettle (*Lamium purpureum*) and Annual stinging nettle (*Urtica urens*)

These spread freely by seeding, but can be controlled by hoeing and forking out. Though an annual, the Red Dead-nettle very often continues flowering and seeding through the winter. The White Dead-nettle also spreads by running roots.

Chemical control: paraquat with diquat repeated.

Stinging nettle (perennial) (*Urtica dioica*). Spreads freely by seeds, and also by running roots. Stout pieces of root if exposed to the air and light will produce growing shoots. Forking out will help.

Chemical control: glyphosate. 2, 4-D; 2, 4, 5-T with 2, 4-D; mecoprop, applied over two seasons. Dichlobenil. Paraquat with diquat, used repeatedly.

SORREL (*Rumex acetosella*)

Spreads by seed, but most freely by running roots, every small portion of which if left in the soil will start life afresh.

Prevalent on poor acid soils. May be forked out or deeply dug, but is very persistent. Enriching and liming the ground will usually help.

Chemical control: glyphosate, 2, 4-D and MCPA, also dichlobenil. Treatment over two seasons may be needed.

COLTSFOOT (*Tussilago farfara*)

Spreads occasionally by seed, but mainly by running roots. Can be forked out in light soils but is usually found in heavy and damp soils, in which case a weedkiller is best.

Chemical control: glyphosate, dichlobenil, 2, 4, 5-T, 2, 4, 5-T with 2, 4-D, aminotriazole and paraquat with diquat are helpful but repeated application may be necessary.

VETCH and TARES (*Vicia cracca, V. sativa* and *V. hirsuta*)

These spread by seeds and also by running roots. Manual control is as for Willow Herb.

Chemical control: repeated treatment with glyphosate, 2, 4-D, MCPA, or paraquat with diquat.

KNOTWEED, GIANT OR JAPANESE (*Polygonum cuspidatum* and *P. sachalinense*)

These spread by underground roots. One thorough digging out of the woody crowns and subsequent pulling of all shoots as soon as they appear will sometimes defeat these otherwise very persistent plants in a few years.

Chemical control: glyphosate.

A weed has been defined as a plant out of place. We cultivate many plants which are weeds in other countries and occasionally one of these takes hold of a suitable piece of soil and becomes a plant out of place. Thus winter heliotrope and certain other ornamental plants and grasses, particularly those with running roots, may need control by weedkillers. Enough has been written I think in earlier chapters and in this one to indicate how best to control unruly plants, whether true weeds or troublesome ornamentals.

There are four ways of controlling the weeds: manually, by hoeing or cultivating; by applying weedkillers; by the use of black polythene sheeting; or by a heavy mulch. If even one to two feet radius of clean soil can be maintained around each shrub for the first season the advantage will be considerable. I need say no more here about the first two methods except to add that in forestry plantations an Arbogard is used for applying weedkillers to save the liquid from wetting young trees. The Arbogard may be of the one-sided type or double-sided, to fit round the young tree. With the double Arbogard a man can, it is claimed, spray up to four acres per day among young trees. This would be a useful machine to use in plantations of shrubs which are perhaps establishing themselves prior to being interplanted with ground-covering plants.

Black polythene not only prevents weed growth but also warms the soil. Fitted as a flat collar around a young shrub with a radius of say two feet it will effectively stop weeds growing. Thin black polythene can also be used in continuous sheeting to cover a large area; young plants can be inserted through it with a pointed dibber into prepared ground, and when they are sufficiently established the sheet can be torn away. The above also applies to small annual weeds.

Sometimes it may be desirable to plant high-growing groundcover shrubs in land which is infested with brambles, coarse weeds and stumps of native shrubs and trees, which persist in growing. The brambles we have already discussed, but for living stumps 2, 4, 5-T or 2, 4, 5-T with 2, 4-D will prove lethal in most cases. For certain difficult genera resistant to 2, 4, 5-T, ammonium sulphamate should be used. It is thus a far cheaper method of dealing with stumps than grubbing them up; moreover, there is no real need to remove them if they are to be covered up. The remaining danger, as from all rotting stumps, is from honey fungus.

WEEDKILLERS

Weedkillers vary in the way they kill weeds. Some attack through the roots, others through the leaves. Some have more than one mode of attack. The above-mentioned weedkillers cause weed death by application as follows:

(a) *to the leaves*

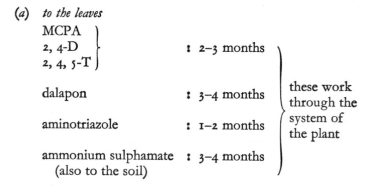

MCPA
2, 4-D   : 2–3 months
2, 4, 5-T

dalapon   : 3–4 months   these work
                                          through the
aminotriazole   : 1–2 months   system of
                                          the plant
ammonium sulphamate : 3–4 months
    (also to the soil)

glyphosate ⎫

⎬ these work through the system
of the plant; no active residues
in soil

alloxydim-sodium ⎭

(b) by contact

paraquat ⎫

⎬ kill by contact with leaves and
other green parts but are trans-
located to a limited extent within
the plant/weed.

paraquat with diquat ⎭

(c) to the soil

atrazine : 12–18 months
simazine : 12–18 months
sodium chlorate : up to 12 months but possibly
longer on heavy soils
lenacil : 3–6 months
ammonium sulphamate : 3–4 months
dichlobenil : up to 12 months
chloroxuron : up to 10 weeks
chlorthal-dimethyl : up to 3 months
propachlor : 7–8 weeks

The time-period given after each chemical refers to the period of persistence in the soil under average conditions.

Proprietary brands are as follows and should be used strictly in accordance with the instructions, taking full precautions in protecting the hands, etc., as directed. The state of growth and the weather or wrong proportions in the solution are often responsible for partial failure, and repeated applications may be necessary. Do not, in any circumstances, exceed manufacturer's recommended rate of application as this may increase risk of damage to nearby garden plants yet may not necessarily help to destroy the weeds. It is a sound plan to keep a separate can or sprayer for weedkillers so that the receptacles are not used inadvertently for insecticides. Fine-rosed watering-cans are useful, but involve greater labour in distributing the liquid than lightweight plastic knapsack sprayers which, with their small nozzles, are extremely useful for spot treatment of specific weeds or small areas among growing plants.

AVAILABILITY AND PROPRIETARY NAMES

MCPA
   Commercial: many, usually with MCPA as part of the name. Amateur: none.

2, 4-D
   Commercial: many, usually with 2, 4-D as part of the name. Amateur: several.

2, 4, 5-T
   Commercial: several, usually with Brushwood Killer as part of the name. Amateur: none.

2, 4, 5-T with 2, 4-D
   Commercial: several. Amateur: 'SBK'; 'Kilnet'.

Mecoprop
   Commercial: many. Amateur: several, e.g. 'Clovotox'.

Dalapon
   Commercial: many. Amateur: several, usually with dalapon as part of the name.

Aminotriazole
   Commercial: 'Weedazol T-L'. Amateur: none.

Ammonium sulphamate
   'Amcide'; available both commercially and to the amateur.

Lenacil
   Commercial: 'Venzar'. Amateur: none.

Paraquat
   Commercial: 'Gramoxone' (liquid formulation). Amateur: none.

Paraquat with diquat
   Commercial: none. Amateur: 'Weedol' (dissolvable solid formulation).

Simazine (for total weed control)
   Several, both commercially and for amateur use.

Simazine (low strength for selective weed control)
   Commercial: several. Amateur: 'Murphy's Weedex'.

Atrazine
   Commercial: several. Amateur: none.

Sodium chlorate
   Several, both commercially and for amateur use. Ensure

product contains an additive to reduce fire risk.

Dichlobenil
'Casoron G' (granular formulation) available both commercially and to amateur.

Chloroxuron
Commercial: 'Tenoran 50 WP'. Amateur: none.

Glyphosate
Commercial: 'Round-up'. Amateur: 'Tumbleweed'.

Alloxydim-sodium
Commercial: 'Clout'. Amateur: 'Weed Out'.

Propachlor
Commercial: several e.g. 'Ramrod'. Amateur: 'Covershield'.

Chlorthal-dimethyl
Commercial: 'Dacthal'. Amateur: none.

For a total kill of almost everything sodium chlorate, atrazine, simazine or dichlobenil can be used at full strength. The first mentioned may, on occasion, have some detrimental effect on the structure of certain soils, is easily leached from the soil and its use can endanger nearby trees or shrubs whose roots approach or underlie treated areas. All can remain active in the soil for up to a full season or more and can be spread to lower ground by heavy rains.

FERTILIZERS AND SOILS

Bonemeal and hoof-and-horn meal are safe, useful, organic fertilizers releasing their nourishment slowly, for a year or more, after being mixed in the soil or sprinkled on the surface and raked in or covered with compost or leaves. As they are slow-acting they are best applied in autumn or winter. Bonemeal is rich in phosphates and is ideal for anything with bulbous roots, but is also suitable as a general fertilizer. Hoof-and-horn meal is richer in nitrogen and may be regarded as a gentle 'pick-me-up' for general use. Dried blood, another organic fertilizer, is also rich in nitrogen, and quicker in action; it can be applied in solution, or watered in during spring and early summer to plants that look starved.

A teacupful of any of the above applied to a square yard is a suitable dose. Used 'in conjunction with any form of compost these fertilizers represent the nearest approach to well-rotted farmyard manure, and have the added advantage of being easily handled. All three contain a little lime.

On very acid soils their action may be extra slow or even negligible; on neutral or limy soils, correspondingly rapid. As mentioned in Chapter 2 soils can be too acid even for rhododendrons; lime in small quantities helps to release nitrogen, which is why on very limy soils nitrogen must be applied in greater quantities.

There are two inorganic nitrogenous fertilizers in general use: sulphate of ammonia and nitro-chalk. Both are quick-acting but not to be recommended, except that the latter is a rapid tonic for plants in too acid soils, and for lime-lovers on neutral or acid soils. A teacupful of either would be beneficial per square yard. Nitro-chalk is very easy to apply since it is coarsely granular and one can see clearly where it lies. It is a great help on sad, acid soils that grow a lot of moss, which it tends to destroy. Both sulphate of ammonia and nitro-chalk are cheaper than the organic fertilizers.

A general compound fertilizer, of which there are many on the market under proprietary names, having a balanced measure of the essential ingredients, is also a good thing to keep in stock, and it should be borne in mind that those with a high potash and phosphate content, especially composed for use on tomatoes and other fruits, are sometimes helpful around shrubs and plants which are chary of producing their ornamental fruits or berries.

HUMUS

A term usually applied to rotting or partly rotted organic matter, though strictly speaking it is a description of organic matter on the point of dissolving into the soil. It is the first and essential ingredient to be added to the inorganic material of the soil to enable plants to live; therefore we should be at pains to conserve everything that will rot down into humus, particularly on limy soils where humus is more quickly absorbed. The following are some well-known examples of materials that will turn into humus (vegetable): leaves, grass mowings, soft prunings, pine needles, straw, bracken, peat, wood shavings, sawdust, spent hops, kitchen refuse (tea leaves, peelings, etc.). The term is also applied to well-rotted manure and soft animal refuse such as skins, leather clippings, wool shoddy and carpet sweepings, etc.

MULCH

A soil-covering of any of the materials listed under 'humus'. This covering has the advantage of enriching the soil, keeping it cool in hot weather, keeping it moist during dry spells (provided the ground was moist when the mulch was applied), preventing heavy soils from 'caking' and cracking, and preventing the germination of weeds. Against all this must be balanced the fact that if showers fall in dry weather the rain will evaporate off the mulch before it reaches the soil and that the presence of a mulch increases the risk of frost near to the soil, particularly in frost pockets in spring.

SOILS AND pH

The pH of a soil is a term used to indicate its lime content; those above 7·0 are termed sweet or limy, and those below 7·0 are termed sour or acid. It is obvious from this that those around 7·0 are also termed neutral. A full-scale soil analysis will shew the presence or absence of other necessities of life, trace elements etc., but a convenient way of determining the pH of the soil is by testing with a British Drug House Soil Tester. By adding an acid to a spoonful of soil the resulting colour indicates whether the soil is acid or limy. Experts can usually judge whether a country (as opposed to a town) soil is limy or not from the native vegetation.

FERTILE SOIL

The weed-growth will usually indicate this!

DRAINAGE

The term 'well-drained' has been used frequently through this book; it refers to a soil which does not remain boggy and moisture-laden after wet periods. Except for moisture-loving plants, free drainage of water through the soil is desirable.

Appendix II

LISTS OF PLANTS FOR SPECIAL CONDITIONS

THE following lists have been prepared to make selection easier for those who are faced with planting in abnormal soils and conditions.

It should be borne in mind that the lists of genera apply only to the species mentioned in this book; other species may require different conditions.

I. PLANTS REQUIRING LIME-FREE SOILS

On limy soils it is wiser not to attempt to grow the genera in the following list. They are mainly woodland plants and thrive best in soil in which humus has been mixed. Species of *Ceanothus, Berberis, Chaenomeles, Cytisus, Iris, Lupinus, Pimelia* and *Myosotideum* are not so dependent on humus so long as the soil is acid or neutral.

Arctostaphylos
Azalea
Berberis thunbergii and
    varieties
Blechnum
Boykinia
Bruckenthalia
Calluna
Camellia
Carex pendula
Cassiope
Chaenomeles
Claytonia sibirica
Clethra
Comptonia

Cornus canadensis
Cyathodes
Cytisus scoparius
    (*Sarothamnus*)
Daboecia
Dicentra
Empetrum
Epigaea
Erica
Galax
Gaultheria
Gaylussacia
Houstonia
Hydrangea macrophylla
Iris douglasiana

Iris innominata
Leiophyllum
Leucothöe
Linnaea
Lithospermum diffusum
Lupinus
Luzula
Meconopsis
Mitchella
Myosotideum
Ourisia
Pachysandra
Pachystima
Pernettya

Philesia
Pieris
Pimelia
Pyrola
Rhododendron
Sarothamnus, see *Cytisus*
Schizocodon
Shortia
Skimmia
Smilacina
Soldanella
Tanakaea
Vaccinium
Woodwardia

2. PLANTS WHICH WILL THRIVE IN LIMY SOILS

While it may be taken that any genus not mentioned in List No. 1 will tolerate lime, many, such as *Rosa*, prefer the soil to be neutral. The following will thrive in soil that is actively limy, even over chalk, though they will grow equally well without lime.

Acaena
Acathus
Achillea
Adiantum
Ajuga
Alchemilla
Alyssum saxatile
Anaphalis
Anchusa
Anemone
Antennaria
Arabis
Armeria
Athyrium
Aubrieta
Aucuba
Ballota

Berberis (except *B. thunbergii*
    and varieties)
Bergenia
Brunnera macrophylla
Caltha
Campanula
Cardamine
Ceanothus
Centaurea
Cerastium
Ceratostigma
Choisya
Cistus
Clematis
Convallaria
Convolvulus
Cornus alba

Cotoneaster
Cotula
Crambe
Crataegus
Cyclamen
Daphne
Dianthus
Dryas
Dryopteris
Epimedium
Erigeron
Erodium
Euonymus fortunei
Euphorbia
Festuca
Forsythia
Fuchsia
Genista hispanica
Geranium
Gymnocarpium
Gypsophila
Halimium
Hebe
Hedera
Helianthemum
Helleborus
Hemerocallis
Houttuynia
Hydrangea villosa
Hypericum
Hyssopus
Iris foetidissima
Jasminum
Juniperus
Lamium
Lathyrus
Lavandula
Liriope
Lonicera

Mahonia
Nepeta
Osmanthus
Othonnopsis
Paeonia
Peltiphyllum
Phlomis
Phlox
Phyllitis
Podocarpus
Polygonatum
Polygonum
Potentilla
Primula
Prunus
Pulmonaria
Pulsatilla
Pyracantha
Pyrus
Ribes
Rodgersia
Rosmarinus
Rubus
Salvia
Sambucus
Santolina
Sarcococca
Scabiosa
Sedum
Senecio
Sorbaria
Spiraea
Stachys
Symphoricarpus
Symphytum
Taxus
Tellima
Teucrium
Thymus

Vancouveria
Viburnum
Vinca

Viola
Waldsteinia
Zauschneria

3. PLANTS WHICH TOLERATE CLAY

Few plants establish quickly on very heavy soils over clay,
though many of the following will luxuriate in maturity, provided
the area is reasonably well drained.

Acanthus
Aesculus
Ajuga
Alchemilla
Anemone × hybrida
—— tomentosa
Aruncus
Asarum
Aucuba
Berberis
Bergenia
Brunnera
Caltha
Chaenomeles
Clematis
Convallaria
Cornus alba
—— stolonifera
Cotoneaster
Crataegus
Daphne
Epimedium
Euonymus fortunei
Forsythia
Geranium
Hedera
Helleborus
Hemerocallis
Hosta
Lamium

Lonicera
Mahonia
Malus
Peltiphyllum
Petasites
Phillyrea
Polygonatum
Polygonum
Prunella
Prunus
Pyrus
Ribes
Rheum
Rodgersia
Rosa
Rubus
Salix
Sambucus
Sarcococca
Sorbaria
Spiraea
Symphoricarpus
Symphytum
Telekia
Tellima
Trachystemon
Vancouveria
Viburnum
Vinca
Waldsteinia

4. PLANTS WHICH WILL GROW SATISFACTORILY IN DRY, SHADY PLACES

Apart from ill-drained clay, this combination of conditions is the most difficult to cope with in the garden. * indicates those which will not tolerate lime.

Alchemilla conjuncta
*Arctostaphylos
Arundinaria
Asperula
Aster macrophyllus
Aucuba
*Blechnum spicant
*Camellia
*Carex
*Cornus canadensis
Cyclamen
Dryopteris filix-mas
Duchesnea
Epimedium
Euphorbia robbiae
Fatshedera
Fragaria
*Gaultheria shallon
Geranium nodosum
Hedera
Hypericum androsaemum
Iris foetidissima
*Linnaea

Lonicera nitida
—— pileata
Lunaria
Mahonia
Myrrhis
Pachyphragma
*Pachysandra
Phyllitis
Phyllostachys
Polypodium
Prunus laurocerasus varieties
Ribes
Rubus
Sarcococca
Skimmia
Thalictrum
Trachystemon
*Vaccinium vitis-idaea
Vancouveria
Vinca minor
Waldsteinia
Xanthorhiza

5. PLANTS WHICH THRIVE ON MOIST SOILS

Genera marked * are suitable for boggy positions.

Ajuga
Aruncus
*Astilbe
Athyrium
Blechnum chilense
*Caltha

Clethra (no lime)
Cornus alba
—— stolonifera
Filipendula palmata
—— purpurea
Gunnera

Heracleum
Houttuynia
*Ligularia
*Lysichitum
Matteuccia
*Onoclea
Osmunda
Peltiphyllum

Petasites japonicus
*Primula florindae
—— various
Ranunculus
Rheum
Rodgersia
*Trollius

6. PLANTS WHICH GROW WELL IN SHADY POSITIONS

The bulk of these are woodland plants, growing well under shrubs and trees, but those marked * are not so satisfactory under trees, though thriving in the shade given by buildings. For those requiring lime-free soil, compare with List No. 1.

Adiantum
Aegopodium
Anemone
*Arabis
Arundinaria
Asarum
Asperula
Athyrium
Aucuba
*Berberis
*Bergenia
Blechnum
Boykinia
Brunnera
Camellia
Cardamine
Carex
Cassiope
Chiastophyllum
*Choisya
Claytonia
Comptonia
Convallaria

Cornus canadensis
Cortusa
Corydalis
*Cotoneaster
Cyathodes
Cyclamen
Cystopteris
Dicentra
Dryopteris
Duchesnia
Epigaea
Epimedium
Euonymus
Euphorbia robbiae
Fragaria
*Fuchsia
Galax
Gaultheria
Gaylussacia
Geranium, most
Gymnocarpium
*Hebe
Hedera

Helleborus
Helxine
Heucherella
Hosta
Houstonia
Hydrangea
Hypericum androsaemum
——— calycinum
*Iberis sempervirens
Iris foetidissima
Jasminum nudiflorum
*——— others
Juniperus × media
Lamium
Leucothöe
Linnaea
Lomaria
Lonicera pileata
Lunaria
Luzula
Lysimachia
Mahonia
Maianthemum
Matteuccia
Meconopsis
Milium
Mitchella
Mitella
Myrrhis
Omphalodes
Onoclea
Osmunda
Ourisia
Oxalis
Pachyphragma
Pachysandra
Pachystima
Patrinia
Petasites

Philesia
Phyllitis
Phyllostachys
Pieris
Polygonatum
Polygonum
Polypodium
Polystichum
Prunus laurocerasus
Pseudosasa
Pulmonaria
Pyrola
Rhododendron, larger-
leaved kinds
Ribes
Rubus
Sarcococca
Saxifraga
Schizocodon
Selaginella
Shortia
Skimmia
Smilacina
*Soldanella
Symphytum
Tanakaea
Tellima
Thalictrum minus
Tiarella
Tolmeia
Trachystemon
Vaccinium macrocarpum
——— vitis-idaea
Vancouveria
*Viburnum davidii
Vinca
Viola
Waldsteinia
Woodwardia

7. PLANTS WHICH WILL THRIVE IN HOT, SUNNY PLACES
ON DRY SOILS

Those marked * require lime-free soil.

Acaena
Acantholimon
Acanthus
Achillea
Alyssum
Ampelopsis
Antennaria
Anthemis
Arabis
*Arctostaphylos
Armeria
Artemisia
Aubrieta
Ballota
Bolax
Bupleurum
Calamintha
Campanula alliariifolia
Campsis
Ceanothus
Centaurea
Cerastium
Ceratostigma
*Chaenomeles
Choisya
Cissus
Cistus
Clematis flammula
—— × jouiniana
Convolvulus
Coronilla
Cotula
Crambe
*Cytisus
Dianthus

Dimorphotheca
Elaeagnus
Elymus
Ephedra
Erigeron glaucus
Erodium
Erysimum
Eschscholtzia
Fascicularia
Festuca
Filipendula hexapetala
Genista
Geranium × magnificum
—— renardii
Gypsophila
Halimiocistus
Halimium
Hebe
Helianthemum
Hypericum calycinum
—— rhodopeum
Hyssopus
Iberis amara
—— sempervirens
Iris graminea
*—— innominata
—— japonica
—— ruthenica
Jasminum parkeri
Juniperus
Lathyrus
Lavandula
Leptospermum
Limonium
Lupinus arboreus

Lychnis coronaria
Moltkia
Muehlenbeckia
Nepeta
Oenothera biennis
Ophiopogon
Osteospermum, see *Dimorphotheca*
Othonnopsis
Oxalis rubra
Paronychia
Parthenocissus
Pennisetum
Pterocephalus
Ptilotrichum
Raoulia
Romneya
Rosmarinus

Ruta
Salvia
Santolina
Saponaria
Satureia
Scabiosa graminifolia
Sedum
Senecio
Silene
Stachys olympica
Teucrium
Thymus
Trachystemon
*Vaccinium oxycoccus
Viola labradorica
Zauschneria

8. PLANTS WHICH THRIVE IN MARITIME DISTRICTS

Many of the following will stand wind and salt-spray, particularly those marked *. Those marked ** will provide shelter for others and shelter is highly important in seaside gardening. For genera requiring lime-free soil, compare with List No. 1.

Acaena
Acantholimon
Achillea
Alchemilla
Alyssum
Antennaria
Anthemis
Arabis
*Arctostaphylos
*Armeria
*Artemisia
Arundinaria
Asperula
Athyrium
Aubrieta

*Aucuba
*Berberis
Bergenia
Beschorneria
Betula
Blechnum
Bolax
Bruckenthalia
**Bupleurum
Calamintha
*Calluna
Camellia
Campanula
Campsis
Ceanothus

Centaurea
*Cerastium
Ceratostigma
Choisya
**Cistus
Clematis
Convolvulus
Coprosma
Cornus alba
—— stolonifera
Coronilla
**Cotoneaster
*Crambe
**Crataegus
*Cytisus
*Daboecia
*Dianthus
*Dimorphotheca
Dryas
Dryopteris
*Elaeagnus
*Elymus
Ephedra
*Erica
*Erigeron glaucus
*Eriogonum
*Eryngium
Erysimum
**Escallonia
*Euonymus
Euphorbia
Fascicularia
Festuca
Filipendula hexapetala
Forsythia
Frankenia
*Fuchsia
Garrya
*Genista

Geranium
*Gypsophila
Halimiocistus
*Halimium
**Hebe
Hedera
Helianthemum
Hemerocallis
Heuchera
*Hydrangea
Hypericum
Hyssopus
Iberis
Ilex
Iris
Jasminum
*Juniperus
Lathyrus
Lavandula
*Leptospermum
*Limonium
Liriope
**Lonicera
*Lupinus arboreus
Mahonia
Myosotideum
Osteospermum, see
Dimorphotheca
*Othonnopsis
Oxalis
Penstemon
Petasites fragrans
Phlox
Phyllitis
Phyllostachys
Polygonum
Polypodium
Polystichum
*Potentilla

Pulsatilla
Pyrus
*Romneya
*Rosa
*Rosmarinus
Rubus
Ruta
**Salix
Salvia
Santolina
Satureia
Saxifraga
*Sedum

**Senecio
Silene
Skimmia
Sorbaria
Spiraea
Stachys
Symphoricarpus
Teucrium
Thymus
Vaccinium
Vinca
Waldsteinia

9. PLANTS WHICH CREATE BARRIERS

The following by their dense or prickly character will deter small animals and human beings as well as weeds.

Arundinaria anceps
Berberis
Chaenomeles
Clematis montana
Clethra
Cornus alba
—— stolonifera
Cotoneaster conspicuus
—— —— 'Decorus'
Crataegus
Forsythia suspensa sieboldii
Gaultheria shallon
Juniperus × media
Lonicera nitida

Mahonia japonica
Pernettya
Pyrus
Rosa 'Macrantha'
—— 'Max Graf'
—— × paulii
—— × polliniana
—— 'Raubritter'
—— rugosa
—— virginiana
—— woodsii fendleri
Spiraea douglasii
—— menziesii

10. PLANTS FOR TOWN GARDENS

Genera marked * prefer acid soil; those marked † will thrive in impoverished soils. Soil in towns is usually deficient in humus.

†Acanthus
†Alchemilla

Anemone
†Asperula odorata

†Aucuba
†Bergenia
 Campanula
 Clematis montana
 Corydalis
*Dicentra
†Epimedium
 Euonymus
†Fatshedera
†Ferns
†Geranium
†Hebe
†Hedera
*Hosta

Nepeta
Parthenocissus
Polygonatum
Polygonum
†Potentilla alba
Ribes
Salix
Saxifraga, Robertsonia
 section
Spiraea
Tellima
†Vancouveria
†Vinca
Waldsteinia

PLANTS SUITABLE FOR COVERING ROSE-BEDS

The following are all small plants that will not be too strong-growing for the purpose, and will help to make the beds more attractive during the seven months when H.T.'s and Floribundas are not in flower. Small spring-flowering bulbs can be grown through them. The more vigorous shrub roses will tolerate many others among the shorter-growing plants in the Alphabetical Tables.

Acaena
Alyssum saxatile
Arabis
Aubrieta
Campanula carpatica
—— portenschlagiana
Cardamine trifolia
Corydalis lutea
—— ochroleuca

Lysimachia nummularia
Phlox subulata
Primula auricula
—— vulgaris sibthorpii
Pulsatilla
Saponaria ocymoides
Saxifraga
Viola

ADDENDA 1977

THE search for good ground-cover continues in Europe and the United States and kinds will continually come onto the market through discerning nurserymen. The following notes cover some of the more attractive species and cultivars to date. Many minor additions have been inserted in earlier pages.

SHRUBS

	Country of Origin	Leaf Height and Planting Distance	Leaf Colour and Character
COTONEASTER			
dammeri 'Coral Beauty'			

A comparatively new form of excellent growth, resembling *C. dammeri* but with coral coloured berries.

CYTISUS			
× praecox	Hybrid	3′ × 2′	Erect grey-green twigs
— 'Allgold'	Hybrid	3′ × 2′	Erect grey-green twigs

C. × *praecox* and its garden forms known as 'Albus' and 'Allgold' are useful 'social' shrubs for close planting; they need to be trimmed over after flowering to keep them compact.

EUONYMUS fortunei is a very variable shrub, and nurserymen continue to propagate forms, many of which are much alike. The normal old variegated form, *E. fortunei* 'Variegata' often sports to green forms with similarly small leaves; named clones are 'Emerald Cushion' and 'Emerald Green'. A green form with much larger rounded leaves is 'Dart's Cardinal'; it bears colourful berries when fully established. All of these should be planted about 2 ft apart and will achieve 1–2 ft in height on open ground.

HEBE			
chathamica	Chatham Islands	4″ × 10″	Light green, oval.

For warmer and maritime districts.

HYPERICUM			
wilsonii	China	2′ × 2′	Bright green, narrow.

This is a useful member of the *H. patulum* group, of arching habit.

LIGUSTRUM			
obtusifolium regelianum	Japan	1½′ × 2′	Fresh green, narrow.

The narrow leaves in their opposite placing on the numerous short ascending stems give an appearance of being pinnate at first glance. Pinkish brown autumn colour. A clone has been named 'Dart's Perfection'.

LONICERA			
nitida 'Elegant'	Hybrid	3′ × 3′	Mid-green, small.

With its mat green leaves and dense low-spreading habit this may rival *L. pileata*.

PERNETTYA			
prostrata	S. America	2′ × 3′	Dark green, narrow.

Vigorous, arching shrub, spreading freely in lime-free, humus-laden soil, by underground shoots.

RHODODENDRON

Further compact hybrids, usually broader than high, are 'Baden Baden', 'Bad Eilsen', 'Elizabeth Lockhart', 'Moerheim's Pink', 'Pink Bountiful', 'Red Carpet' and 'Tidbit'; in a larger, looser vein are the forms of 'Fabia'.

ROSA			
'Nozomi'	Hybrid	1½′ × 3′	Dark green, small.

A useful carpeter with tiny leaves, but the single flowers are of a nondescript tone of washy pink.

'Sanders' White'	Hybrid	1½′ × 6′	Dark green, small, glossy

An old rambler of dense trailing habit with very fragrant flowers.

Deciduous or Evergreen	Flower Height and Colour and Fruits (if any)	Flowering Season	Habit	Propagation
D	Primrose yellow.	Spring	Hummock	C
D	Bright yellow.	Spring	Hummock	C
E			Hummock	CL
E	Lilac, small, in small heads.	Summer	Carpet	CL
E/D	Soft yellow.	Summer	Hummock	CS
D	White in small heads.	Summer	Carpet	CL
E	Inconspicuous.		Hummock, rooting	CL
E	Small, white; black or pink fruits.	Spring	Spreader	CLS
D	Pale pink to off white.	Summer	Carpet	CL
D	White, double.	Summer	Carpet	CL

SHRUBS

	Country of Origin	Leaf Height and Planting Distance	Leaf Colour and Character
SALIX			
× **finnmarchica**	Hybrid	1′ × 2′	Grey-green, small.

Not the least of its attractions is the red-brown colouring of the twigs in winter. A good, dense cover.

uva-ursi	N. America	1′ × 3′	Dark green, small.

Bearberry Willow, *S. apoda* of gardens.

yezo-alpina	Japan	1′ × 3′	Large, rounded.

Vigorous species with remarkable leaves.

SANTOLINA

The nomenclature is confused. *S. neapolitana* appears to be referable to *S. chamaecyparissus insularis*. *S. pectinata* appears to be referable to *S. chamaecyparissus tomentosa* and two cultivars have been named, 'Edward Bowles', ivory-white, and 'Sulphurea', pale primrose-yellow. *S. viridis* (*S. virens*) has a primrose yellow cultivar, 'Primrose Gem'.

HERBACEOUS PLANTS

	Country of Origin	Leaf Height and Planting Distance	Leaf Colour and Character
HEUCHERA			
cylindrica	W. North America	8″ × 1′	Dark green, rounded.

Any soil. 'Alba', with creamy white flowers, and 'Hyperion', rosy red, are to be preferred; division.

ORIGANUM			
vulgare	Europe, Britain	6″ × 1′	Small, hairy, rounded.

The Marjoram has a useful variant, 'Aureum', whose growth is more compact, with brilliant yellow-green leaves in spring. CD. It is easily suited regarding soil.

PULMONARIA			
mollis	Europe, N. Asia	9″ × 1½′	Long, dark velvety.

picta (*P. saccharata* of gardens). See page 186.

'Margery Fish' was the most beautiful in flower and leaf of many forms and hybrids in the Trials at Wisley.

PACHYPHRAGMA			
macrophyllum	S. Europe	9″ × 1′	Round; rich green.

A useful early flower, tolerant of shade; any fertile soil. Wrongly described as *Cardamine asarifolia* in the first edition of this book.

...duous r green	Flower Height and Colour and Fruits (if any)	Flowering Season	Habit	Propagation
Ɔ	Grey-green female catkins.	Spring	Carpet, rooting	CL
Ɔ	Yellow catkins.	Spring	Carpet, rooting	CL
D	Yellow catkins.	Spring	Carpet, rooting	CL

...iduous or ...rgreen	Flower Height and Colour and Fruits (if any)	Flowering Season	Habit	Propagation
E	2–3′. Stiff spikes, brownish.	E. Summer	Clump	DS
D	1½′. Tiny, rosy purple in sprays.	Summer	Clump	CDS
D	1½′. Vivid blue, in sprays.	Spring	Clump	DS
D	White, small in heads.	E. Spring	Clump	DS

GRASS

	Country of Origin	Leaf Height and Planting Distance	Leaf Colour and Character
HAKONECHLOA			
macra	Japan	9″ × 9″	Narrow, dark green.

'Aureola' is a spectacular form with yellow-striped leaves slowly making a dense cover. Division in spring.

FERN

	Country of Origin	Leaf Height and Planting Distance	Leaf Colour and Character
HYPOLEPIS			
millefolia	New Zealand	9″ × 1½′	Dark green branching.

A rapid coloniser for shade or part-shade, like a miniature Bracken. *Dennstaedtia punctilobula* is often confused with this but, though a similar coloniser, it has bright green, erect, narrower fronds.

iduous or ergreen	Flower Height and Colour and Fruits (if any)	Flowering Season	Habit	Propagation
D	1'. Yellowish.	Summer	Spreader	DS

ciduous or ergreen	Flower Height and Colour and Fruits (if any)	Flowering Season	Habit	Propagation
D			Spreader	D

BOOKS FOR FURTHER STUDY

Flowering Earth, Donald Culross Peattie, 1948, Phoenix House.

Taking the Ache out of Gardening, Stuart Dudley, 1962, Phoenix House.

Weed Control Handbook, Edited by J. D. Fryer and S. A. Evans, Vol. 1, *Principles*, 1968; Vol. 2, *Recommendations*, 1973, Blackwell.

Weatherwise Gardening, S. A. Searle and L. P. Smith, 1958, Blandford.

A Chalk Garden, F. C. Stern, 1960, Nelson.

Gardening on Lime, Judith M. Berrisford, 1963, Faber.

Gardening on Clay, Howard Hamp Crane, 1963, Collingridge.

Seaside Gardening, Christine Kelway, 1962, Collingridge.

Gardening on Sand, Christine Kelway, 1965, Collingridge.

Approved Products for Farmers and Growers, The Ministry of Agriculture, Fisheries and Food.

Gardening Chemicals, The Royal Horticultural Society.

Manual of Trees and Shrubs, Hillier & Sons, Winchester, 1971 and later editions.

Gardening on Chalk and Lime, Ronald Dyson, 1977, Dent.

GENERAL INDEX

including Common Names of Plants

Anglesey Abbey, garden, xx
Annuals, classification of, 228 *et seq.*
Arbogard, 238
Associations of plants in nature, 1
Azalea, see *Rhododendron*

Bamboos, various, 224
Banks and slopes, 11, 222
Bellvine, 234
Biennials, classification of, 228 *et seq.*
Bindweed, 234
Birch, dwarf, see *Betula*
Bishop's Weed, 235
Bouncing Bet, see *Saponaria*
Bowles, E. A., xix
Bracken, 233
Bramble, 233
Broom, see *Cytisus* and *Genista*
Bugle, see *Ajuga*
Bulbs and bulb planting, 13
Butter Burr, see *Petasites*
Buttercup, 234

Californian Fuchsia, see *Zauschneria*
Californian Poppy, see *Romneya*
Camomile, see *Anthemis*
Candytuft, see *Iberis*
Cape Gooseberry, see *Physalis*
Catmint, see *Nepeta*
Chestnut, dwarf, see *Aesculus*
Chinese Lantern, see *Physalis*
Christmas Rose, see *Helleborus*
Climbing plants, classification of, 96 *et seq.*
Coltsfoot, 237
Comfrey, see *Symphytum*
Conifers, classification of, 108 *et seq.*
—, cultivation of, 112
Cotton Lavender, see *Santolina*
Cranesbill, see *Geranium*
Cultivation, 5
Cydonia, see *Chaenomeles*
Cypress, see *Chamaecyparis*

Dandelion, 234

Day Lily, see *Hemerocallis*
Design of borders, 26
Disadvantages of ground-cover plants, xxiii
Dock, 234
Dogwood, see *Cornus*
Drainage, 7, 243
Dutchman's Pipe, see *Aristolochia*
Dwarf 'social' shrubs in border, Plate IVb

Elder, see *Sambucus*
Everlasting Pea, see *Lathyrus*

Fair Maids of France, see *Ranunculus*
Ferns, classification of, 208 *et seq.*
Fertility of soil, 9
—, restoring, 10
Fertilizers, 241
Foliage, value of, xiv, 19, 134
Formal designs, ground-cover for, 4, 226
Foxglove, see *Digitalis*
Funkia, see *Hosta*
Furnishing the garden, xxiv

Gardening in four layers, 3
Globe Flower, see *Trollius*
Goat's Beard, see *Aruncus*
Gout weed, 235
Grass (weeds), 235
—, value of, xxi
Grasses, classification of, 202 *et seq.*
Graves, ground-cover for, 226
Green, importance as a colour, xiv
Ground Elder, 235

Heath and Heather, see *Ca una*, *Erica*, *Daboecia*
Heath gardens, Plate Ia and b
Herbaceous plants, classification of, 116 *et seq.*
— —, evergreen, 117
Heronsbill, see *Erodium*

History of gardening concerning ground-cover, xviii
Holly, see *Ilex*
Honesty, see *Lunaria*
Honeysuckle, see *Lonicera*
Horsetail, 235
Humus, 8, 242

Ivy, see *Hedera*
—, Irish (*Hedera helix hibernica*), 221 Plate XXIXA

'Japonica', see *Chaenomeles*
Jekyll, Gertrude, xix
Johnson, A. T., writer, xvi, xix
Johnston, Lawrence, xix

Knotweed, see *Polygonum*

Labour-saving beds at Killerton, Plate IIIA
Labour-saving borders, Fig. 77
Lady's Mantle, see *Alchemilla*
Lamb's Ears, see *Stachys lanata*
Laurel, see *Prunus laurocerasus*
Lavender, see *Lavendula*
Leaves, value of, xiv, 2, 3, 19
Lenten Rose, see *Helleborus*
Lily of the Valley, see *Convallaria*
Lime, 6
Lungwort, see *Pulmonaria*
Lyme Grass, see *Elymus*

Manuring, 9
Mare's Tail, 236
Marjoram, see *Origanum*
Marsh Marigold, see *Caltha*
Megasea, see *Bergenia*
Mexican Orange, see *Choisya*
Michaelmas Daisies, see *Aster*
'Mind your own business', see *Helxine*
Mint, see *Mentha*
Moss gardens, 211
Mouse plant, see *Arisarum*
Mulches, 8, 243
Municipal gardening, xx, xxi, 216 *et seq.*
Myrtle, see *Myrtus*

Names of plants, popular, 17
Nasturtium, see *Tropaeolum*

Nature's ground-cover, 1
Nettles, 236
Nomenclature, 16
Nutrition, 10

Onion, wild, 235
Oregon Grape, see *Mahonia aquifolium*

Partridge Berry, see *Mitchella*
Pasque Flower, see *Pulsatilla*
Pea, Perennial or Everlasting, see *Lathyrus latifolius*, 104
Periwinkle, see *Vinca*
pH content of soils, 7, 243
Pinks, see *Dianthus*
Plantain Lily, see *Hosta*
Planting programme, 8, 21
— rules, 22
Plume, Poppy, see *Macleaya*
Polythene, black, 238
Poppy, Harebell, see *Meconopsis*
Preparation of ground, 5
Propagation of clones, 19; general propagation, 22
Pruning, 14

Ramsons, 235
Rhubarb, see *Rheum*
Robinson, William, xix
Rosemary, see *Rosmarinus*
Roses, Shrub, books on, 36
Rue, see *Ruta*, 41
Rushes, classification of, 202 *et seq.*

Sage, see *Salvia*
St Bernard's Lily, see *Anthericum*
St John's Wort, see *Hypericum*
Seakale, see *Crambe*
Shade in the garden, 13
Shrubs, classification of, 26 *et seq.*
Skunk Cabbage, see *Lysichitum*
Snow in Summer, see *Cerastium*
Snowberry, see *Symphoricarpus*
Soapwort, see *Saponaria*
'Social' Shrubs, 36
Soil testing, 7, 243
Soils, 239
Solomon's Seal, see *Polygonatum*
Sorrel, 236
Spiraea, see *Astilbe, Aruncus, Filipendula, Spiraea*

Spruce Fir, see *Picea*
Spurge, see *Euphorbia*
Stonecrop, see *Sedum*
Strawberry, see *Duchesnia* and *Fragaria*
Sun Rose, see *Helianthemum*, 41
Sweet Cicely, see *Myrrhis*

Tares, 237
Terms, descriptive, 20, 24
Thistle, 236
Thorn, see *Crataegus*
Thrift, see *Armeria*

Variegated leaves, positions for, 12

Verges of borders and beds, 14
Veronica, shrubby, see *Hebe*
Vetch, 237
Violet, see *Viola*
Virginian Creeper, 96, 98

Weedkillers, 238
Weeds, classification of, 231 *et seq.*
Willmott, Ellen, xix
Willow, see *Salix*
Willow Herb, 235
Woodruff, see *Asperula*
Wood Sorrel, see *Oxalis*

INDEX OF LATIN NAMES
OF PLANTS

Acaena adscendens, 136
— *anserinifolia*, 136
— *buchananii*, 136
— *caesiglauca*, 136
— *hirsutula*, 136
— *inermis*, 136
— *microphylla*, 136
— *novae-zelandiae*, 136
— *sanguisorbae*, see *A. anserinifolia*, 136
— *splendens*, 136
Acantholimon glumaceum, 136
Acanthus mollis latifolius, 131, 136, 217
— *spinosissima*, 136
— *spinosus*, 131, 136, 217, Pl. IVB
Achillea ageratifolia, 136
— *chrysocoma*, 136
— × *kellereri*, 136
— *millefolium*, 136
— — 'Cerise Queen', 136
— *tomentosa*, 136
Acorus gramineus, 124, 138
— — 'Variegatus', 138
Adiantum pedatum, 210, 212
— — 'Klondyke', 212
— *venustum*, 210, 212
Aegopodium podagraria, 218, 234
— — 'Variegata', 218
Aesculus parviflora, 223
Ajuga pyramidalis, 126, 138
— *reptans*, 138
— — 'Atropurpurea', 126, 138
— — 'Jungle Beauty', 126, 138
— — 'Pink Spire', 126, 138
— — 'Variegata', 126, 138
Akebia quinata, 99
Alchemilla alpina, see under *A. conjuncta*, 120
— *conjuncta*, 120, 138
— *mollis*, 119, 138, 220, Figs. 40, 41, Pl. XV
Alyssum maritimum, see *Lobularia maritima*, 229

Alyssum saxatile, 127, 138, Fig. 38
— *saxatile* 'Citrinum' ('Silver Queen'), 127, 138
— *spinosum*, see *Ptilotrichum spinosum*, 41
— Sweet, see *Lobularia*, 229
Ampelopsis sempervirens, see *Cissus striata*, 102
— *veitchii*, see *Parthenocissus tricuspidata*, 106
Anaphalis margaritacea, 138
— *triplinervis*, 120, 138, Pl. XIV
— *yedoensis*, 138
Anchusa myosotidiflora, see *Brunnera macrophylla*, 120, 148
Andromeda, see *Leucothöe*, 37, 49, 74
Androsace lanuginosa, 140
— — *leichtlinii*, 140
Anemone apennina, 140
— × *elegans*, see *A.* × *hybrida*, 140
— *hupehensis*, see under *A.* × *hybrida*, 140
— × *hybrida* 'Honorine Jobert', 140
— — 'Louise Uhink', 140
— — 'Prince Henry' ('Profusion'), 140
— — 'Queen Charlotte', 140
— — 'September Charm', 140
—, Japanese, see *A.* × *hybrida*, 140
— *nemorosa*, 140
— *pulsatilla*, see *Pulsatilla vulgaris*, 186
— *tomentosa*, 131, 140, 217, Fig. 71
— *vitifolia*, see *A. tomentosa*
Angelica archangelica, 229
Antennaria aprica, 140
— *dioica*, 140
— — 'Hyperborea Rosea', 140
— *plantaginifolia*, 125, 140
Anthemis cupaniana, 140
— *nobilis*, 126, 140
— — 'Plena', 140
— — 'Treneague', 126, 140
Anthericum liliago, 124, 140

Arabis albida, 127, 142
— — 'Flore Pleno', 127, 142
— — 'Variegata', 127, 142
Arctostaphylos nevadensis, 42, 52, 221, 226, Fig. 12
— *officinalis*, see *A. uva-ursi*, 52
— *uva-ursi*, 42, 52
Arenaria balearica, 142
— *ledebouriana*, 142
— *montana*, 142
Arisarum proboscideum, 142
Aristolochia durior and *A. sipho*, see *A. macrophylla*, 102
— *macrophylla*, 102
— *sempervirens*, 52
Armeria corsica, 126, 142
— *maritima*, 126, 142, 227
— — *alba*, 142
— — 'Laucheana', 126, 142
Artemisia stellerana, 142
Aruncus dioicus, 119, 142, 220
— — 'Kneiffii', 142
— *sylvester*, see *A. dioicus*, 119, 142, 220
Arundinaria anceps, 225
— *japonica* ('Metake'), see *Pseudosasa japonica*, 224
— *palmata*, see *Sasa senanensis*, 224
— *ragamowskii*, see *Sasa tessellata*, 224
— *veitchii*, see *Sasa veitchii*, 224
Asarum canadense, 144
— *caudatum*, 144
— *europaeum*, 132, 144, 227, Fig. 47
— *shuttleworthii*, 144
Asperula odorata, 132, 144, 227, Fig. 64
Asplenium scolopendrium, see *Phyllitis*
Aster, dwarf Michaelmas Daisies, 144
— 'Climax', 144
— *macrophyllus*, 142
Astilbe × *arendsii*, 119, 144, Figs. 42, 73
— 'Betsy Cuperus', 144
— 'Bridal Veil', 144
— 'Erica', 144
— 'Fanal', 144
— 'Jo Ophorst', 144
— 'King Albert', 144
— 'Koblenz', 144
— 'Ostrich Plume', 144
— 'Peach Blossom', 144
— 'Professor van der Wielen', 144
— 'Red Sentinel', 144

Astilbe 'Rheinland', 144, Pl. XIXв
— 'Salland', 144
— *rivularis*, 144
— *simplicifolia*, 144
— — 'Atrorosea', 144
— — 'Bronze Elegance', 144
— — 'Hybrida Rosea', 144
— *sinensis*, 144
— — *pumila*, 146
— — — 'Gnome', 'Kobold', and 'Perkeo', 146
— *taquetii* 'Superba', 146
Astilboides tabularis, see *Rodgersia tabularis*, 188
Astrantia helleborifolia, see *A. maxima*, 146
— *major*, 146
— — 'Sunningdale Variegated', 146
— *maxima*, 146
Athyrium filix-femina, 209, 212
— — 'Minor', 209, 212, Fig. 69
Aubrieta 'Bressingham Red', 146
— 'Carnival', 146
— *deltoides*, 127, 146
— 'Lilac Time', 146
— 'Maurice Prichard', 146
Aucuba japonica 'Crassifolia', 30
— — 'Hillieri', 30
— — 'Nana Rotundifolia', 52, 227
Aurinia saxatilis, see *Alyssum saxatile*, 127, 138
Azalea, Japanese and other species and varieties, see under *Rhododendron*, 82, 84
Azorella trifurcata, see *Bolax gummifera*, 148

Bahia lanata, see *Eriophyllum lanatum*, 158
Ballota acetabulosa, 146
— *pseudodictamnus*, 124
Bambusa pygmaea, see *Phyllostachys viridi-striatus vagans*, 224
Begonia evansiana, 146
Bellium minutum, 125, 146
Berberis, see also under *Mahonia*
— *calliantha*, 48, 52
— *candidula*, 33, 52
— *coxii*, 48, 52
— *darwinii prostrata*, see *B.* × *stenophylla* 'Prostrata'
— *hookeri*, 33, 48, 52

Berberis sargentiana, 29
— × *stenophylla* 'Corallina', 52
— — 'Prostrata', 52
— *thunbergii,* 52
— — 'Atropurpurea', 52
— — 'Atropurpurea Nana', 52
— *verruculosa,* 33, 52
— *wallichiana pallida,* see *B. candidula,* 52
— *wilsoniae,* 33, 52
Bergenia 'Abendglut', 148
— 'Ballawley', 146, 148
— *ciliata,* 146
— — *ligulata,* 146, 148, Pl. XIV
— *cordifolia,* 146, 148
— — 'Purpurea', 127, 146, 148, Fig. 44
— *crassifolia,* 148
— *delavayi,* see *B. purpurascens,* 148
— *delbees,* see *B.* 'Ballawley', 146, 148
— 'Evening Glow', see 'Abendglut', 148
— 'Morgenröte', 148
— 'Morning Blush', see 'Morgenröte', 148
— *purpurascens,* 37, 148
— × *schmidtii* 'Ernst Schmidt', 148
— 'Silberlicht', 148
— 'Silver Light', see 'Silberlicht', 148, Pl. XIVD
— 'Sunningdale', 37, 148, Pl. XIVB
Beschorneria yuccoides, 116
Betula nana, 54
Bignonia, see *Campsis,* 99
Blechnum chilense, 209, 212
— *penna-marina,* 210, 212, Fig. 67
— *spicant,* 210, 212
— *tabulare,* see *B. chilense,* 209, 212
Bocconia, see *Macleaya,* 117, 217
Bolax glebaria, see *B. gummifera,* 148
— *gummifera,* 148
Borago laxiflora, 229
Bruckenthalia spiculifolia, 54
Brunnera macrophylla, 120, 148, 220, Fig. 58
Buphthalmum salicifolium, 148
— *speciosum,* see *Telekia speciosa,* 117
Bupleurum fruticosum, 54

Calamintha grandiflora, 123, 150
Calluna vulgaris, 37, 54

Calluna vulgaris 'Blazeaway', 54
— — 'County Wicklow', 54
— — 'Foxii Nana', 54
— — 'Golden Feather', 54
— — 'Goldhaze', 54
— — 'J. H. Hamilton', 54
— — 'Hirsuta Typica', 54
— — 'Minima' *see* 'Pyrenaica', 54
— — 'Mullion', 54
— — 'Multicolor', 54
— — 'Pyrenaica', 54
— — 'Rigida', 54
— — 'Robert Chapman', 54
— — 'Sister Anne', 54
— — 'Sunset', 54
Caltha palustris, 119, 150
— — 'Plena', 150
— *polypetala,* 150
Camellia japonica, 31
— — 'Apple Blossom', 31
— — 'Asuniyovense', 31
— — 'Elegans', 31
— — 'Gloire de Nantes', 31
— — 'Lady Clare', 31
— — 'Latifolia', 31
— — 'Nagasaki', 31
— — 'Preston Rose', 31
— — 'Tsukimiguruma', 31
— *sasanqua,* 32
— — 'Shishi-gashira', 32
— × *williamsii,* 31
Campanula alliariifolia, 150
— *carpatica,* 150
— —*turbinata,* 150
— *latiloba,* 150
— — 'Alba', 150
— — 'Hidcote Amethyst', 150
— — 'Highcliffe', 150
— — 'Percy Piper', 150
— *muralis,* see *C. portenschlagiana* 'Bavarica', 133, 150
— *portenschlagiana* 'Bavarica', 133, 150
— *poscharskyana,* 133, 150
— — 'Stella', 150
Campsis grandiflora, 99, 102
— *radicans,* 99, 102
— × *tagliabuana* 'Madame Galen', 99, 102
Cardamine asarifolia, see under *Pachyphragma macrophyllum*
— *latifolia,* see *C. raphanifolia,* 150

Cardamine raphanifolia, 150
— *trifolia*, 125, 150
Carex pendula, 202, 204
Carpobrotus, see *Mesembryanthemum*, 176
Cassiope hypnoides, 54
— *lycopodioides*, 42, 54
— *selaginoides*, 54
— *stellerana*, 54
Ceanothus divergens, 54, 56
— *gloriosus*, 54, 56
— *prostratus*, 43, 54, 56
— *thyrsiflorus repens*, 54
Celastrus scandens, 99
Centaurea hypoleuca 'John Coutts', 133, 150, Pl. XXVI
— *montana*, 152
— — 'Alba', 152
— — 'Parham Variety', 152
— — 'Rosea', 152
— *simplicicaulis*, 150, 152
Cerastium tomentosum, 133, 152, 217
Ceratostigma plumbaginoides, 133, 152
Chaenomeles 'Crimson Gold', 56
— *japonica*, 40, 48, 56, 221
— — *alpina*, 56
Chamaecyparis lawsoniana 'Knowe-fieldensis', 112
— — 'Nidiformis', 112
— — 'Tamariscifolia', 112
Chamaemelum nobile, 126
Chamaepericlymenum canadense, see *Cornus canadensis*, 56, 227
Chiastophyllum oppositifolium, 152
Choisya ternata, 30
Chrysanthemum haradjanii, 152
— *yezoense*, 133, 152
Cissus striata, 102
Cistus, see also *Halmiocistus* and *Halimium*, 40
— × *corbariensis*, 56
— *lusitanicus decumbens*, 56
— *salviifolius*, 56
Claytonia alsinoides, see *C. sibirica*, 229
— *perfoliata*, 152, 229
— *sibirica*, 152, 229
Clematis armandii, 98, 102
— *flammula*, 98, 102
— *glauca*, 98, 102
— — *akebioides*, 102
— × *jouiniana*, 98, 102
— *montana*, 98, 102

Clematis montana, 'Elizabeth', 102
— — 'Tetrarose', 102
— — *wilsonii*, 102
— *orientalis*, 98, 102
— *paniculata*, 98
— *rehderana*, 98, 102, 104
— *tangutica*, 98, 102, 104
— — *obtusiuscula*, 102
— × *vedrariensis*, 102
— *veitchiana*, 98, 102
— *viticella* varieties, 224
Clethra alnifolia, 223
— *tomentosa*, 223
Convallaria majalis, 132, 152
— — 'Fortin's Giant', 132, 152
— — 'Prolificans', 152
— — 'Rosea', 152
Convolvulus cneorum, 41, 56
Coprosma petriei, 43, 56
Cornus alba, 221
— *canadensis*, 47, 56, 227, Pl. XXVIIA
— 'Sibirica' ('Westonbirt'), 222
— *stolonifera* 'Flaviramea', 222
Coronilla varia, 131, 154, 218, Fig. 77
Corydalis cheilanthifolia, 154
— *lutea*, 124, 125, 154
— *ochroleuca*, 125, 154
— *scouleri*, 154
Cotinus coggygria, 31
Cotoneaster 'Autumn Fire', see 'Herbstfeuer'
— *adpressus*, 58
— *congestus*, 43, 58
— *conspicuus*, 58
— — 'Decorus', 58, 221
— *dammeri*, 44, 58, Pl. XXVIIIA
— 'Gnome', 51
— 'Herbstfeuer', 51, 58
— *horizontalis*, 44, 51, 58
— — 'Little Gem', 58
— — 'Saxatilis', 58
— *humifusa*, see *C. dammeri*, 44, 58
— 'Hybridus Pendulus', 44, 58
— *microphyllus*, 58, Fig. 15
— — *cochleatus*, 43, 58, 227
— — *glacialis*, see *C. congestus*, 58
— 'Nan Shan', see *C. adpressus praecox*, 58
— 'Parkteppich' ('Park Carpet'), 51, 58
— *pyrenaicus*, see *C. congestus*, 58
— 'Repens', 51, 58

Cotoneaster 'Saldam', 51, 58
— *salicifolius*, hybrids of, 51, 58
— 'Skogholm', 51, 58
Cotula potentillina, 154
— *reptans*, 154
— *squalida*, 154
Cotyledon oppositifolia (*C. simplicifolia*
   of gardens), see *Chiastophyllum
   oppositifolium*, 152
Crambe cordifolia, 120, 154
— *maritima*, 120, 154
Crataegus oxyacantha 'Punicea', 224
— *prunifolia*, 224
Crocosmia crocosmiiflora, 154
— *masonorum*, 154
Cyathodes colensoi, 38, 58
Cyclamen hederifolium, 156, 228
— *neapolitanum*, see *C. hederifolium*,
   156, 228
Cydonia maulei, see *Chaenomeles japonica*,
   40, 48, 56, 221
Cystopteris bulbifera, 210, 212
— *fragilis*, 210, 212
Cytisus × *beanii*, 40, 58
— *decumbens*, 43, 58
— *demissus*, 58
— *hirsutus demissus*, see *C. demissus*, 58
— × *kewensis*, 43, 58
— *leucanthus*, 58
— × *praecox*, 31, 33
— *prostratus*, see *C. decumbens*, 43, 58
— *schipkaensis*, see *C. leucanthus*, 58
— *scoparius* 'Andreanus Prostratus',
   60
— — *pendulus*, 60
— — *prostratus*, see *C. s. pendulus*, 43,
   60

Daboecia, 37
— *azorica*, 60
— *cantabrica*, 60
— *polifolia*, see *D. cantabrica*
Daphne cneorum × *burkwoodii*, 60
— 'Eximia', 60
— *odora* 'Aureo Marginata', 60
Dennstaedtia punctilobula, 260
Dianthus arenarius, 156
— *caesius*, see *D. gratianopolitanus*, 156
— *deltoides*, 156
— — 'Superbus', 156
— 'Emperor', 156
— 'Enid Anderson', 156

Dianthus fragans, 156
— *gratianopolitanus*, 156
— — 'Baker's Variety', 156
— — 'Flore Pleno', 156
— 'Grenadier', 156
— 'Highland Hybrids', 124, 156
— 'C. T. Musgrave', 124, 156
— 'White Ladies', 124, 156
Dicentra formosa, 130, 156, 227
— — 'Adrian Bloom', 156
— — *alba*, 130, 156
— — 'Bountiful', 130, 156
— *oregana*, 156
Dicentra spectabilis, 156
Dielytra, see *Dicentra*
Digitalis purpurea, 230
Dimorphotheca barberiae, 156
Doronicum 'Miss Mason', 156
Dorycnium hirsutum, 41, 60
Dryas octopetala, 43, 60
— × *suendermannii*, 43, 60, 227
Dryopteris carthusiana, 212
— *dilatata*, 212
— *filix-mas*, 209, 212
— *spinulosa*, see *D. carthusiana*, 212
Duchesnea indica, 128, 158

Elaeagnus × *ebbingei*, 30
— *macrophylla*, 30
Elymus arenarius, 203, 204, 218
Empetrum nigrum, 60
Ephedra gerardiana, 33, 62, 221, Fig. 9
Epigaea asiatica, 62
— × *intermedia* 'Aurora', 62
— *repens*, 42, 62
Epimedium, 30, Pl. XXV
— *perraldierianum*, 158, 226
— *pinnatum colchicum*, 158, Fig. 50
— *pubigerum*, 158
— × *rubrum*, 158
— × *versicolor*, 131, 158
— — 'Sulphureum', 158
— × *warleyense*, 158
Erica carnea, 37, 39, 43, 62, 226
— — 'Myretoun Ruby', 62
— — 'Ruby Glow', 62
— — 'Springwood Pink', 62, Pl. IIB
— — 'Springwood White', 62, Pl. IIB
— — 'Vivellii', 62
— *ciliaris*, 62
— *cinerea*, 37, 62
— — 'Alba Minor', 62

Erica cinerea 'C. D. Eason', 62
—— 'Glasnevin Red', 62
—— 'Golden Drop', 62
—— 'Golden Hue', 62
—— 'Rosea', 62
— × *darleyensis*, 37, 39, 62
—— 'Arthur Johnson', 62
—— 'Molten Silver', see 'Silber-schmelze', 62
—— 'Silberschmelze', 62
— *mediterranea*, 62
—— 'Brightness', 62
—— 'W. T. Rackliffe', 62
— *tetralix*, 62
— *vagans*, 37, 62
—— 'Cream', 62
—— 'Holden's Pink', 62
—— 'Mrs D. F. Maxwell', 62
—— 'Pallida', 62
—— 'St Keverne', 62
— *vulgaris*, see *Calluna vulgaris*
— × *williamsii*, 62
Erigeron glaucus, 158
—— 'Elstead Rose', 158
—— 'Four Winds', 158
Eriogonum umbellatum 'Major', 158
Eriophyllum caespitosum, see *E. lanatum*, 158
— *lanatum*, 158
Erodium chrysanthum, 41, 64
— *guttatum*, 64
— *macradenum*, 41, 64
— *manescavii*, 158
— *trichomanefolium*, 41, 64
Erysimum linifolium, 229
Escallonia 'Edinensis', 30
— 'Langleyensis', 30
Euonymus fortunei, 50, 64, 221
—— *carrierei*, 50, 64
—— 'Coloratus', 50, 64
—— 'Emerald and Gold', 64
—— 'Emerald Cushion', 256
—— 'Emerald Green', 256
—— 'Gracilis', 64
—— 'Kewensis', 64
—— *radicans*, see *E. fortunei*
—— 'Silver Queen', 64
—— 'Variegatus', 64
— *radicans*, see *E. fortunei*, 50, 64
— *vegetus*, 64, Fig. 17
Euphorbia epithymoides, see *E. poly-chroma*, 160

Euphorbia griffithii 'Fireglow', 160
— *polychroma*, 160
— *robbiae*, 131

Fascicularia pitcairnifolia, 116
Fatshedera lizei, 50, 64, 221
Festuca crinum ursi, see *F. eskia*, 202, 204
— *eskia*, 202, 204, Fig. 60
— *glauca*, 202, 204
— *ovina glauca*, see *F. glauca*, 202, 204
Ficus pumila 'Minima', 64
Filipendula hexapetala 'Flore Pleno', 160
— *palmata*, 160
— *purpurea*, 160
Forsythia 'Arnold Dwarf', 64
— 'Bronxensis', 64
— *ovata*, 34, 64
— *suspensa sieboldii*, 64
Fragaria 'Baron Solemacher', 128, 160
— *chiloense*, 128
— *indica*, see *Duchesnea indica*, 128
— *vesca semperflorens*, 128, 160
Frankenia laevis, 125, 160
— *thymifolia*, 160
Fuchsia 'Corallina', see *F.* 'Exonien-sis', 43, 66
— 'Exoniensis', 43, 66
— *magellanica* 'Prostrata', 66
— *procumbens*, 66

Galax urceolata (*G. aphylla*), 160, 226
Galeobdolon argentatum, see *Lamium galeobdolon*, 172
Garrya elliptica, 29
Gaulnettya wisleyensis, 49
Gaultheria adenothrix, 66
— *cuneata*, 38, 66
— *nummularioides*, 42, 66
— *procumbens*, 47, 66
— *shallon*, 49, 66, 223, Fig. 24
Gaylussacia brachycera, 66
Genista hispanica, 40, 66
— *lydia*, 66
— *pilosa*, 43, 66, Pl. VIA
— *sagittalis*, 66, Pl. VIB
— *tinctoria* 'Flore Plena', 66
Geranium armenum, see *G. psilostemon*, 162
— *bergeranum*, 160

Geranium 'Claridge Druce', 122, 220
— *endressi*, 122, 160, 220, Pl. XVIIA
—— 'Wargrave Pink', 122
— *grandiflorum*, 123, 133, 160, Fig. 56, and cultivars see *G. himalayense*
— *himalayense*, 123, 133, 160, Fig. 56
—— 'Gravetye' ('Alpinum'), 162
— *ibericum*, see *G.* × *magnificum*, 122, 160
— 'Johnson's Blue', 122, 160
— *macrorrhizum*, 123, 160, 162, 219, 226, Pl. XVIA, Pl. XXXII
—— *album*, 160, 162
— *maculatum*, 122
— × *magnificum*, 122, 160, Pl. XVIIB
— *nodosum*, 160
— *phaeum*, 160
— *platypetalum*, see *G.* × *magnificum*
— *pratense*, 123, 160, 162, 229
—— 'Albo Plenum', 162
—— 'Caeruleum Plenum', 162
—— 'Violaceum Plenum', 162
— *procurrens*, 128
— *psilostemon*, 160, 162, Fig. 42
— *punctatum*, 162
— *rectum album*, 160
— *renardii*, 122, 160, 162, Fig. 38
— 'Russell Prichard', 122, Pl. XVIB
— *sanguineum*, 123, 133, 160, 162
—— *album*, 123, 162
—— 'Glenluce', 123, 162
—— *lancastriense*, 123, 162
— *sylvaticum*, 122, 162
—— 'Mayflower', 162
— *vlassovianum*, 162
— *wallichianum* 'Buxton's Variety', 122, 160, 162
Geum × *borisii*, 162
— *rivale*, 162
Glechoma, see *Nepeta hederacea*, 176, 220
Glyceria maxima (*G. aquatica*), 204, Pl. XXVB
Gunnera chilensis, 164
— *magellanica*, 126, 164
— *manicata*, 118, 164
— *scabra*, see *G. chilensis*, 164
Gymnocarpium dryopteris, 210, 212, 227, Fig. 68
— *phegopteris*, see *Thelypteris phegopteris*, 210

Gymnocarpium robertianum, 212
Gypsophila repens, 127, 164, Fig. 55
—— *rosea*, 165
— 'Rosy Veil', 127

Hakonechloa macra 'Aureola', 260
Halimiocistus, 40
— *ingwersenii*, 68
— *sahucii*, 68
Halimium, 40
— *algarvense*, see *H. ocymoides*, 68
— *alyssoides*, 68
— *formosum*, see *H. lasianthum formosum*, 68
— *lasianthum concolor*, 68
—— *formosum*, 68
— *ocymoides*, 68
Harrimanella stellerana, see *Cassiope stellerana*, 54
Hebe albicans, 40, 68
— 'Aoira', 40, 68
— 'Autumn Glory', 68
— 'Carl Teschner', 68
— *carnosula*, 68
— *catarractae*, 68
— *chathamica*, 256
— *colensoi*, 68
— *elliptica* 'Blue Gem', 68
— *gibbsii*, 68
— *pageana*, see *H. pinguifolia* 'Pagei', 68
— *pinguifolia*, 68
—— 'Pagei', 40, 68, Pl. IIA
— *rakaiensis*, 68
— *subalpina*, see *H. rakaiensis*, 68
Hedera canariensis, 97, 104
—— 'Variegata' ('Gloire de Marengo'), 97, 104, Fig. 20
— *colchica*, 104
—— 'Dentata', 97, 104, 221, Fig. 21
—— 'Dentato Variegata', 97, Pl. VIIIB
— *helix*, 70, 104
—— 'Angularis Aurea', 97, 104
—— 'Buttercup', 104, Pl. VIIIA
—— 'Caenwoodiana', 104
—— 'Conglomerata', 70
—— 'Cristata', 104
—— 'Feastii', 70, 227
—— 'Glacier', 104
—— 'Gold Heart', *see* 'Jubilee', 97, 104

Hedera helix hibernica, 97, 104, Pl. XXIX
— — 'Jubilee', 97, 104
— — 'Little Diamond', 70
— — 'Lobata Major', 97, 104
— — 'Marginata Major', 97
— — 'Marmorata', 97, 104, 227
— — 'Minima', 70
— — 'Sagittaefolia', 70, 227, Fig. 20
— — 'Silver Queen', 97, 227
— — 'Très Coupé', 70
— — 'Tricolor', 97
— *poetica* 'Emerald Green', 97, 104
Helianthemum alpestre, 43, 70
— 'Butter and Eggs', 70
— 'Jubilee', 70
— 'Mrs Earl', 70
— *nummularium*, 41, 70
— 'Rhodanthe Carneum', 41, 70, Pl. IIIB
— 'Wisley Primrose', 70
Helichrysum bellidioides, 166
Helleborus abschasicus, see under *H. orientalis*, 164
— *antiquorum*, see under *H. orientalis*, 164
— *atrorubens*, see under *H. orientalis*, 164
— *cyclophyllus*, 164
— *foetidus*, 123, 164, Fig. 45
— *guttatus*, see under *H. orientalis*, 164
— *kochii*, see under *H. orientalis*, 164
— *niger*, 123, 164
— *olympicus*, see under *H. orientalis*, 164
— *orientalis*, 123, 164
— *purpurascens*, see under *H. orientalis*, 164
— *viridis*, 164
Helxine soleirolii, 166, 219, Fig. 79
Hemerocallis 'Bold Courtier', 166
— 'Dorothy McDade', 166
— *dumortieri*, 166
— *flava*, 166
— *fulva*, 134, 166
— — 'Kwanso Flore Pleno', 134, 166, Fig. 61
— 'J. S. Gaynor', 166
— *middendorfiana*, 166
— 'Pink Damask', 166
— 'Spanish Gold', 166

Heracleum mantegazzianum, 124, 166, 220, Pl. XXXA
Heuchera americana, 168
— × *brizoides*, 166
— *cylindrica*, 258
— *micrantha*, 166
— *pilosissima*, 168
— *rubescens*, see *H. americana*, 168
— *sanguinea*, 168
Heucherella tiarelloides, 168
— — 'Bridget Bloom', 168
Hosta species and varieties, 120
— *albomarginata*, 168, Fig. 29
— — 'Alba', 168
— *crispula*, 168, Pl. XIIB, Pl. XIIIA
— *decorata*, 168
— *elata*, 168
— *fortunei*, 168
— — 'Albopicta', 168, Pl. XIA
— — 'Aurea', 168, Pl. XIB
— — *hyacinthina*, 168, Fig. 32
— — 'Marginato Alba', 168, Fig. 30
— — 'Obscura', 170
— — 'Obscura Marginata', 170, Fig. 31
— *glauca*, see *H. sieboldiana*, 170
— *lancifolia*, 170, 227, Fig. 28
— — *fortis*, see *H. undulata* 'Erromena', 170
— — *medio-variegata*, see *H. undulata*, 170
— *minor alba*, see *H. albomarginata* 'Alba', 168
— *plantaginea*, 170
— — *grandiflora*, 170, Figs. 34, 35
— *rectifolia*, 170
— *sieboldiana*, 170
— — 'Elegans', 170, Pl. XIIA, Pl. XXXII, Fig. 32
— — 'Frances Williams' ('Gold Edge'), 170, Fig. 33
— *subcordata*, see *H. plantaginea*, 170
— *tardiflora*, 170
— 'Thomas Hogg', 168, 170, Pl. XIB
— *tokudama*, 170
— — 'Variegata', 170
— *undulata*, 170
— — *erromena*, 170
— — *univittata*, 170, 227, Fig. 27
— *ventricosa*, 170
— — 'Aureomaculata', 170
— — 'Variegata', 170, Fig. 34

Houstonia caerulea, 170
— *serpyllifolia*, 126, 170
Houttuynia cordata, 170
— — 'Flore Pleno', 133, 170
Hydrangea anomala petiolaris, 99, 104
— *macrophylla* 'Blue Wave', 30, Fig.
    2
— *petiolaris*, see *H. anomala*, 99, 104
— *villosa*, 30
Hypericum androsaemum, 70
— *buckleyi*, 70
— *calycinum*, 47, 70, 221, 226, Pl.
    XXXIB
— × *moseranum*, 70
— *olympicum grandiflorum*, 70
— *polyphyllum* of gardens, see *H.
    olympicum grandiflorum*, 70
— *reptans*, 172
— *rhodopeum*, 70, 172, 227
— — 'Sunspot', 172
Hypolepis millifolia, 155
Hyssopus officinalis, 72

Iberis amara, 228
— *saxatilis*, 39, 72
— *sempervirens*, 'Snowflake', 39, 72,
    Fig. 11
Ilex aquifolium 'Pendula', 44, 72
Impatiens glandulifera, 229
— *roylei*, see *I. glandulifera*, 229
Iris douglasiana, 172
— *flavescens*, 172
— *florentina*, 172
— *foetidissima*, 172
— — 'Chinese Form', see *I. f. citrina*,
    172
— — *citrina*, 172
— *graminea*, 124, 172
— — 'Hort's Variety', 172
— *innominata*, 172, Fig. 37
— *japonica*, 124, 172
— — 'Ledger's Variety', 172
— *kochii*, 172
— *pallida*, 172
— *ruthenica*, 172
— *unguicularis* (*I. stylosa*), 172

Jasminum nudiflorum, 44, 50, 72, 221
— *parkeri*, 42, 72
Juniperus chinensis 'Glauca', 113
— — 'Parsonii', 110, 112
— — 'San José', 113

Juniperus chinensis sargentii, 113
— *communis*, 109, 113
— — *depressa*, 109, 113
— — 'Depressa Aurea', 113
— — *depressa* 'Depressed Star', 109,
    113
— — — 'Dumosa', 113
— — — 'Gimbornii', 113
— — — 'Vase', 109, 113
— — 'Effusa', see under *J. c.*
    'Repanda', 113
— — 'Hornibrookii', 109, 113, Pl.
    X
— — 'Prostrata', 109
— — 'Repanda', 109, 113
— — *saxatilis*, 113
— *conferta*, 110, 113
— *horizontalis*, 109, 113, Pl. XA
— — 'Bar Harbour', 110, 113
— — 'Black Hills Creeper', see *J. h.*
    'Emerson', 114
— — 'Douglasii', 110, 113, Pl. XB
— — 'Emerson', 114
— — 'Glauca', 110, 113
— — 'Plumosa', 114
— — 'Prostrata', 109, 113
— — 'Viridis', 114
— — 'Wiltonii' ('Wilton Carpet' or
    'Blue Rug'), 110, 114
— 'Knaphill Savin', see *J.* × *media*
    'Pfitzerana', 110, 114
— × *media*, 110, 114
— — 'Pfitzerana', 51, 110, 111, 114,
    220, Fig. 72
— — 'Pfitzerana Aurea', 114
— — 'Pfitzerana Glauca', 110, 114
— *procumbens*, 114, 227
— — 'Bonin Island', 110, 114
— — 'Nana', 114
— *sabina*, 110, 114
— — 'Arcadia', 114
— — 'Hicksii', 114
— — 'Skandia', 114
— — 'Tamariscifolia', 110, 114, Fig.
    10
— *scopulorum*, 114
— — 'Repens', 114
— *taxifolia*, 114
— — *lutchuensis*, 110, 114
— *virginiana* 'Chamberlaynii', 111,
    115
— — 'Tripartita', 115

Kalmia angustifolia rubra, 50

Lamium galeobdolon 'Variegatum', 172, 219, 221, Fig. 52
— *maculatum*, 129, 172, 219, Fig. 53
Pl. XXIVв
— — 'Album', 172
— — 'Aureum', 172
— — 'Roseum', 172
Lathyrus latifolius, 99, 104
Lavandula 'Dutch', 40, 72
— 'Hidcote Giant', 72
— 'Twickel Purple', 72
Leiophyllum buxifolium, 38, 72
— — *prostratum*, 72
Leptospermum humifusum, 42, 74
— *scoparium* 'Prostratum', see *L. humifusum*
Leucothöe catesbaei, see *L. fontanesiana*, 37, 49, 74
— *fontanesiana*, 37, 49, 74, Fig. 22
— *keiskii*, 49, 74
Ligularia clivorum, see *L. dentata*, 117
— *dentata*, 117
— — 'Desdemona', 117
— *veitchiana*, 117
Ligustrum obtusifolium regelianum, 256
— — — 'Dart's Perfection', 256
Limonium latifolium, 174
— — 'Blue Cloud', 172
Linnaea borealis, 74
— — *americana*, 74
Liriope exiliflora, 174
— *graminifolia densiflora*, see *L. muscari*, 174
— — *minor*, see *L. spicata*, 174
— *muscari*, 124, 174
— *spicata*, 134, 174
Lithospermum diffusum, 42, 74, Fig. 76
— — 'Grace Ward', 74
— — 'Heavenly Blue', 42, 74
— *prostratum*, see *L. diffusum*, 74
— *purpureo-caeruleum*, 174
Lobularia maritima, 229
Lomaria alpina, see *Blechnum pennamarina*, 210, 212
— *magellanica*, see under *Blechnum chilense*, 209, 212
Lonicera × *americana*, 99
— 'Early Dutch' and 'Late Dutch', see under *L. periclymenum*, 99, 106

Lonicera etrusca 'Superba', 99
— *henryi*, 99
— *japonica*, 106
— — *aureo-reticulata*, 106
— — *halliana*, 99, 106
— *nitida*, 221
— *periclymenum belgica*, 99, 106
— — *serotina*, 99, 106, Pl. XXVIIв
— *pileata*, 44, 74, 221, Pl. VIIв
Lunaria annua, 230
Lupinus angustifolius, 230
— *arboreus*, 230
— *hartwegii*, 229
— *luteus*, 230
— *polyphyllus*, 230
Luzula maxima, 203, 204, 219, Fig. 59
— *sylvatica*, see *L. maxima*, 203, 204, 219
— — 'Variegata', 204
Lychnis coronaria, 229
Lysichitum americanum, 119, 174, Pl. XXA
— *camtschatcense*, 119, 174
Lysimachia nummularia, 126, 174
— — 'Aurea', 174

Macleaya cordata, 117
— *microcarpa*, 117, 217
— — 'Coral Plume', 117
Mahonia aquifolium, 37, 48, 74
— *japonica*, 29
— *nervosa*, 48, 74
— *repens*, 48, 74
— — *rotundifolia*, 74
Maianthemun bifolium, 132, 174, Fig. 63
Malus floribunda, 224
Matteuccia struthiopteris, 209, 214, Pl. XXI
Meconopsis quintuplinervia, 176
Megasea, see *Bergenia*, 121
Melianthus major, 30
Mentha, various, 125, 176
Menziesia polifolia, see *Daboecia cantabrica*, 60
Mesembryanthemum, 219
— *acinaciforme*, 176
— *edule*, 176
Milium effusum 'Aureum', 203, 204
Mitchella repens, 42, 74
— *undulata*, 74

Mitella breweri, 176
— *diphylla*, 176
Moltkia × *intermedia*, 43, 76
Montia sibirica, see *Claytonia alsinoides*,
   229
Muehlenbeckia axillaris, 47, 76
Myosotideum hortensia, 116
— *nobile*, see *M. hortensia*, 116
Myrrhis odorata, 229
Myrtus nummularia, 43, 76

Nepeta × *faassenii*, 176
— *gigantea*, of gardens, 176
— *hederacea*, 176, 220
— — 'Variegata', 176
— *mussinii*, see *N.* × *faassenii*, 176 ,
— 'Six Hills Giant', see *N. gigantea*,
   176

Oenothera biennis, 229
Omphalodes cappadocica, 178
— *verna*, 133, 178
Onoclea sensibilis, 209, 214, Pl. XXIV
Ophiopogon intermedius, 178
— *japonicus*, 134, 178
Origanum vulgare 'Aureum', 127, Pl.
   XVIIIA
Osmanthus delavayi, 30
Osmunda regalis, 214
Osteospermum jucundum, see *Dimor-
   photheca barberiae*, 156
Othonna, see *Othonnopsis*, 178
Othonnopsis cheirifolia, 178
Ourisia coccinea, see *O. elegans*, 178
— *elegans*, 178
— *macrophylla*, 178
Oxalis acetosella, 129, 178
— — 'Rosea', 129, 178, 227, Fig.
   48
— *oregana*, 129, 178, 219, 227, Pl.
   XXIIA
— *rosea*, 228
— *rubra*, 178

Pachyphragma macrophyllum, 125, Fig.
   36
Pachysandra axillaris, 76
— *terminalis*, 47, 76, 221, 226, 227,
   Fig. 19, Pl. XXXB
Pachystima, 43
— *canbyi*, 76
— *myrsinites*, 76

Paronychia argentea, 178
— *capitata* (*P. nivea*), 178
Parthenocissus henryana, 98
— *himalayana*, 106
— *inserta*, 98, 106
— *quinquefolia*, 98, 106
— *tricuspidata*, 106
— *vitacea*, see *P. inserta*, 98, 106
Patrinia triloba (*P. palmata*), 178
Peltiphyllum peltatum, 118, 180
— — 'Nanum', 180
Pennisetum alopecuroides, 202, 204
Penstemon newberryi, 76, Pl. XXVIIIB
— *scouleri*, 76
Pernettya mucronata, 49, 76, 223
— — 'Bell's Seedling', 49, 76
— — 'Davis' Hybrids', 49, 76
— *prostrata*, 256
— *tasmanica*, 42, 76
Petasites albus, 180, 218, Fig. 75
— *fragrans*, 180, 218
— *hybridus*, 180, 218, Fig. 74
— *japonicus*, 180
— — *giganteus*, 180, 218
Phalaris arundinacea 'Picta', 206
Philadelphus 'Beauclerk', 31
Philesia magellanica, 78
Phillyrea decora, 30
Phlomis russeliana, 129, 180
— *samia*, see *P. russeliana*, 129, 180
— *viscosa*, see *P. russeliana*, 129, 180
Phlox amoena, 180
— 'Benita', 180
— *bifida*, 180
— *douglasii*, 180
— — 'Boothman's Variety', 180,
   Fig. 54
— — 'May Snow', 180
— 'Margery', 180
— 'Sprite', 180
— *stolonifera*, 180
— *subulata*, 180
— 'Temiscaming', 180
Phyllitis scolopendrium, 210, 214
Phyllostachys viridi-striatus vagans, 224
Physalis alkekengii, 180
— *franchetii*, 180
Phytolacca americana, 229
Picea abies 'Pendula', see *P. a.*
   'Reflexa', 115
— — 'Procumbens', 115
— — 'Reflexa', 115, Pl. XC

Pieris taiwanensis, 32
Pimelia, 43
— *coarctata*, 78
— *prostrata*, 78
Pittosporum humifusum, 42
— *scoparium* 'Prostratum', see *P. humifusum*
Plumbago larpentae, see *Ceratostigma plumbaginoides*, 152
Poa annua, 228
Podocarpus nivalis, 115
Polygonatum falcatum of gardens, 182
— × *hybridum*, 182
— *multiflorum*, 182
— *odoratum*, 180
Polygonum affine, 128, 182, Pl. XXIIIB
— — 'Darjeeling Red', 182
— — 'Superbum', 128, 182
— *amplexicaule*, 182
— — 'Atrosanguineum', 182
— — 'Firetail', 182
— *campanulatum*, 182, 217
— *cuspidatum*, 182, 214
— — *compactum*, see under *P. reynoutria* of gardens, 131, 182
— *equisetiforme*, 182
— *molle*, see *P. rude*, 182
— *polystachyum*, 182, 217
— *reynoutria*, of gardens, 131, 182, 217
— *rude*, 182
— *sachalinense*, 217
— *tenuicaule*, 182
— *vacciniifolium*, 128, 182
Polypodium dryopteris, see *Gymnocarpium dryopteris*
— *phegopteris*, see *Thelypteris phegopteris*
— *vulgare*, 210, 214, 227, Fig. 66
— — *cornubiense*, 210, 214
Polystichum aculeatum, 210, 214
— *munitum*, 214
— *setiferum*, 210, 214
— — 'Divisilobum' and 'Plumosum', 214
— — 'Proliferum' 210, 214
Potentilla alba, 127, 182, 227, Fig. 57
— *ambigua*, see *P. cuneata*, 184
— *argyrophylla*, 184
— *cuneata*, 184
— *cuneifolia*, see *P. cuneata*, 184
— *fruticosa*, 39, 78
— — 'Abbotswood', 78

Potentilla fruticosa arbuscula, of gardens, see *P. f.* 'Elizabeth', 78
— — 'Beesii', 78
— — 'Clotted Cream', 78
— — 'Donard Orange', see *P. f.* 'Tangerine', 80
— — 'Elizabeth', 39, 78
— — *farreri*, 78
— — — *prostrata*, see *P. f. farreri*, 78
— — 'Katherine Dykes', 78
— — 'Longacre', 78
— — *mandschurica*, 78
— — 'Nana Argentea', see *P. f.* 'Beesii', 78
— — *parvifolia* 'Farreri', 78
— — 'Primrose Beauty', 39, 78
— — 'Red Ace', 78
— — 'Tangerine', 80, Pl. IVA
— — 'Walton Park', 80
— *montana*, 184
— *parvifolia*, 78
— — *farreri*, see *P. fruticosa farreri*, 78
— *rigida*, 78
— *splendens*, see *P. montana*, 184
— *verna*, 184
Primula altaica of gardens, see *P. vulgaris sibthorpii*
— *auricula*, 184
— *beesiana*, 184
— × *bullesiana*, 184
— *bulleyana*, 184
— *denticulata*, 184
— — *cashmiriana*, 184
— *edgworthii*, 184
— *florindae*, 119, 184, Pl. XIXA
— 'Garryarde', 184
— — 'Guinevere', 184
— *helodoxa*, 184
— *japonica*, 184
— *juliana*, see *P. pruhoniciana*, 184
— *poissonii*, 184
— *prolifera*, 184
— × *pruhoniciana*, 184
— *pulverulenta*, 184
— *vulgaris*, 184
— — *sibthorpii*, 184
— 'Wanda', see under *P. pruhoniciana*, 184
Prunella grandiflora, 128, 184
— 'Loveliness', 128, 184
Prunus laurocerasus 'Otto Luyken', 33, 80

Prunus laurocerasus 'Zabeliana', 32, 80, Fig. 3
— *nana*, see *P. tenella*, 80
— *tenella*, 48, 80
— — 'Fire Hill' ('Gessleriana'), 80
Pseudosasa japonica, 224
Pterocephalus parnassi, 184
Ptilotrichum spinosum, 41, 80
Pulmonaria angustifolia, 186, 203
— — 'Azurea', 186
— — 'Mawson's Variety', 186
— — 'Munstead Variety', 186
— *mollis*, 155
— *officinalis*, 186
— *picta*, 186
— — 'Margery Fish', 155
— *rubra*, 186, Pl. XXIV
— *saccharata*, see *P. picta*, 186, Pl. XXIV
— — 'Mrs Moon', 186
Pulsatilla montana, 186
— *vulgaris*, 186
Pyracantha 'Santa Cruz', 51
Pyrola asarifolia incarnata, 186
— *rotundifolia*, 186
Pyrus salicifolia 'Pendula', 224

Ranunculus aconitifolius, 186
— — 'Flore Pleno', 186
Raoulia australis, 186
— *glabra*, 186
Rheum officinale, 118, 186
— *palmatum*, 118, 188
— — 'Atrosanguineum', 188, Fig. 26
— *rhaponticum*, 186
Rhododendron (Azalea) Japanese, 35, 82, Fig. 5
— *atlanticum*, 50
— 'Baden Baden', 256
— 'Bad Eilsen', 256
— 'Blue Peter', 31
— 'Britannia', 31
— *calostrotum*, 38, 80, 82
— 'Camillo Schneider', 82
— *campylogynum myrtilloides*, 38, 82
— 'Carmen', 38, 82
— 'Christmas Cheer', 31
— 'Cowslip', 31
— 'Creeping Jenny', see R. 'Jenny', 38, 82
— 'Elizabeth', var. 'Jenny', see R. 'Jenny', 38, 82

Rhododendron 'Elizabeth Hobbie', 82
— 'Elizabeth Lockhart', 256
— 'Ems', 82
— 'Fabia', 256
— *ferrugineum*, 38, 80, 82
— *forrestii repens*, 42, 82
— 'Gertrude Schale', 82
— *hanceanum* 'Nanum', 38, 82
— 'Harvest Moon', 31
— 'Humming Bird', 31
— 'Impeanum', 38, 82
— *impeditum*, 38, 82
— *imperator*, 42, 82
— *indicum* and varieties, 35, 84
— 'Jenny', 38, 82
— *kaempferi*, 35, 84
— *keleticum*, 38, 82
— *kiusianum*, 82
— 'Lava Flow', 42, 82
— *leucaspis*, 38, 82
— 'Malvatica' of gardens, 35, 84
— 'Moerheim's Pink', 256
— 'Moerheim's Scarlet', 82
— 'Mucronatum', 35, 82, 84
— — 'Bulstrode', 82, Fig. 7
— — 'Ripense', 82
— 'Myrtifolium', 80
— *nobleanum* 'Venustum', 31
— *obtusum* 'Amoenum', 82
— — 'Amoenum Coccineum', 31
— *ovatum*, of gardens, 80, 82
— *pemakoense*, 50, 80, 82, Fig. 6
— 'Pink Bountiful', 256
— × *prostigiatum*, 38, 82
— *prostratum*, 42, 82
— *radicans*, 42, 82
— 'Red Carpet', 256
— *saluenense*, 37, 38, 80, 82
— *scintillans*, 38, 82
— *simsii*, 35, 84
— 'Snow Queen', 31
— 'Temple Belle', 31
— 'Tidbit', 256
— 'Ursula Siems', 82
— *viscosum* and varieties, 50
— 'Vulcan', 31
— *williamsianum*, 82
— *wilsonii*, 80
Rhus cotinus, 31
Ribes alpinum, 84
— 'Aureum', 34, 84
— 'Pumilum', 84

Rodgersia aesculifolia, 188, Fig. 25
— *pinnata* 'Superba', 188
— *podophylla*, 188, Pl. XXB, Pl. XXI
— *sambucifolia*, 188
— *tabularis*, 188
Romneya coulteri, 49, 84
— × *hybrida*, 49, 84
— *trichocalyx*, 49, 84
Rosa foliolosa, 222
— 'Macrantha', 84
— 'Max Graf', 45, 84, 221, Pl. VIIA
— *moyesii*, 39
— *nitida*, 49, 84
— 'Nozomi', 256
— × *paulii*, 45, 84, 221
— — 'Rosea', 45, 86, Fig. 18
— × *polliniana*, 86, Pl. XV
— 'Raubritter', 86
— *rugosa*, 222
— — 'Alba', 222
— — 'Blanc Double de Coubert',
222
— — 'Fru Dagmar Hastrup', 222
— — 'Roseraie de l'Haÿ', 222
— 'Sanders' White', 256
— *virginiana*, 222
— *wichuraiana*, 45, 86, 221, 226
Rose 'Nevada', 31
Rosmarinus lavandulaceus, 43, 86, 227,
Fig. 16
— *officinalis*, 50, 86
— — *prostratus*, see R. *lavandulaceus*,
43, 86, 227
Rubus calycinoides, 86
— *fockeanus*, see R. *calycinoides*, 86
— *nutkanus*, 223
— *odoratus*, 223, Pl. XXXIA
— *tricolor*, 45, 86, 221, Fig. 13
Ruta graveolens 'Jackman's Blue', 41,
86, Fig. 41

Sagina glabra, see S. *pilifera*
— *pilifera*, 184, 188, 219, Fig. 78
— — 'Aurea', 188
Salix alba 'Chrysostella', 222
— — 'Vitellina', 222
— *arbuscula*, 86
— *caprea* 'Pendula', 44, 86
— — 'Kilmarnock', 44
× *finnmarchica*, 258
— *gracilistyla*, 222
— × *grahamii*, 86

Salix lanata, 86
— — 'Stuartii', 34, Fig. 4
— *myrtilloides*, 86
— *uva-ursi*, 258
— *vitellina* 'Britzensis', see S. *alba*
vitellina, 222
— *yezo-alpina*, 258
Salvia glutinosa, 188
— *officinalis*, 40, 88
— — 'English Broad Leaf', 88
— — *icterina*, 88, Pl. VA
— — 'Purpurascens', 40, 88, Fig. 38,
Pl. VB
— — 'Variegata', 88
Sambucus ebulus, 188, 217
Santolina chamaecyparissus, 41, 88, Pl.
VB
— — *nana*, 88
— *incana*, see S. *chamaecyparissus*, 41,
88
— 'Italica Sulphurea', see S. *neapolitana*, 88
— *neapolitana*, 88
— *pectinata*, 88
— *virens*, 88
— *viridis*, see S. *virens*, 88
Saponaria ocymoides, 127, 188
— *officinalis*, 131, 188
Sarcococca hookerana digyna, 88
— *humilis*, 88, 227
— *ruscifolia*, 88
Sarothamnus scoparius, see *Cytisus
scoparius*
Sasa species, 224
Satureia montana, 41, 88
Saxifraga × *andrewsii*, 190
— *caespitosa*, 190
— *cuneifolia*, 190
— — *infundibulum*, see S. *cuneifolia*
subintegra, 190
— — *subintegra*, 190
— 'Edie Campbell', 190
— *geranioides*, 190
— *geum* 'Monstrosa', 129, 190, 219,
226, Fig. 46
— — *hirsuta*, 190
— *hypnoides*, 127, 190
— 'Letchworth Beauty', 190
— *muscoides*, 190
— *peltata*, see *Peltiphyllum peltatum*,
180
— *sarmentosa*, see S. *stolonifera*, 190

Saxifraga stolonifera, 190
— *trifurcata*, 127, 190
— *umbrosa*, 127, 190, Pl. XIIIA
— — *primuloides*, 190
Scabiosa graminifolia, 123, 190
— *pterocephalus*, see *Pterocephalus parnasii*, 184
Schizocodon soldanelloides, 130, 190
Schizophragma hydrangeoides, 106
— *integrifolia*, 100, 106
Scolopendrium vulgare, see *Phyllitis scolopendrium*, 210, 214
Sedum alboroseum, 192
— — 'Variegatum', 192
— *album*, 192
— — 'Murale', 192
— *anacampseros*, 192
— 'Autumn Joy', 120, 190, 192
— *ewersii*, 190, 192
— *kamtschaticum*, 190, 192
— *oreganum*, 190, 192
— *populifolium*, 192
— *rhodiola*, see *S. roseum*, 190, 192
— *rosea*, 190, 192
— 'Ruby Glow', 190, 192
— *spathulifolium*, 190, 192
— — 'Capa Blanca', 192
— — *purpureum*, 192
— *spectabile*, 190, 192
— — 'Brilliant', 192
— — 'Meteor', 192
— *spurium*, 127, 192
— — 'Album', 192
— — 'Green Mantle', 192, 219, 227
— — 'Schorbuser Blut', 192
— — 'Splendens', 192
Selaginella helvetica, 126, 192, 219
Senecio cineraria, 190
— *clivorum*, see *Ligularia dentata*, 117
— *greyi*, see *S. laxifolius*, 41, 90
— *laxifolius* of gardens, 41, 90, 221, Fig. 8
Shortia galacifolia, 130, 192
— *uniflora*, 192
Silene acaulis, 194
— — *saxatilis*, 194
— *armeria*, 228
Skimmia 'Foremanii', see under *S. japonica*, 90
— *japonica*, 33, 90, Pl. IVB
— — 'Bronze Knight', 90
— — 'Foremanii', 90

Skimmia japonica 'Rogersii', 90
— — 'Rubella', 33, 90
— *laureola*, 90
— *reevesiana* 'Rubella', see *S. japonica* 'Rubella', 90
— 'Rogersii', see under *S. japonica*, 90
Smilacina racemosa, 194
— *stellata*, 194
Soldanella villosa, 130, 194
Sorbaria aitchisonii, 223
— *arborea*, 223
— *assurgens*, 223
— *lindleyi*, see *S. tomentosa*, 223
— *sorbifolia*, 223
— *tomentosa*, 223
Spiraea arborea, see *Sorbaria arborea*, 223
— *aruncus*, see *Aruncus dioicus*, 119, 220
— × *bumalda*, 34, 90
— — 'Anthony Waterer', 90
— — 'Anthony Waterer Improved', 90
— — 'Walluffii', 90
— *callosa alba*, see *S. japonica alba*, 90
— *decumbens*, 34, 90
— *douglasii*, 222
— *hacquetii*, see *S. decumbens*, 90
— herbaceous, see *Aruncus*, 119, 220, *Astilbe*, 119, and *Filipendula*, 160
— *japonica*, 34, 90
— — *alba*, 90
— — 'Froebellii', 90
— — 'Macrophylla', 90
— — 'Ruberrima', 90
— *menziesii* 'Triumphans', 223
— *nana alpina*, see *S. japonica* 'Ruberrima', 90
Stachys betonica 'Superba', see *S. macrantha*, 129, 194
— *lanata*, see *S. olympica*, 129, 194
— *macrantha*, 129, 194, Fig. 62
— *olympica*, 129, 194
— — 'Silver Carpet', 129, 194, Pl. XVIIIB
Statice, see *Limonium*, 174
Stephanandra incisa 'Crispa', see *S. i. 'Prostrata'*, 34, 90
— — 'Prostrata', 34, 90
Stipa calamagrostis, 202, 206
— *gigantea*, 202, 206

Struthiopteris, see *Matteuccia*, 209, 214
— *germanica*, see *Matteuccia struthiopteris*, 209, 214
Symphoricarpus albus (*S. racemosus*), 223
— — *laevigatus*, 223
— — — 'Constance Spry', 223
— 'Hancock', 92
Symphytum grandiflorum, 129, 194, 219, 226, Pl. XXIIIA
— 'Hidcote Pink', 129, 194
— 'Hidcote Blue', 129, 194
— *peregrinum*, see under *S.* × *uplandicum*, 124, 194, 219
— × *uplandicum*, 124, 194, 219
— — 'Variegatum', 124, 194, Fig. 62

Tanakaea radicans, 194
Taxus baccata 'Dovastonii', 115
— — 'Dovastonii Aurea', 115, 220, Fig. 73
— — 'Repandens', 115
Telekia speciosa, 117
Tellima grandiflora, 196, 220
— — 'Purpurea', or 'Rubra', 37, 196
Teucrium chamaedrys, 196, 227
— *pyrenaicum*, 196
Thalictrum adiantifolium, see *T. minus*, 131, 196
— *minus*, 131, 196
Thelypteris phegopteris, 214
Thymus citriodorus, 92
— *drucei*, see *T. serpyllum*, 196
— *herba-barona*, 196
— *hirsutus doerfleri*, 196
— *nummularius*, 43, 92
— *pseudolanuginosus*, 196
— *serpyllum*, 196
— — 'Albus', 196
— — 'Coccineus', 196
— — *lanuginosus*, see *T. pseudolanuginosus*, 196
— — 'Pink Chintz', 196
— *vulgaris*, 40, 92
— — 'Aureus', 40, 92
— — 'Variegatus', 92
Tiarella cordifolia, 128, 196, 227, Fig. 49, Pl. XXVA
— *wherryi*, 196

Tolmeia menziesii, 128, 198
Trachystemon orientale, 132, 198, 217, 226, Fig. 70
Trollius 'Canary Bird', 198
— × *cultorum*, 198
— *europaeus*, 198
— *ledebouri*, 198
— 'Orange Princess', 198
Tropaeolum ('Nasturtium'), 228
Tsuga canadensis 'Pendula', 115

Vaccinium macrocarpum, 92
— *oxycoccus*, 42, 92, Pl. IXA
— *vitis-idaea*, 92
Vancouverias, 130
— *hexandra*, 198, Fig. 51
— *planipetala*, 198
Verbascum nigrum, 230
Verbena corymbosa, 198, 221
Veronica, shrubby, evergreens, see *Hebe*, 68
— *gentianoides*, 200
— — 'Variegata', 198
— *incana*, 123, 200
— — 'Wendy', 198
— × *whittleyi*, 200
Viburnum davidii, 33, 38, 92
— *plicatum* varieties, 29, Fig. 1
— *tomentosum* varieties, see *V. plicatum tomentosum*, 29
Vinca acutiloba, see *V. difformis*, 45, 92
— *difformis*, 45, 92
— *major*, 45, 94
— — 'Elegantissima', 46, 94, Pl. IXB
— — *hirsuta*, 45, 94, 221, Fig. 14
— — *oxyloba*, see *V. m. hirsuta*, 46, 94
— — *pubescens*, see *V. m. hirsuta*, 46, 94
— — *variegata*, see *V. m.* 'Elegantissima', 46, 94
— *minor*, 46, 94, Pl. XIIA
— — 'Alba', 94
— — 'Argentea Variegata', 94
— — 'Bowles' Variety', 46, 94, Pl. IXC
— — 'Caerulea Plena', 94
— — 'Gertrude Jekyll', 46, 94
Vinca minor 'La Graveana', see *V. m.* 'Bowles' Variety', 46, 94

Vinca minor 'Multiplex', 94
—— 'Variegata Aurea', 94
Viola alba, 200
— *cornuta*, 129, 200
—— 'Alba', 129, 200
—— 'Lilacina', 129, 200
— *cucullata*, 200
— 'Huntercombe Purple', 200
— *labradorica*, 133, 200
— *odorata*, 200
— *papilionacea*, 200
— *riviniana*, 200
— *septentrionalis*, 200, Fig. 43
Vitis coignetiae, 98, 106
— *davidii*, 98, 106
— *hederacea*, see *Parthenocissus quinquefolia*, 98, 106

Vitis inconstans, see *Vitis tricuspidata*, 106
— *tricuspidata*, 106

Waldsteinia sibirica, see *W. ternata*, 130, 200
— *ternata*, 130, 200, 219, 227, Pl. XXIIB
— *trifolia*, see *W. ternata*, 130, 200
Woodwardia radicans, 209, 214

Xanthorhiza apiifolia, see *X. simplicissimus*, 48, 94
— *simplicissimus*, 48, 94, Fig. 23

Zauschneria californica, 133, 200
—— *mexicana*, 200
— *cana*, 200

NOTES